The Wild Duck
Hedda Gabler

THE PLAYS OF HENRIK IBSEN
(1828-1906)

WITH THEIR DATES OF COMPOSITION

HENRIK IBSEN, the most influential dramatist since Shakespeare, was born at Skien, Norway, in 1828. After years of failure and poverty, he emigrated at the age of thirty-six to Italy, and there wrote *Brand*, which brought him immediate fame. He remained in self-imposed exile for twenty-seven years, living in Rome, Dresden, and Munich. In 1891 he returned to Norway, and spent the last fifteen years of his life in Christiania (now Oslo). He died there in 1906 at the age of seventy-eight. Ibsen wrote twenty-six plays, sixteen of which are still performed in England and America.

MICHAEL MEYER, the translator, was born in London in 1921. After studying at Oxford he was for three years lecturer in English Literature at Upsala University in Sweden and now lives partly in Stockholm and partly in London. Author of one novel, two plays, and one television play, he is best known as a translator from the Scandinavian languages and has established a unique reputation for himself in this field in England.

HENRIK IBSEN

The Wild Duck
Hedda Gabler

TRANSLATED FROM THE NORWEGIAN
BY MICHAEL MEYER

W. W. Norton & Company
New York • London

Library of Congress Cataloging in Publication Data

Ibsen, Henrik, 1828-1906
  The wild duck

  (The Norton Library)
  Translation of Vildanden and Hedda Gabler.
  "Originally published as part of a volume entitled
'Hedda Gabler" and three other plays."
  I. Ibsen, Henrik, 1828-1906. Hedda Gabler. English.
1977. II. Meyer, Michael Leverson, 1921-
III. Title.
PT8854.M44 1977   839.8'2'26   76-49433

ISBN 0-393-31449-9 pbk.

W. W. Norton & Company, Inc.
500 Fifth Avenue, New York, N.Y. 10110
www.wwnorton.com

W. W. Norton & Company Ltd.
Castle House, 75/76 Wells Street, London W1T 3QT

3 4 5 6 7 8 9 0

ACKNOWLEDGMENTS

Permission to quote from Ibsen's letters has been kindly granted by Gyldendal Norsk Forlag of Oslo, Norway.

Permission to use material by George Bernard Shaw has been granted by the Public Trustees, London, England, and The Society of Authors, London, England.

CONTENTS

The Wild Duck

INTRODUCTION

On January 11, 1883, Ibsen wrote from Rome to his publisher, Frederik Hegel: "I am already at work again planning a new play about contemporary life. It will be in 4 acts, and I hope to be able to get down to the actual writing within a couple of months at most. The Italian air, and the pleasant way of life down here, greatly increase my eagerness to create. I find it much easier to work here than in Germany."

Ibsen was now fifty-four, and the reception of *Ghosts* in Scandinavia a year earlier might well have deterred a less resilient spirit than his from setting pen to paper for some while. It had been reviled, not merely by the conservative press, which he had expected, but also by the radical press; even such an old admirer as Henrik Jaeger had lectured against it, and Hegel had been forced to take back large quantities of the book from booksellers who refused to stock it; indeed, it was thirteen years before the first printing of 10,000 copies was sold out. The theatres of Christiania, Copenhagen and Stockholm had been unanimous in declaring it unfit for public presentation.

So far from being silenced by this reception, however, Ibsen had reacted swiftly with the most buoyant play he had written since *Peer Gynt. An Enemy of the People* was immediately accepted by the Christiania Theatre, the management of which seems not to have appreciated, or to have been insensitive to, the fact that its theme was the unworthiness of "those who do not dare" and its conclusion: "The strongest man is he who stands alone." The play was in its last days of rehearsal when Ibsen wrote to Hegel with plans for its successor.

In the event, it was to be another fifteen months before he began the actual writing of THE WILD DUCK, and a further eleven weeks of intensive revision before he completed it. The slowness and difficulty with which it took shape contrasts markedly with the swiftness and ease with which he had written *An Enemy of the People.* THE WILD DUCK represented yet another departure into new country. Just as he had abandoned poetic drama as soon as he had mastered it in *Peer Gynt,* so now he threw aside almost contemptuously the new anti-poetic, anti-symbolic form which he had perfected in *A Doll's House, Ghosts* and *An Enemy of the People.* He explained his restlessness and passion for experiment in a letter to Georg Brandes that summer (June 12, 1883):

"An intellectual pioneer," he wrote, "can never gather a majority about him. In ten years the majority may have reached that standpoint which Dr. Stockmann had reached when the people held their meeting. But during those ten years the Doctor has not remained stationary; he still stands at least ten years ahead of the others. The majority, the masses, the mob, will never catch him up; he can never rally them behind him. I myself feel a similarly unrelenting compulsion to keep pressing forward. A crowd now stands where I stood when I wrote my earlier books. But I myself am there no longer. I am somewhere else—far ahead of them—or so I hope. At present I am struggling with the draft of a new play in four acts. As time passes, various odd ideas settle in one's head, and one must find some outlet for them. Though since it won't deal with the High Court, or the absolute veto, or even the 'pure' flag,* it is hardly likely to arouse any interest in Norway. However, I hope it may obtain a hearing in other quarters."

Ibsen does not seem to have made any progress with THE WILD DUCK during the remainder of 1883, apart from a few pages of rough notes and a provisional list of characters. On January 22, 1884, he wrote to Laura Grundtvig: "I have been having one of those periods when I can only with the greatest

---

* I.e., without the mark of union with Sweden.

reluctance sit down to my desk." On April 21, however, he was able to send better tidings to his publisher. "The political complications in Norway," he wrote to Hegel, "have prevented me all this winter from working seriously, and with undivided attention, on my new play. But now at last I have managed to free my mind from this chaos, and am writing at full stretch. The first act will be finished this week, and I reckon that by the middle of June I should be able to let you know that the play is ready."

He completed Act 1 according to schedule; his manuscript draft of this act is dated April 20–28, 1884. On May 2 he began Act 2; but when he was halfway through it, he stopped, and started to rewrite the play from the beginning. By May 24 he had completed Acts 1 and 2 in their new form. Act 3 occupied him from May 25–30; Act 4 from June 2–8; and Act 5 from June 9–13. The following day, June 14, 1884, he wrote to Hegel:

"I am glad to be able to tell you that yesterday I completed the draft of my new play. It comprises five acts and will, as far as I can calculate, occupy some 200 printed pages, possibly a little more. It still remains for me to make the fair copy and I shall start on that tomorrow. As usual, however, this will involve not just copying the draft but a comprehensive rewriting of the dialogue. So it will take time. Still, unless some unforeseen obstacle presents itself I reckon that the whole manuscript should be in your hands by mid-September. The play doesn't touch on political or social problems, or indeed any matters of public import. It takes place entirely within the confines of family life. I dare say it will arouse some discussion; but it can't offend anyone."

On June 30, he left Rome for the little mountain resort of Gossensass in the Tyrol—that village that was later to prove so fateful to him. There he settled down in his usual strictly methodical manner to revise the play.

"My routine," he wrote to his wife on July 4, 1884, "has so far been as follows. Rise at 6.30; breakfast brought up half an hour later; then I go out while they do the room; then write from 9 to 1. Then lunch, with a ravenous appetite. In the afternoons, too, I have managed to write a little, or at any rate do groundwork. The second act will be ready in 5–6 days. I am not drinking any beer; which suits me well. But I am drinking milk, and a little—not much—white wine, with water. A light evening meal at 7.30. Up to now I have been in bed each evening by 10, and have been sleeping well."

Ibsen's wife and son were holidaying in Norway, and his fairly frequent letters to them enable us to date the progress of his revision. He finished Act 2 in its final form on July 12. Act 3 took him from July 14 until either July 29 or 30; Act 4 was ready by August 17. On August 27 he wrote to his son Sigurd: "My play is now fast nearing its conclusion. In 3–4 days it will be ready; then I shall read it through carefully and send it off. I take great joy in working on this play; it grows all the time in little details, and I shall miss it when I have to part from it; though, at the same time, I shall be glad . . . The German sculptor Professor Kopf, from Rome, has with him a 13-year-old daughter who is the most perfect model for my Hedvig that could be imagined; she is pretty, has a serious face and manner, and is a little *gefräsig*." Three days later, on August 30, he wrote to his wife: "Although I don't know when or where my letters reach you, while you continue to move from town to town, I must nevertheless send you the good news that I have just finished my manuscript. The play will be very rich in content, and bigger than any other of my recent works. I have said everything I wanted to say; and I don't think it could easily have been said better. Now to the business of reading it through, which will take 2–3 days; then off it goes to Hegel."

On September 2 he wrote to Hegel (still from Gossensass): "I enclose the manuscript of my new play, THE WILD DUCK, which has occupied me daily for the past 4 months, and from which I cannot now part without a certain feeling of loss. The characters in it have, despite their many failings, grown dear to me as a result of this long daily association. But I cherish the hope that they will also find good friends and well-wishers among the great reading public and, not least, among theatre folk; for they all, without exception, offer rewarding opportunities. But the study and representation of them will not be found easy. . . . This new play occupies, in some ways, a unique position among my dramatic works. Its method differs in certain respects from that which I have previously employed. However, I don't wish to enlarge on that subject here. The critics will, I trust, see this for themselves; at any rate, they will find something to argue about, something to construe. I believe, too, that THE WILD DUCK may possibly tempt some of our younger dramatists to explore new territories, and this I regard as a desirable thing."

Hegel's firm, Gyldendals of Copenhagen, published THE WILD DUCK on November 11, 1884, in a printing of 8000 copies. This sold so quickly that a new edition appeared on December 1. The play received its première on January 9, 1885, at Bergen; before the month was out it had also been staged in Christiania, Helsinki and Stockholm, and the following month it was presented in Copenhagen. Germany, surprisingly, had to wait three years to see the play; its German première was on March 4, 1888, at the Residenztheater, Berlin. Berne, Wiesbaden and Dresden saw it in 1889, and Paris in 1891, when Antoine staged it at the Théâtre Libre (the only Ibsen play, apart from *Ghosts*, which he presented there). William Archer had not yet begun his association with Janet Achurch and J. T. Grein, and it was not performed in London until 1894.

THE WILD DUCK greatly perplexed Norwegian readers when it first appeared. "The public does not know what to make of it," commented the *Christiania Intelligentssedler.* "One paper says one thing and the other just the opposite." *Aftenposten* complained: "One may study and study to find what Ibsen wants to say, and not find it." *Morgenbladet* found the plot "as queer as it is thin . . . The total impression can hardly be other than a strong sense of emptiness and unpleasantness." *Bergens Tidende* thought the play proved Ibsen's inferiority to Bjoernson. "He does not speak from the depths of his heart as does Bjoernson. He does not make demands of the individual with the same strength, he has no faith in his own ability to ennoble humanity by means of his writings. He states the

problems excellently as he sees them, but makes no attempt
to show the way beyond them; he chastises as one who has
authority, but makes no demand for improvement." The only
newspaper critic in Norway who seemed to appreciate the
point of the play was Irgens Hansen in *Dagbladet;* he recognised that Ibsen "here stands on humanity's ground and speaks
humanity's cause, even though it be the cause of a very shabby
humanity."

Across the North Sea, Ibsen's admirers were equally baffled.
His earliest English champion, Edmund Gosse, condemned it
in the *Fortnightly Review* as "a strange, melancholy and pes-
simistic drama, almost without a ray of light from beginning
to end . . . There is really not a character in the book that
inspires confidence or liking . . . There can be no doubt that
it is by far the most difficult of Ibsen's dramas for a reader to
comprehend." Gosse himself does not seem to have compre-
hended it very well, for he concluded that "the ideal spirit
of goodness is the untamed bird in its close and miserable
garret, captive to circumstances and with no hope of escape."
William Archer also failed to understand it at first, though he
later came to admire it greatly, and named it "Ibsen's greatest
play." Arthur Symons thought it "a play of inferior quality,"
and Havelock Ellis dismissed it as "the least remarkable of
Ibsen's plays." Almost the only critic to see the point of the
play during the next ten years was Bernard Shaw, who de-
voted to it one of his most penetrating passages in *The Quintes-
sence of Ibsenism:*

"After *An Enemy of the People,* Ibsen . . . left the vulgar
ideals for dead and set about the exposure of those of the
choicer spirits, beginning with the incorrigible idealists who
had idealized his very self, and were becoming known as Ib-
senites. His first move in this direction was such a tragi-comic
slaughtering of sham Ibsenism that his astonished victims
plaintively declared that THE WILD DUCK, as the new play
was called, was a satire on his former works; while the pious,
whom he had disappointed so severely by his interpretation of
Brand . . . began to hope that he was coming back repentant
to the fold."

Shaw concluded: "The busybody [i.e., Gregers] finds that people cannot be freed from their failings from without. They must free themselves."

THE WILD DUCK at first received a mixed reception on the stage. It was admired in Christiania, thanks largely to Arnoldus Reimers's rendering of Hjalmar; but it was hissed in Helsinki. In Stockholm, at that time the most theatrically enlightened of the Scandinavian capitals, it aroused deep interest, not least because the production was so daringly realistic as to include real doors with actual handles and even, which caused a great buzz, a commode in Hjalmar's studio. When it was staged in Rome in January 1892, the audience became so irritated by Gregers's behaviour that they harassed the unfortunate actor who played him with shouts of "Basta!" and "Imbecile!", while at the Paris première at the Théâtre Libre some of the spectators showed their displeasure by quacking like ducks. As an illustration of how little people understood the play, Francisque Sarcey, the famous critic of *Le Temps*, thought that Hedvig had shot herself out of grief because the wild duck was dead. The first London performance, in 1894, was only moderately good, but in 1897 there was a much better one, directed by Charles Charrington with Laurence Irving (Sir Henry's younger son) as Hjalmar. Bernard Shaw paid the play a memorable tribute in the *Saturday Review*:

"Where shall I find an epithet magnificent enough for THE WILD DUCK? To sit there getting deeper and deeper into that Ekdal home, and getting deeper and deeper into your own life all the time, until you forget that you are in a theatre; to look on with horror and pity at a profound tragedy, shaking with laughter all the time at an irresistible comedy; to go out, not from a diversion, but from an experience deeper than real life ever brings to most men, or often brings to any man; that is what THE WILD DUCK was like last Monday at the Globe."

Subsequent generations proved similarly receptive, and THE WILD DUCK now shares with *A Doll's House, Ghosts, Hedda Gabler* and *The Master Builder* the honour of being the most frequently staged of Ibsen's plays.

A rich quantity of Ibsen's draft material for the play has survived: nine sets of notes, the unfinished first draft (comprising one and a half acts) and the full second draft, which differs considerably from the final version. The first set of notes, undated but probably written in late 1882 or early 1883, contains a quantity of aphorisms, often rather vapid, but is chiefly of interest in that it shows Ibsen making his first sketches for the characters of Hjalmar and Gregers. Hjalmar seems to have been originally based on a photographer named Edvard Larsen with whom Ibsen had lodged in earlier days, and who had taken the oldest known photograph of him (in 1861–62).

"E.L. . . . is a naïve and pretentious pessimist, devoid of energy, an idle dreamer. . . . [His] marriage with a simple wife has, in one way, been a 'true' marriage, in that it has caused him to shrink, or at any rate stopped him developing. Now he can't manage without her; or she without him . . . He has to spend the evening with people of quality. It bores and irritates him. He longs to get back to his own narrow, homely surroundings . . . Like A. the printer [Aslaksen of *The League of Youth* and *An Enemy of the People*] he has been afforded a glimpse into a higher world; that is his tragedy. . . . 'The sixth sense.' Magnetic [i.e., hypnotic] influence is E.L.'s favourite subject. . . . Photographer, failed poet, dreams of a socialist revolution, the revolution of the future, of science. Poison in the breakfast . . . Is a socialist at heart but dares not admit it; he has a family, and so is not free."

Gregers was at first based on the Norwegian novelist and playwright, Alexander Kielland (1849–1906), whose radicalism Ibsen appears to have regarded as bogus:

"A.K., the sybarite, enjoys an aesthetic indignation at poverty and misery. Enjoys his visits to his old schoolfriend who has come down in the world, without realizing why he enjoys them. . . . A.K-d.: to lie tucked up in a soft bed with a well-filled belly and hear the rain pouring down and think of difficult journeys in the wet and cold, is a great pleasure."

As Ibsen's plans developed, however, Hjalmar and Gregers became more and more different from the E.L. and A.K-d. of these first notes. The Gregers we know has little in common with the character of A.K-d. as sketched here. It is the contrast between the two characters rather than the characters themselves that has survived into the play. The rich man's son visiting his old schoolfellow who has come down in the world seems to have been the idea which first ignited Ibsen's imagination. Gregers gradually developed into a kind of *reductio ad absurdum* of Dr. Stockmann, the hero of Ibsen's previous play—a living illustration of the danger of a single-minded pursuit of truth if not tempered by common sense and an understanding of human limitations. Similarly, Ibsen soon found Edvard Larsen inadequate as a model for Hjalmar, and borrowed characteristics from two other Norwegians of his acquaintance, a poet named Kristofer Janson and, especially, a failed artist, Magnus Bagge, from whom Ibsen had taken drawing lessons around 1860. Halvdan Koht has said of Bagge that he had "a constant longing to lift himself above everyday prose"; it was typical of him that when he went to live in Germany he called himself von Bagge. Hjalmar's mode of speech was fairly ordinary at first; it is only in the final (third) draft that it acquires its peculiarly florid quality and its excess of adjectives. He is perhaps the most difficult of all Ibsen's characters to translate, at any rate in the prose dramas.

Hedvig, in Ibsen's early notes, is described as being "drawn to the sea." There is a reference to "the first time she saw a big expanse of water looking down from a height," and a note that "Human beings are sea-creatures—like the wild duck—not land creatures. Gregers was made for the sea. In time, all people will live on it, when the land becomes swallowed up. Then family life will cease." Ibsen discarded these ideas from THE WILD DUCK, but returned to them two plays later in *The Lady from the Sea.* Hedvig's impending blindness was an afterthought. There is no reference to it until the final draft; indeed, until that draft she is rather a commonplace child. Hjalmar's "invention," too, which figures so largely in the play as we know it, is barely touched on in the preliminary drafts. Ibsen, in a letter to Georg Brandes (June 25, 1884) described his revisionary work as "polishing the language and

giving a sharper individuality to the characters and dialogue"
and, as William Archer remarked: "Everywhere, on a close
comparison of the texts, we see an intensive imagination lighting up, as it were, what was at first somewhat cold and colour-
less. In this case, as in many others, the draft suggests a trans-
parency before the electricity has been switched on."

THE WILD DUCK is full of echoes from Ibsen's own child-
hood. The family home at Venstoep had contained a library
of old books left, like the ones in the Ekdals' loft, by a previous
owner of the house known as "The Flying Dutchman," a Norwegian who had been a prison convict in England and a slave
in the Barbary States, and had died the year Ibsen was born.
These books had included *Harrison's* (or, as Ibsen originally
wrote it, *Harryson's*) *History of London* (1775), which so
delighted Hedvig. Hedvig herself seems to have got her name,
and probably some of her character, from Ibsen's sister Hedvig; and Old Ekdal contains many traits of the playwright's
father, Knud Ibsen, who had been a lieutenant in the militia
and a great huntsman before he went bankrupt and brought
the family name into disgrace. Ibsen also borrowed certain
details from a trial which had caused a sensation during his
student days in Christiania, when an army officer accused of
embezzlement tried unsuccessfully to shoot himself. (He was
to return to this source for much of his material for *John
Gabriel Borkman*.) And, perhaps the most significant echo
from Ibsen's past, at the age of sixteen he had, like Haakon
Werle, given a servant girl an illegitimate child.

Wherein does the "method" of THE WILD DUCK differ, as
Ibsen told Hegel, from that which he had previously employed? At first sight there is no immediately obvious difference; it seems, like *A Doll's House, Ghosts* and *An Enemy of
the People,* to be a realistic play about realistic people, and
the method seems to be his old method of raking over apparently dead ashes and exposing the live embers beneath. The
symbolism? But Ibsen had used symbolism at least as freely
in *Brand*.

Nevertheless, I think there is little doubt that it was the

symbolism in THE WILD DUCK to which Ibsen was referring
when he wrote of a new method. In *Brand* the symbols are
incidental to the play, or at any rate are not fully integrated
into it. The Ice Church and the hawk are left deliberately im-
precise; there is room for intelligent argument about their
meaning; perhaps, indeed, they are intended to mean different
things to different people. In THE WILD DUCK, however, there
is a single and precise symbol, that of the bird itself; and, so
far from being incidental to the play, it is the hub and heart
of it. *Brand* is a play into which symbols have worked their
way; THE WILD DUCK is a play dependent on, and held together by, a symbol, as though the wild duck were a magnet
and the characters in the play so many iron filings held together by this centripetal force. This was not a method that
Ibsen was to use invariably in his subsequent plays; *Rosmersholm*, for example, and *Hedda Gabler* seem to me to have
more in common with *Ghosts* than with THE WILD DUCK. But
we find him returning to it in the later plays; the towers and
spires in *The Master Builder* and the crutch in *Little Eyolf*
serve a structural purpose similar to the wild duck. They are
images from which the characters cannot escape, any more
than the iron filings can escape the magnet.

Ibsen probably borrowed the image of the wild duck from a
poem called "The Sea Bird" by Johan Sebastian Welhaven
which describes how a wild duck is wounded and dives down
to die on the sea-bed; and Professor Francis Bull suggests that
he may also have been influenced by Darwin's account in *The
Origin of Species* of how wild ducks degenerate in captivity.
Some astonishing theories have been advanced as to what the
bird is intended to stand for. Surely Ibsen makes it abundantly
clear that he intended it as a double symbol with two precise
and obvious references. Firstly, it is, like Hedvig, a by-product
of Haakon Werle's fondness for sport which has been rejected
by him and is now cared for by the Ekdal family. Secondly,
with a more general application, it represents the refusal of
most people, once they have been wounded, to go on living
and face reality. Both Hjalmar and his father have sought to
hide themselves in the deep blue sea of illusion, and Gregers,

like the "damned clever dog" trained by his father, hauls them back to the surface. The cynics (Relling and Haakon Werle) watch this operation; so do the two sensible, earthbound women, Gina and Mrs. Soerby. These women, Ibsen seems to imply, offer the only real refuge: love. Mrs. Soerby can save Haakon Werle, despite Gregers's cynicism, just as she could have saved Relling, who had also once loved her; Relling knows this, and it is hinted that the loss of her is partly responsible for his having turned into a drunkard. And Gina, if Gregers had not intervened, could have saved Hjalmar. Yet Ibsen leaves a question mark here; is love simply another illusion, like the Ekdals' loft? And if so, then is not the illusion of the loft justified, just as much as the illusion of love?

At the same time, while the wild duck has these two specific significances within the play, it is possible that, consciously or unconsciously, it also reflects Ibsen's impression of himself when he wrote it; one who has forgotten what it means to live wild, and has grown plump and tame and content with his basket; as unlike the author of *Brand* as the duck is unlike the hawk of the earlier play, of which, too, the climax had been a shot fired at (or supposedly at) a bird by a girl of fourteen. How far, Ibsen must have asked himself—and he was to ask the question again, through Allmers in *Little Eyolf* and Rubek in *When We Dead Awaken*—does the artist, like the Ekdals, shut himself off from life? Is his world so very different from their loft with its imitations of reality? Which is the more cowardly refuge, the Ekdals' loft or Brand's Ice Church?

Hjalmar and Gregers both represent different aspects of Ibsen; on the one hand the evader of reality, on the other the impractical idealist who pesters mankind with his "claims of the ideal" because he has a sick conscience and despises himself. How far, one wonders, did Ibsen identify himself with Gregers in that curious episode when the latter, finding that the stove smokes, throws water on it to put out the fire and only makes the stink worse? He had already portrayed these two conflicting aspects of himself in *Brand* and *Peer Gynt*, and the conflict between Gregers and Hjalmar is as though Brand and Peer Gynt had been brought face to face.

Two main dangers confront anyone who produces THE
WILD DUCK: the temptation to play Hjalmar as ridiculous and
farcical, and the temptation to play Gregers as spiteful. A perusal of the notices of London productions of the play during
the past seventy years reveals how often actors and producers
have fallen into these traps. Ibsen foresaw the danger of
Hjalmar being made a figure of fun, and warned against it
in a letter which he wrote to H. Schroeder, the manager of
the Christiania Theatre, on November 14, 1884. Hjalmar, he
wrote, "must not be played with any trace of parody. The
actor must never for a moment show that he is conscious that
there is anything funny in what he says. His voice has, as
Relling observes, something endearing about it, and this quality must be clearly brought out. His sentimentality is honest,
his melancholy, in its way, attractive; no hint of affectation.
Between ourselves, I would suggest you cast your mind towards Kristofer Janson, who still contrives to give an effect of
beauty whatever drivel he may be uttering. There is a pointer
for whoever plays the part. . . . Where can one find a Hedvig?
I don't know. And Mrs. Soerby? She must be beautiful and
witty, *not* vulgar. . . . Gregers is the most difficult part in the
play, from the acting point of view. Sometimes I think Ham-
mer would be best, sometimes Bjoern B. . . . I hope you will
spare me Isachsen, as he always carries on like some strange
actor instead of like an ordinary human being. However, I
suppose he might possibly make something out of Molvik's few
lines. The two servants must not be cast too casually; Pettersen
might possibly be played by Bucher, and Jensen by Abelsted,
if the latter is not required for one of the dinner guests. Yes,
those guests! What about them? You can't just use ordinary
extras; they'd ruin the whole act. . . . This play demands
absolute naturalness and truthfulness both in the ensemble
work and in the staging. The lighting, too, is important; it is
different for each act, and is calculated to establish the particular atmosphere of that act. I just wanted to pass on these
random reflections. As regards everything else, please do as you
think best."

Further evidence of Ibsen's anxiety that his actors should

not overstep the boundary dividing comedy from farce is given in an account by P. A. Rosenberg of a conversation he and some acquaintances had with Ibsen in Copenhagen fourteen years later (April 3, 1898). "Ibsen spoke also of the Royal Theatre's presentation of THE WILD DUCK, of which strangely enough he did not approve. The rest of us were unanimous in praising Bloch's masterly *mise-èn-scene*, Mrs. Henning's enchanting Hedvig, Olaf Poulsen's Old Ekdal and Miss Anthonsen's incomparable Gina. But Ibsen declared it had been played too much for farce. "It must be played as tragicomedy," he said; "otherwise Hedvig's death makes no sense."

As a postscript, one may remark how in THE WILD DUCK, as in almost every play he wrote, Ibsen anticipated one of the main discoveries of modern psychology. "Liberation," he had noted in his preliminary jottings, "consists in securing for individuals the right to free themselves, each according to his particular need." To free *themselves;* how many of Ibsen's contemporaries who regarded themselves as revolutionaries realised that? Ibsen understood that the demand must come from within, and that truth, if it comes from without, is often regarded as an attack on the defensive system which the "life-lie" represents.

M. M.

CHARACTERS

HAAKON WERLE, a wholesale merchant
GREGERS WERLE, his son
OLD EKDAL
HJALMAR EKDAL, his son, a photographer
GINA EKDAL, HJALMAR's wife
HEDVIG, their daughter, aged 14
MRS. SOERBY, housekeeper to HAAKON WERLE
RELLING, a doctor
MOLVIK, sometime student of theology
GRAABERG, a clerk
PETTERSEN, servant to HAAKON WERLE
JENSEN, a hired waiter
A PALE, FLABBY GENTLEMAN
A BALDING GENTLEMAN
A SHORT-SIGHTED GENTLEMAN
SIX OTHER GENTLEMEN, dinner guests of HAAKON WERLE
SEVERAL HIRED WAITERS

The first act takes place in HAAKON WERLE's *house, the remaining acts in* HJALMAR EKDAL's *studio.*

ACT ONE

The home of HAAKON WERLE, *a wholesale merchant. A study, expensively and comfortably furnished; bookcases, upholstered furniture. A desk, with papers and ledgers on it, stands in the middle of the room. Lighted lamps with green shades throw a soft light. In the rear wall folding doors stand open; the curtains across the entrance are drawn aside, and within can be seen a large and elegant room, brilliantly lit by lamps and candelabra. Downstage right in the study a small concealed door leads to the offices. Downstage left, a fireplace with coals glowing in it. Upstage of this a double door leads to the dining room.*

WERLE'S *servant,* PETTERSEN, *in livery, and a hired waiter,* JENSEN, *in black, are arranging the study. In the larger room two or three other hired waiters are moving around putting things in order and lighting more lamps. From the dining room can be heard the buzz of conversation and laughter. Someone taps a knife against a glass; silence; a toast is proposed; cries of "Bravo!"; then the buzz of conversation begins again.*

PETTERSEN *lights a lamp on the mantelpiece above the fireplace, and puts a shade over it.* You hear that, Jensen? Now the old man's at it, proposing a toast to Mrs. Soerby.

JENSEN *moves a chair forward.* Is it true what they say, that there's something between them?

PETTERSEN. I wouldn't know.

JENSEN. They say he's been a regular old billy goat in his time.

PETTERSEN. Could be.

JENSEN. Did you say he's giving this party for his son?

PETTERSEN. Yes. He came home yesterday.

JENSEN. I never knew old Werle had a son.

PETTERSEN. Oh yes, he's got a son. The boy spends all his time up at the sawmill, though, out at Hoydal. He's never set foot in town all the years I've worked in this house.

A HIRED WAITER, *in the doorway to the large room.* Pettersen, there's an old fellow here who wants to—

PETTERSEN, *beneath his breath.* What the devil—oh, not now!

OLD EKDAL *enters from the large room, right. He is wearing a threadbare coat with a high collar, and woollen gloves, and carries a stick and a fur hat in his hand and a brown paper parcel under his arm. He has a dirty, reddish-brown wig and small grey moustaches.*

Goes towards him.

Oh, Jesus! What do *you* want here?

EKDAL, *in the doorway.* Got to get into the office, Pettersen. It's very important.

PETTERSEN. The office has been shut for an hour—

EKDAL. They told me that downstairs, my boy. But Graaberg's still in there. Be a good lad, Pettersen, and let me nip in this way.

Points at the concealed door.

I've been this way before.

PETTERSEN. Oh, all right.

Opens the door.

But make sure you leave by the proper way. We've got company.

EKDAL. Yes, I know that—hm! Thanks, Pettersen, my boy. You're a good pal.

Mutters quietly.

Damn fool!

Goes into the office. PETTERSEN *shuts the door after him.*

JENSEN. Does he work in the office, too?

PETTERSEN. No, he just takes stuff home to copy, when they've more than they can manage. Mind you, he's been quite a gentleman in his time, has old Ekdal.

JENSEN. Yes, he looked as if he might have been around a bit.

PETTERSEN. Oh, yes. He was a lieutenant.

JENSEN. What—him a lieutenant?

PETTERSEN. That's right. But then he went into timber or something of that sort. They say he did the dirty on old Werle once. The two of them used to work together at Hoydal. Oh, I know old Ekdal well. We often have a nip and a bottle of beer together down at Madame Eriksen's.

JENSEN. But he can't have much to spend, surely?

PETTERSEN. I'm the one who does the spending. The way I look at it is, it's only right to lend a helping hand to gentry who've come down in the world.

JENSEN. What, did he go bankrupt?

PETTERSEN. Worse. He went to prison.

JENSEN. Went to prison!

PETTERSEN. Ssh, they're getting up now.

The doors to the dining room are thrown open from inside by waiters. MRS. SOERBY *comes out, engaged in conversation by two gentlemen. A few moments later, the rest of the company follow,* HAAKON WERLE *among them. Last come* HJALMAR EKDAL *and* GREGERS WERLE.

MRS. SOERBY, *as she goes through.* Pettersen, have the coffee served in the music room.

PETTERSEN. Very good, Mrs. Soerby.

She and the two gentlemen go into the large room and out towards the right. PETTERSEN *and* JENSEN *follow them.*

A PALE, FLABBY GENTLEMAN, *to one with little hair.* Whew—that dinner! Pretty exhausting work, eh?

BALDING GENTLEMAN. Ah, it's remarkable what one can get through in three hours, when one puts one's mind to it.

FLABBY GENTLEMAN. Yes, but afterwards, my dear sir! Afterwards!

A THIRD GENTLEMAN. I hear the—er—mocha and maraschino are to be served in the music room.

FLABBY GENTLEMAN. Capital! Then perhaps Mrs. Soerby will play something for us.

BALDING GENTLEMAN, *sotto voce.* Let's hope it isn't a marching song!

FLABBY GENTLEMAN. No fear of that. Berta won't give her old friends the shoulder.

They laugh and pass into the large room.

WERLE, *quietly, unhappily.* I don't think anyone noticed, Gregers.

GREGERS *looks at him.* What?

WERLE. Didn't you notice, either?

GREGERS. Notice what?

WERLE. We were thirteen at table.

GREGERS. Thirteen? Oh, really?

WERLE *glances at* HJALMAR EKDAL. We're usually twelve.

To the others.

Gentlemen—please!

He and the rest, except for HJALMAR *and* GREGERS, *go out upstage right.*

HJALMAR, *who has overheard their conversation.* You shouldn't have invited me, Gregers.

GREGERS. What! But this dinner is said to be in my honour. So why shouldn't I invite my one and only friend?

HJALMAR. I don't think your father approves. I mean, I never get invited to this house.

GREGERS. No, so I've heard. But I had to see you and speak with you; I'm not staying very long, you know. Yes, we've lost touch with each other since we were at school, Hjalmar.

We haven't seen each other for—why, it must be sixteen or seventeen years.

HJALMAR. Is it as long as that?

GREGERS. I'm afraid so. Well, how is everything with you? You look well. You've filled out a bit; you're quite stout now.

HJALMAR. Oh—I wouldn't say stout. I dare say I'm a bit broader across the shoulders than I used to be. After all, I'm a man now.

GREGERS. Oh, yes. You're as handsome as ever.

HJALMAR, *sadly*. But within, Gregers! There has been a change there. You must know how disastrously my world has crashed about me—and my family—since we last met.

GREGERS, *more quietly*. How is your father now?

HJALMAR. My dear friend, let us not talk about it. My poor unfortunate father lives with me, of course. He has no one else in the world to lean on. But all this is so distressing for me to talk about. Tell me now, how have things been for you up at the sawmill?

GREGERS. Oh, I've been wonderfully lonely. I've had plenty of time to brood over things. Come, let's make ourselves comfortable.

He sits in an armchair by the fire and motions HJALMAR *into another beside him.*

HJALMAR, *softly*. Thank you all the same, Gregers. I'm grateful to you for inviting me to your father's house. I know now that you no longer have anything against me.

GREGERS, *amazed*. What makes you think I have anything against you?

HJALMAR. You did at first.

GREGERS. At first?

HJALMAR. After the great disaster. Oh, it was only natural that you should. It was only by a hairsbreadth that your father himself escaped being dragged into all this—this dreadful business.

GREGERS. And I should hold that against you? Who gave you this idea?

HJALMAR. I know—I know you did, Gregers. Your father himself told me so.

GREGERS. Father! I see. Hm. Was that why you never wrote me a line?

HJALMAR. Yes.

GREGERS. Not even when you went and became a photographer?

HJALMAR. Your father said there would be no purpose in my writing to you about anything whatever.

GREGERS, *thoughtfully.* No, no; perhaps he was right. But, tell me, Hjalmar—are you quite satisfied the way things are now?

HJALMAR, *with a little sigh.* Oh yes, indeed I am. I can't complain. At first, you know, I found it a little strange. It was such a different way of life from what I'd been used to. But everything had changed. The great disaster that ruined my father—the disgrace and the shame, Gregers—

GREGERS, *upset.* Yes, yes, of course, yes.

HJALMAR. Naturally, I had to give up any idea of continuing with my studies. We hadn't a shilling to spare—quite the reverse in fact. Debts. Mostly to your father, I believe—

GREGERS. Hm—

HJALMAR. Well, so I thought it'd be best, you see, to make a clean break. Cut myself off from everything that had to do with my old way of life. In fact, it was your father who advised me to do it—and as he was being so very helpful to me—

GREGERS. Father?

HJALMAR. Yes, surely you must know? How else could I have found the money to learn photography and equip a studio and set myself up? That costs a lot of money, you know.

GREGERS. And Father paid for all this?

HJALMAR. Yes, my dear fellow, didn't you know? I understood him to say he'd written to you.

GREGERS. He never said he was behind it. He must have forgotten. We never write to each other except on business. So it was Father—

HJALMAR. Why, yes. He's never wanted people to know about it; but it was he. And of course it was he who made it possible for me to get married. But—perhaps you don't know that either?

GREGERS. I had no idea.

Shakes him by the arm.

But, my dear Hjalmar, I can't tell you how happy I feel—and guilty. Perhaps I've been unjust to Father after all—in some respects. This proves that he has a heart, you see. A kind of conscience—

HJALMAR. Conscience?

GREGERS. Yes, or whatever you like to call it. No, I can't tell you how happy I am to hear this about Father. Well, and you're married, Hjalmar! That's more than I shall ever dare to do. Well, I trust you've found happiness in marriage.

HJALMAR. Oh, indeed I have. She's as capable and good a wife as any man could wish for. And she's not by any means uncultured.

GREGERS, *a little surprised.* I'm sure she isn't.

HJALMAR. Yes. Life is a great teacher. Being with me every day—and we have a couple of very gifted friends who visit us daily. I can assure you, you wouldn't recognise Gina.

GREGERS. Gina?

HJALMAR. Yes, my dear fellow, don't you remember? Her name's Gina.

GREGERS. Whose name is Gina? I have no idea what you're—

HJALMAR. But don't you remember? She used to work here once.

GREGERS *looks at him.* You mean Gina Hansen?

HJALMAR. Of course I mean Gina Hansen.

GREGERS. Who kept house for us when my mother was ill? The year before she died?

HJALMAR. Yes, that's right. But, my dear fellow, I'm absolutely certain your father wrote and told you I'd got married.

GREGERS *has got up.* Yes, he told me that. But what he didn't tell me was that—

Begins to pace up and down.

Ah, but wait a minute. Perhaps he did after all, now I think about it. But Father always writes such brief letters. *Half sits on the arm of his chair.*

Look, tell me now, Hjalmar—this is very funny—how did you come to meet Gina—I mean, your wife?

HJALMAR. Oh, it was quite straightforward. As you know, Gina didn't stay long with your father—everything was so upside down at that time—your mother's illness—it was all too much for Gina, so she gave notice and left. It was the year before your mother died. Or was it the same year?

GREGERS. The same year. And I was up at the sawmill. But then what happened?

HJALMAR. Yes, well, then Gina went home to live with her mother, a Mrs. Hansen, a very excellent hard-working woman who ran a little café. Well, she had a room to let; a very nice, comfortable room.

GREGERS. And you were lucky enough to find out about it?

HJALMAR. Yes—in fact, it was your father who suggested it. And it was there, you see, that I really got to know Gina.

GREGERS. And the engagement followed?

HJALMAR. Yes. Well, you know how quickly young people become fond of each other—hm—

GREGERS *gets up and walks up and down for a little.* Tell me —when you were engaged—was that when Father got you to—I mean, was that when you began to take up photography?

HJALMAR. Yes, that's right. I was very keen to get married as soon as possible. And your father and I both came to the conclusion that photography would be the most convenient profession for me to take up. And Gina thought so too. Oh, and there was another thing. By a lucky chance, Gina had learned how to retouch photographs.

GREGERS. What a fortunate coincidence.

HJALMAR, *pleased, gets up.* Yes, wasn't it? Amazingly lucky, don't you think?

GREGERS. I certainly do. Father seems almost to have been a kind of fairy godfather to you.

HJALMAR, *emotionally.* He did not forget his old friend's son in his time of need. He's got a heart, you see, Gregers.

MRS. SOERBY *enters with* HAAKON WERLE *on her arm.* Not another word, now, Mr. Werle. You mustn't walk around any longer in there with all those bright lights. It's not good for you.

WERLE *lets go of her arm and passes his hand over his eyes.* Yes, I think you may be right.

PETTERSEN *and* JENSEN *enter with trays.*

MRS. SOERBY, *to the guests in the other room.* Gentlemen, please! If anyone wants a glass of punch, he must come in here.

FLABBY GENTLEMAN *comes over to* MRS. SOERBY. Dammit, madame, is it true that you have deprived us of our sacred privilege, the cigar?

MRS. SOERBY. Yes. This is Mr. Werle's sanctum, sir, and here there is no smoking.

BALDING GENTLEMAN. When did you introduce this austere edict, Mrs. Soerby?

MRS. SOERBY. After our last dinner, sir; when certain persons permitted themselves to overstep the mark.

BALDING GENTLEMAN. And it is not permitted to overstep the mark a little, Madame Berta? Not even an inch or two?

MRS. SOERBY. No. Not in any direction, my dear Chamberlain. *Most of the guests have come into the study. The* SERVANTS *hand round glasses of punch.*

HAAKON WERLE, *to* HJALMAR, *who is standing apart, by a table.* What's that you're looking at, Ekdal?

HJALMAR. It's only an album, sir.

BALDING GENTLEMAN, *who is wandering around*. Ah, photographs! Yes, that's rather down your street, isn't it?

FLABBY GENTLEMAN, *in an armchair*. Haven't you brought any of your own with you?

HJALMAR. No, I haven't.

FLABBY GENTLEMAN. You should have. It's so good for the digestion to sit and look at pictures.

BALDING GENTLEMAN. Adds to the fun. We've each got to contribute our mite, haven't we?

A SHORT-SIGHTED GENTLEMAN. All contributions will be gratefully received.

MRS. SOERBY. I think the gentlemen mean that if one is invited out one should work for one's dinner, Mr. Ekdal.

FLABBY GENTLEMAN. Where the table is so exquisite, that duty becomes a pleasure.

BALDING GENTLEMAN. Yes, by God! Particularly when it's a question of fighting for survival—

MRS. SOERBY. *Touché!*

They continue amid joking and laughter.

GREGERS, *quietly*. You must join in, Hjalmar.

HJALMAR *twists uncomfortably*. What should I talk about?

FLABBY GENTLEMAN. Wouldn't you agree, Mr. Werle, that Tokay may be regarded as a comparatively safe drink for the stomach?

WERLE, *by the fireplace*. I'd guarantee the Tokay you drank tonight, anyway. It's an exceptional year, quite exceptional. But of course you would have noticed that.

FLABBY GENTLEMAN. Yes, it had a remarkably *soigné* bouquet.

HJALMAR, *uncertainly*. Is there some difference between the various years?

FLABBY GENTLEMAN *laughs*. I say, that's good!

WERLE *smiles*. It's a waste to offer you good wine.

BALDING GENTLEMAN. Tokay's like photography, Mr. Ekdal. It needs sunshine. Isn't that right?

HJALMAR. Oh yes, light is important, of course.

MRS. SOERBY. But that's like you, gentlemen. You're drawn towards the sun, too.

BALDING GENTLEMAN. For shame! That's not worthy of you.

SHORT-SIGHTED GENTLEMAN. Mrs. Soerby is displaying her wit.

FLABBY GENTLEMAN. At our expense.

Threateningly.

Oh, madame, madame!

MRS. SOERBY. But it's perfectly true. Vintages do differ greatly. The oldest are the best.

SHORT-SIGHTED GENTLEMAN. Do you count me among the old ones?

MRS. SOERBY. By no means.

BALDING GENTLEMAN. Indeed? And what about me, dear Mrs. Soerby?

FLABBY GENTLEMAN. Yes, and me. What vintage are we?

MRS. SOERBY. A sweet vintage, gentlemen!

She sips a glass of punch. The GENTLEMEN *laugh and flirt with her.*

WERLE. Mrs. Soerby always finds a way out—when she wants to. Fill your glasses, gentlemen! Pettersen, look after them. Gregers, let us take a glass together.

GREGERS *does not move.*

Won't you join us, Ekdal? I didn't get a chance to drink with you at dinner.

GRAABERG, *the bookkeeper, looks in through the concealed door.*

GRAABERG *to* HAAKON WERLE. Excuse me, sir, but I can't get out.

WERLE. What, have you got locked in again?

GRAABERG. Yes. Flakstad's gone off with the keys.

WERLE. Well, you'd better come through here, then.

GRAABERG. But there's someone else—

WERLE. Well, let him come, too. Don't be frightened.

GRAABERG and OLD EKDAL *come out of the office.*

Involuntarily.

Oh, God!

The laughter and chatter of the GUESTS *dies away.* HJALMAR *shrinks at the sight of his father, puts down his glass and turns away towards the fireplace.*

EKDAL *does not look up, but makes little bows to either side as he walks, mumbling.* Beg pardon. Come the wrong way. Door locked. Beg pardon.

He and GRAABERG *go out upstage right.*

WERLE, *between his teeth.* Damn that Graaberg!

GREGERS *stares open-mouthed at* HJALMAR. Surely that wasn't—?

FLABBY GENTLEMAN. What's all this? Who was that?

GREGERS. Oh, no one. Just the bookkeeper and someone else.

SHORT-SIGHTED GENTLEMAN, *to* HJALMAR. Did you know that man?

HJALMAR. I don't know—I didn't notice—

FLABBY GENTLEMAN *gets up.* What the devil's going on?

He goes over to some of the others, who are talking quietly amongst themselves.

MRS. SOERBY *whispers to* PETTERSEN. Take something out to him. Something really nice.

PETTERSEN *nods.* Very good, ma'am.

Goes out.

GREGERS, *quietly, emotionally, to* HJALMAR. Then it *was* he!

HJALMAR. Yes.

GREGERS. And you stood here and denied him!

HJALMAR *whispers violently.* What could I do?

GREGERS. You denied your own father?

HJALMAR, *in pain.* Oh—if you were in my place, you'd—

The talk among the GUESTS, *which has been carried on in a low tone, now switches over to a forced loudness.*

BALDING GENTLEMAN *goes amiably over to* HJALMAR *and* GREGERS. Hullo, reviving old college memories, what? Don't you smoke, Mr. Ekdal? Want a light? Oh, I'd forgotten—we mustn't—

HJALMAR. Thank you, I won't.

FLABBY GENTLEMAN. Haven't you some nice little poem you could recite to us, Mr. Ekdal? You used to recite so beautifully.

HJALMAR. I'm afraid I can't remember one.

FLABBY GENTLEMAN. Pity. What else can we find to amuse ourselves with, Balle?

The TWO GENTLEMEN *walk into the next room.*

HJALMAR, *unhappily.* Gregers, I want to go. You know, when a man has been as buffeted and tossed by the winds of Fate as I have— Say good-bye to your father for me.

GREGERS. I will. Are you going straight home?

HJALMAR. Yes?

GREGERS. In that case I may drop in on you later.

HJALMAR. No, don't do that. You mustn't come to my home. It's a miserable place, Gregers; especially after a brilliant gathering like this. We can always meet somewhere in town.

MRS. SOERBY *has come over to them, and says quietly.* Are you leaving, Ekdal?

HJALMAR. Yes.

MRS. SOERBY. Give my regards to Gina.

HJALMAR. Thank you.

MRS. SOERBY. Tell her I'm coming out to see her one of these days.

HJALMAR. I will. Thank you.

To GREGERS.

Stay here. I don't want anyone to see me go.

Saunters into the other room and out to the right.

MRS. SOERBY, *to* PETTERSEN, *who has returned.* Well, did you give the old man something?

PETTERSEN. Yes, I put a bottle of brandy into his pocket.

MRS. SOERBY. Oh, you might have found him something nicer than that.

PETTERSEN. Why no, Mrs. Soerby. Brandy's what he likes best.

FLABBY GENTLEMAN, *in the doorway, with a sheet of music in his hand.* Shall we play a duet together, Mrs. Soerby?

MRS. SOERBY. Yes, with pleasure.

GUESTS. Bravo, bravo!

She and all the GUESTS *go out to the right.* GREGERS *remains standing by the fireplace.* HAAKON WERLE *starts looking for something on his desk, and seems to wish that* GREGERS *would go. Seeing that* GREGERS *does not move, he goes towards the door.*

GREGERS. Father, would you mind waiting a moment?

WERLE *stops.* What is it?

GREGERS. I've got to speak with you.

WERLE. Can't it wait till we're alone together?

GREGERS. No, it can't. We may never be alone together.

WERLE *comes closer.* What does that mean?

During the following scene, piano music can be heard distantly from the music room.

GREGERS. How has that family been allowed to sink into this pitiable condition?

WERLE. You mean the Ekdals, I presume?

GREGERS. Yes, I mean the Ekdals. Lieutenant Ekdal and you used to be such close friends.

WERLE. Unfortunately, yes. Too close. All these years I've had to pay for it. It's him I have to thank for the stain I have suffered on my name and reputation.

GREGERS, *quietly.* Was he really the only one who was guilty?

WERLE. Who else?

GREGERS. You and he bought those forests together.

WERLE. But it was Ekdal who drew up that misleading map. It was he who had all that timber felled illegally on government property. He was in charge of everything up there. I was absolutely in the dark as to what Lieutenant Ekdal was doing.

GREGERS. Lieutenant Ekdal seems to have been pretty much in the dark himself.

WERLE. Quite possibly. But the fact remains that he was found guilty and I was acquitted.

GREGERS. Oh yes, I know nothing was proved against you.

WERLE. An acquittal means not guilty. Why do you rake up these old troubles, which turned me grey before my time? Is that what you've been brooding about all these years up there? I can assure you, Gregers, in this town the whole business has been forgotten long ago, as far as my reputation is concerned.

GREGERS. But what about those wretched Ekdals?

WERLE. What would you have had me do for them? When Ekdal was released he was a broken man, past help. There are some people in this world who sink to the bottom the moment they get a couple of pellets in their body, and never rise to the surface again. Upon my honour, Gregers, I did everything I could short of exposing myself to gossip and suspicion—

GREGERS. Suspicion? Oh, I see.

WERLE. I've arranged for Ekdal to do copying for the office, and I pay him a great deal more than the work's worth—

GREGERS, *without looking at him*. I don't doubt it.

WERLE. You laugh? You don't think it's true? Oh, you won't find anything about it in the books. I don't keep account of that kind of payment.

GREGERS *smiles coldly*. No, there are certain payments of which it's best to keep no account.

WERLE. What do you mean by that?

GREGERS, *screwing up his courage.* Have you any account of what it cost you to have Hjalmar Ekdal taught photography?

WERLE. Why should I have any account of that?

GREGERS. I know now that it was you who paid for it. And I also know that it was you who so generously enabled him to set himself up.

WERLE. And still you say I've done nothing for the Ekdals? I can assure you, that family's cost me a pretty penny.

GREGERS. Have you accounted any of those pennies in your books?

WERLE. Why do you ask that?

GREGERS. Oh, I have my reasons. Tell me—when you began to take such a warm interest in your old friend's son—wasn't that just about the time he was about to get married?

WERLE. Yes, how the devil—how do you expect me to remember after all these years—?

GREGERS. You wrote me a letter at the time—a business letter, of course—and in a postscript you said—quite briefly—that Hjalmar Ekdal had married a Miss Hansen.

WERLE. Yes, so he did. That was her name.

GREGERS. But what you didn't say was that this Miss Hansen was Gina Hansen—our former maid.

WERLE *laughs scornfully, but with an effort.* No. It didn't occur to me that you were particularly interested in our former maid.

GREGERS. I wasn't. But—

Lowers his voice.

—there was someone else in this house who was interested in her.

WERLE. What do you mean?

Angrily.

You're not referring to me?

GREGERS, *quietly but firmly.* Yes, I am referring to you.

WERLE. You dare to—you have the impertinence—! That ungrateful—that photographer—how dare he make such insinuations!

GREGERS. Hjalmar has never said a word about this. I don't think he suspects anything.

WERLE. Where do you get it from, then? Who has said such a thing to you?

GREGERS. My unhappy mother told me. The last time I saw her.

WERLE. Your mother! I might have known it. She and you always clung together. She turned you against me from the first.

GREGERS. No. It was all the suffering and humiliation she had to endure before she finally succumbed and came to such a pitiful end.

WERLE. Oh, she didn't have to suffer. Not more than most people, anyway. But one can't do anything with people who are oversensitive and romantic. I've learned that much. And you nurse these suspicions and go around rooting up all kinds of old rumours and slanders about your own father! At your age, Gregers, it's time you found something more useful to do.

GREGERS. Yes, it's about time.

WERLE. It might enable you to be a little more at peace with yourself than you seem to be now. What good can it do for you to stay up at the sawmill, year after year, drudging away like a common clerk and refusing to accept a penny more than the standard wage? It's absolutely idiotic.

GREGERS. I wish I was sure of that.

WERLE. I understand how you feel. You want to be independent, you don't want to be in my debt. But now there is an opportunity for you to become independent, and be your own master in everything.

GREGERS. Oh? How?

WERLE. When I wrote and told you it was necessary for you to travel here at once—hm—

GREGERS. Yes, what do you want me for? I've been waiting all day to find out.

WERLE. I want to suggest that you become a partner in the firm.

GREGERS. I? Your partner?

WERLE. Yes. It wouldn't mean we'd have to be together all the time. You could take over the business here, and I'd move up to the mill.

GREGERS. You?

WERLE. Yes. You see, I'm not able to work as hard as I used to. I've got to take care of my eyes, Gregers. They've begun to grow a little weak.

GREGERS. They always were.

WERLE. Not like now. Besides—circumstances might make it desirable for me to live up there. For a while, anyway.

GREGERS. I hadn't imagined anything like this.

WERLE. Listen, Gregers. I know there are so many things that stand between us. But we're father and son. It seems to me we must be able to come to an understanding.

GREGERS. You mean, we must appear to come to an understanding?

WERLE. Well, that is something. Think it over, Gregers. Don't you think it might be possible? Well?

GREGERS *looks at him coldly.* What's behind all this?

WERLE. How do you mean?

GREGERS. You want to use me, don't you?

WERLE. In a relationship as close as ours, one can always be useful to the other.

GREGERS. That's what they say.

WERLE. I should like to have you living at home with me for a while. I'm a lonely man, Gregers. I've always felt lonely, all my life, but especially now that I'm growing old. I need to have someone near me—

GREGERS. You've got Mrs. Soerby.

WERLE. Yes; I have her. And she's become—well, almost indispensable to me. She's witty and good-humoured; she brightens the house for me. I need that—badly.

GREGERS. Well, then you have things the way you want them.

WERLE. Yes, but I'm afraid it can't continue like this. A woman in her situation may easily find herself compromised in the eyes of the world. Yes; and I dare say it's not very good for a man's reputation, either.

GREGERS. Oh, when a man gives dinners like this, he needn't worry about what people think.

WERLE. Yes, but what about her, Gregers? I'm afraid she won't want to put up with this for much longer. And even if she did—even if, for my sake, she were to set herself above the gossip and the slander— Don't you think then, Gregers—you with your stern sense of right and wrong—that—?

GREGERS *interrupts*. Answer me one thing. Are you thinking of marrying her?

WERLE. Suppose I were? Would you be so insuperably opposed to that?

GREGERS. Not in the least.

WERLE. I didn't know if perhaps—out of respect to your late mother's memory—

GREGERS. I'm not a romantic.

WERLE. Well, whatever you are, you've taken a great weight from my mind. I'm delighted that I may count on your agreement to the action I propose to take.

GREGERS *looks at him*. Now I see what you want to use me for.

WERLE. Use you? What kind of talk is that?

GREGERS. Oh, let's not be squeamish. Not when we're alone together.

Gives a short laugh.

I see. So that's why, at all costs, I had to come along and show myself here. So as to have a nice family reunion in Mrs. Soerby's honour. Father and son—*tableau!* That's something new, isn't it?

WERLE. How dare you take that tone?

GREGERS. When has there been any family life here? Not for as long as I can remember. But now of course there's got to be a little. It'll look splendid if people can say that the son of the family has flown home on the wings of filial piety to attend his ageing father's wedding feast. What'll become then of all those dreadful rumours about the wrongs his poor dead mother had to put up with? They will vanish. Her son will dissipate them into thin air.

WERLE. Gregers—I believe there's no one in the world you hate as much as you do me.

GREGERS, *quietly*. I've seen you at close quarters.

WERLE. You have seen me with your mother's eyes.

Lowers his voice a little.

But you should remember that her vision was sometimes a little—blurred.

GREGERS, *trembling*. I know what you're trying to say. But who was to blame for that? You were! You and all those—! And the last of them you palmed off on to Hjalmar Ekdal, when you no longer—oh!

WERLE *shrugs his shoulders*. Word for word as though I were listening to your mother.

GREGERS, *not heeding him*. And there he sits, childlike and trusting, caught in this web of deceit—sharing his roof with a woman like that, never suspecting that what he calls his home is built upon a lie!

Comes a step closer.

When I look back on your career, I see a battlefield strewn with shattered lives.

WERLE. It seems the gulf between us is too wide.

GREGERS *bows coldly*. I agree. Therefore I take my hat and go.

WERLE. Go? Leave the house?

GREGERS. Yes. Because now at last I see my vocation.

WERLE. And what is that vocation?

GREGERS. You'd only laugh if I told you.

WERLE. A lonely man does not laugh easily, Gregers.

GREGERS *points upstage*. Look, Father. The gentlemen are

playing blind man's buff with Mrs. Soerby. Good night, and
good-bye.

*He goes out upstage right. Sounds of laughter and merri-
ment are heard from the* GUESTS, *as they come into sight in
the other room.*

WERLE *mutters scornfully after* GREGERS. Hm! Poor wretch!
And he says he's not a romantic!

ACT TWO

HJALMAR EKDAL's *studio. It is quite a large room, and is evidently an attic. To the right is a sloping ceiling containing large panes of glass, which are half covered by a blue curtain. In the corner upstage right is the front door. Downstage of this is a door to the living room. In the left-hand wall are two more doors, with an iron stove between them. In the rear wall are broad double sliding doors. The studio is humbly but comfortably furnished. Between the doors on the right, a little away from the wall, stands a sofa, with a table and some chairs. On the table is a lighted lamp, with a shade. In the corner by the stove is an old armchair. Here and there, various pieces of photographic apparatus are set up. Against the rear wall, to the left of the sliding doors, is a bookcase, containing some books, boxes, bottles containing chemicals, various tools, instruments and other objects. Photographs and small articles such as brushes, sheets of paper and so forth, lie on the table.*

GINA EKDAL *is seated on a chair at the table, sewing.* HEDVIG *is seated on the sofa with her hands shading her eyes and her thumbs in her ears, reading a book.*

GINA *glances at her a couple of times, as though with secret anxiety.* Hedvig!

HEDVIG *does not hear.* GINA *repeats more loudly.*

Hedvig!

HEDVIG *drops her hands and looks up.* Yes, Mother?

GINA. Hedvig darling, don't read any more.

HEDVIG. Oh, but Mother, can't I go on a little longer? Just a little?

GINA. No, no; put the book away. Your father doesn't like it. He never reads in the evenings.

HEDVIG *closes the book.* No, Father doesn't bother much about reading, does he?

GINA *puts down her sewing and picks up a pencil and a small notebook from the table.* Can you remember how much we paid for that butter?

HEDVIG. One crown sixty-five öre.

GINA. That's right.

Makes a note of it.

It's shocking how much butter gets eaten in this house. Then there was the sausages, and the cheese—let me see—

Writes.

And the ham—hm—

Adds it up.

Mm, that makes nearly—

HEDVIG. Don't forget the beer.

GINA. Oh yes, of course.

Writes.

It mounts up. But we've got to have it.

HEDVIG. But you and I didn't have to have a proper meal this evening, as Father was out.

GINA. Yes; that helped. Oh, and I got eight and a half crowns for those photographs.

HEDVIG. I say! As much as that?

GINA. Exactly eight and a half crowns.

Silence. GINA *takes up her sewing again.* HEDVIG *picks up a pencil and paper and starts to draw, her left hand shading her eyes.*

HEDVIG. Isn't it lovely to think of Father being invited by Mr. Werle to that big dinner?

GINA. He wasn't invited by Mr. Werle. It was his son who sent the invitation.

Short pause.

You know we've nothing to do with Mr. Werle.

HEDVIG. I'm so looking forward to Father coming home. He promised he'd ask Mrs. Soerby for something nice to bring me.

GINA. Yes, there's never any shortage of nice things in that house.

HEDVIG, *still drawing.* I think I'm beginning to get a bit hungry.

OLD EKDAL, *his package of papers under his arm and another parcel in his coat pocket, comes in through the front door.*

GINA. Hullo, Grandfather, you're very late tonight.

EKDAL. They'd shut the office. Graaberg kept me waiting. I had to go through the—hm.

HEDVIG. Did they give you anything new to copy, Grandfather?

EKDAL. All this. Look!

GINA. Well, that's good.

HEDVIG. And you've another parcel in your pocket.

EKDAL. Have I? Oh, nonsense—that's nothing.

Puts down his stick in a corner.

This'll keep me busy for a long time, this will, Gina.

Slides one of the doors in the rear wall a little to one side. Ssh!

Looks inside for a moment, then closes the door again carefully.

He, he! They're all asleep. And she's lied down in her basket. He, he!

HEDVIG. Are you sure she won't be cold in that basket, Grandfather?

EKDAL. What an idea! Cold? With all that straw?

Goes towards the door upstage left.

Are there any matches?

GINA. They're on the chest-of-drawers.

EKDAL *goes into his room.*

HEDVIG. Isn't it splendid Grandfather getting all that stuff to copy again, after so long?

GINA. Yes, poor old Father. It'll mean a bit of pocket money for him.

HEDVIG. And he won't be able to spend all morning down at that horrid Mrs. Eriksen's restaurant, will he?

GINA. Yes, there's that too.

Short silence.

HEDVIG. Do you think they're still sitting at table?

GINA. God knows. It wouldn't surprise me.

HEDVIG. Think of all that lovely food Father's getting to eat! I'm sure he'll be in a good humour when he comes back. Don't you think, Mother?

GINA. Oh, yes. But if only we were able to tell him we'd managed to let that room.

HEDVIG. But we don't have to worry about *that* tonight.

GINA. It wouldn't do any harm. It's no use to us standing empty.

HEDVIG. No, I mean we don't have to worry about it because Father'll be jolly anyway. It'll be better if we can save the news about the room for another time.

GINA *glances across at her.* Does it make you happy to have good news to tell Father when he comes home in the evening?

HEDVIG. Yes, it makes things more cheerful here.

GINA. Yes, there's something in that.

OLD EKDAL *comes in again and goes towards the door downstage left.*

Half turns in her chair.

Do you want something out of the kitchen, Grandfather?

EKDAL. Er—yes, yes. Don't get up.

Goes out.

GINA. He's not messing about with the fire, is he?

Waits a moment.

Hedvig, go and see what he's up to.

EKDAL *returns with a little jug of steaming water.*

HEDVIG. Are you getting some hot water, Grandfather?

EKDAL. Yes, I am. Need it for something. Got some writing to do; and the ink's like porridge—hm!

GINA. But, Grandfather, you should eat your supper first. I've put it in there for you.

EKDAL. Can't be bothered with supper, Gina. I'm busy, I tell you. I don't want anyone to disturb me. Not anyone—hm!

He goes into his room. GINA *and* HEDVIG *look at each other.*

GINA, *quietly.* Where do you think he's got the money from?

HEDVIG. From Graaberg, I suppose.

GINA. No, he can't have. Graaberg always sends the money to me.

HEDVIG. He must have got a bottle on tick somewhere, then.

GINA. Poor Grandfather! No one'll give him anything on credit.

HJALMAR EKDAL, *wearing an overcoat and a grey felt hat, enters right.*

GINA *drops her sewing and gets up.*

Why, Hjalmar, are you here already?

HEDVIG, *simultaneously, jumping to her feet.* Oh Father, fancy your coming back so soon!

HJALMAR *takes off his hat.* Yes, well, most of them had begun to leave.

HEDVIG. As early as this?

HJALMAR. Yes. It was a dinner party, you know.

Begins to take off his overcoat.

GINA. Let me help you.

HEDVIG. Me too.

They take off his coat. GINA *hangs it up on the rear wall.*
Were there many people there, Father?

HJALMAR. Oh no, not many. We were, oh, twelve or fourteen at table.

GINA. And you talked to them all?

HJALMAR. Oh yes, a little. But Gregers monopolised me most of the time.

GINA. Is he still as ugly as ever?

HJALMAR. Well, he's not very much to look at. Hasn't the old man come home?

HEDVIG. Yes, Grandfather's in his room, writing.

HJALMAR. Did he say anything?

GINA. No, what should he say?

HJALMAR. Didn't he mention anything about—? I thought I heard someone say he'd been up to see Graaberg. I'll go in and have a word with him.

GINA. No, no—don't.

HJALMAR. Why not? Did he say he didn't want to see me?

GINA. I don't think he wants to see anyone this evening.

HEDVIG *makes signs to* HJALMAR. GINA *does not notice.*

He's been out and fetched some hot water.

HJALMAR. Oh. He's—?

GINA. Yes.

HJALMAR. Dear God! Poor old Father! Bless his white hairs! Let him have his little pleasure.

OLD EKDAL, *wearing a dressing gown and smoking a pipe, enters from his room.*

EKDAL. So you're home? I thought I heard your voice.

HJALMAR. Yes, I've just got back.

EKDAL. You didn't see me, did you?

HJALMAR. No. But they said you'd been through, and so I thought I'd follow you.

EKDAL. Hm. Decent of you, Hjalmar. Who were all those people?

HJALMAR. Oh, all sorts. There was Mr. Flor—the Chamberlain—and Mr. Balle—he's one, too—and so's Mr. Kaspersen—

and Mr.—what's his name, I don't remember what they were all called—

EKDAL *nods.* You hear that, Gina? People from the palace—and Hjalmar!

GINA. Yes, they're very grand up there nowadays.

HEDVIG. Did the Chamberlains sing, Father? Or recite anything?

HJALMAR. No, they just chattered. They tried to get me to recite something. But I said: "No."

EKDAL. You said "No," did you?

GINA. Oh, you might have obliged them.

HJALMAR. No. One can't go round pandering to everyone.

Begins to walk up and down the room.

I won't, anyway.

EKDAL. No, no. You won't get round Hjalmar as easily as that.

HJALMAR. I don't see why *I* should have to provide the entertainment on the few occasions when I go out to enjoy myself. Let the others do some work for a change. Those fellows go from one dinner table to the next stuffing themselves every night. Let them work for their food and drink.

GINA. You didn't say all this?

HJALMAR *hums to himself.* I gave them a piece of my mind.

EKDAL. You said this to their faces?

HJALMAR. Could be.

Nonchalantly.

Afterwards we had a little altercation about Tokay.

EKDAL. Tokay, did you say? That's a fine wine.

HJALMAR *stops walking.* It *can* be a fine wine. But, let me tell you, all vintages are not equally fine. It depends on how much sunshine the grapes have had.

GINA. Oh, Hjalmar! You know about everything!

EKDAL. And they tried to argue about that?

HJALMAR. They tried. But they soon learned that it's the same as with Chamberlains. All vintages are not equally fine.

GINA. The things you think of!

EKDAL *chuckles.* He, he! And they had to put that in their pipes and smoke it?

HJALMAR. Yes. It was said straight to their faces.

EKDAL. You hear that, Gina? He said it straight to the Chamberlains' faces.

GINA. Just fancy! Straight to their faces!

HJALMAR. Yes, but I don't want it talked about. One doesn't repeat such things. It was all very friendly, of course. They're decent, friendly people. Why should I hurt them?

EKDAL. But straight to their faces!

HEDVIG, *trying to please him.* What fun it is to see you in tails! You look splendid in tails, Father!

HJALMAR. Yes, I do, don't I? And it fits me perfectly; almost as though it had been made for me. Just a little tight under the arms, perhaps. Give me a hand, Hedvig.

Takes them off.

I think I'll put my jacket on. Where's my jacket, Gina?

GINA. Here it is.

Brings the jacket and helps him on with it.

HJALMAR. That's better! Don't forget to let Molvik have the tails back tomorrow morning.

GINA *puts them away.* I'll see he gets them.

HJALMAR *stretches.* Ah, now I feel more at home. Loose-fitting clothes suit my figure better. Don't you think, Hedvig?

HEDVIG. Yes, Father.

HJALMAR. When I loosen my tie so that the ends flow like this— Look! What do you think of that?

HEDVIG. Oh yes, that looks very good with your moustache and those big curls of yours.

HJALMAR. I wouldn't call them curls. Waves.

HEDVIG. Yes, they're such big curls.

HJALMAR. They are waves.

HEDVIG, *after a moment, tugs his jacket.* Father!

HJALMAR. Well, what is it?

HEDVIG. Oh, you know quite well what it is.

HJALMAR. No, I don't. Really.

HEDVIG *laughs and whimpers.* Oh yes, you do, Father. You mustn't tease me!

HJALMAR. But what *is* it?

HEDVIG. Oh, stop it! Give it to me, Father! You know! All those nice things you promised me!

HJALMAR. Oh, dear! Fancy my forgetting that!

HEDVIG. Oh, no, you're only teasing, Father! Oh, it's beastly of you! Where have you hidden it?

HJALMAR. No, honestly, I forgot. But wait a moment! I've something else for you, Hedvig.

Goes over to the tails and searches in the pockets.

HEDVIG *jumps and claps her hands.* Oh, Mother, Mother!

GINA. There, you see. Just be patient, and—

HJALMAR *holds out a card.* Look, here it is.

HEDVIG. That? That's only a piece of paper.

HJALMAR. It's the menu, Hedvig. The whole menu. Look here. It says *Déjeuner.* That means menu.

HEDVIG. Is that all?

HJALMAR. Well, I forgot the other things. But believe me, Hedvig, they're not much fun really, all those sickly sweet things. Sit over there at the table and read this menu, and then I'll describe to you how each dish tasted. Here you are, now, Hedvig.

HEDVIG *swallows her tears.* Thank you.

She sits down but does not read. GINA *makes a sign to her.* HJALMAR *notices.*

HJALMAR *starts walking up and down.* Really, it's incredible the things a breadwinner's expected to remember. If one forgets the slightest little thing, there are sour faces all round one. Well, one gets used to it.

Stops by the stove, where OLD EKDAL *is sitting.*

Have you looked in there this evening, Father?

EKDAL. Yes, of course I have. She's gone into the basket.

HJALMAR. Gone into the basket, has she? She's beginning to get used to it, then.

EKDAL. What did I tell you? Well, now, you see, there are one or two little—

HJALMAR. Little improvements, yes.

EKDAL. We've got to have them, Hjalmar.

HJALMAR. Yes. Let's have a word about those improvements, Father. Come along, let's sit on the sofa.

EKDAL. Yes, let's. Er—I think I'll fill my pipe first. Oh, I'd better clean it, too. Hm.

Goes into his room.

GINA *smiles at* HJALMAR. Clean his pipe!

HJALMAR. Oh, Gina, let him. Poor, shipwrecked old man! Yes, those improvements—I'd better get them done tomorrow.

GINA. But you won't have time tomorrow, Hjalmar.

HEDVIG *interrupts.* Oh, yes, he will, Mother!

GINA. Don't forget those prints have to be retouched. They've sent for them so many times.

HJALMAR. Oh, are you on about those prints again? They'll be ready. Have there been any new orders at all?

GINA. No, I'm afraid not. I've nothing tomorrow but those two portraits I told you about.

HJALMAR. Is that all? Well, if one doesn't put one's mind to it—

GINA. But what can I do? I advertise as much as I can—

HJALMAR. Advertise, advertise! You see what good that does. I don't suppose anyone's come to look at the room either?

GINA. No, not yet.

HJALMAR. I might have known it. If one doesn't bother to keep one's eyes and ears open— One must try to make an ' effort, Gina.

HEDVIG *goes towards him.* Can I bring your flute, Father?

HJALMAR. No. No flute. *I* don't need the pleasures of this world.

Starts walking again.

Yes, I'm going to work tomorrow. Don't you worry about that. I'll work as long as there's strength in these arms—

GINA. But my dear Hjalmar, I didn't mean it like that.

HEDVIG. Father, would you like a bottle of beer?

HJALMAR. Certainly not. I want nothing of anyone.

Stops.

Beer? Did you say beer?

HEDVIG, *alive.* Yes, Father. Lovely, cool beer.

HJALMAR. Well—if you want to, bring in a bottle.

GINA. Yes, do. That's a nice idea.

HEDVIG *runs towards the kitchen door.*

HJALMAR, *by the stove, stops her, looks at her, takes her head in his hands and presses her to him.* Hedvig! Hedvig!

HEDVIG, *happy, crying.* Oh, dear, kind, Father!

HJALMAR. No, don't call me that. I have been eating at the rich man's table. Gorging my belly at the groaning board. And yet I could—

GINA, *sitting at the table.* Oh, nonsense, nonsense, Hjalmar.

HJALMAR. It's true. But you mustn't judge me too harshly. You know I love you both. In spite of everything—

HEDVIG *throws her arms round him.* And we love you very, very much, Father.

HJALMAR. And if I should, once in a while, be unreasonable— dear God!—remember that I am a man besieged by a host of sorrows. Oh, well.

Dries her eyes.

This is not the moment for beer. Give me my flute.

HEDVIG *runs to the bookcase and fetches it.*

Thank you. Ah, this is better. With my flute in my hand, and you two by my side—ah!

HEDVIG *sits at the table by* GINA. HJALMAR *walks up and*

down, then begins to play a Bohemian folk dance, with spirit, in a slow and mournful tempo, and sensitively. Stops playing, stretches out his left hand to GINA *and says emotionally.*

Life may be poor and humble under our roof. But it is home. And I tell you, Gina—it is good to be here.

He begins to play again.

After a few moments, there is a knock on the front door.

GINA *gets up.* Hush, Hjalmar. I think there's someone at the door.

HJALMAR *puts the flute away in the bookcase.* Oh, here we go again.

GREGERS WERLE, *outside on the landing.* Excuse me, but—

GINA *starts back slightly.* Oh!

GREGERS. Doesn't Mr. Ekdal live here? The photographer.

GINA. Yes, he does.

HJALMAR *goes over to the door.* Gregers! Are you here? Well, you'd better come in.

GREGERS *enters.* But I told you I'd visit you.

HJALMAR. But—tonight? Have you left the party?

GREGERS. Yes. I have left the party. And my home, too. Good evening, Mrs. Ekdal. I don't suppose you recognise me?

GINA. Why, yes, Mr. Gregers. I recognise you.

GREGERS. Yes. I'm like my mother. And I've no doubt you remember her.

HJALMAR. Did you say you had left your father's house?

GREGERS. Yes. I've moved to a hotel.

HJALMAR. Oh, I see. Well, since you've come, take off your coat and sit down.

GREGERS. Thank you.

He takes off his coat. He has changed into a simple grey suit of a provincial cut.

HJALMAR. Here, on the sofa. Make yourself comfortable.

GREGERS *sits on the sofa,* HJALMAR *on a chair by the table.*

GREGERS *looks around.* So this is it, Hjalmar. This is where you live.

HJALMAR. This room is my studio, as you see.

GINA. We usually sit here, because there's more space.

HJALMAR. We had a nicer place before, but this apartment has one great advantage. The bedrooms—

GINA. And we've a spare room on the other side of the passage that we can let.

GREGERS *to* HJALMAR. Oh, I see. You take lodgers as well?

HJALMAR. No, not yet. It takes time, you know. One's got to keep one's eyes and ears open.

To HEDVIG.

Let's have that beer now.

HEDVIG *nods and goes out into the kitchen.*

GREGERS. So that's your daughter?

HJALMAR. Yes, that is Hedvig.

GREGERS. Your only child?

HJALMAR. Yes, she is the only one. Our greatest joy.

Drops his voice.

And also our greatest sorrow, Gregers.

GREGERS. What do you mean?

HJALMAR. There is a grave risk that she may lose her eyesight.

GREGERS. Go blind?

HJALMAR. Yes. As yet there are only the first symptoms, and she may be all right for some while. But the doctor has warned us. It will happen in the end.

GREGERS. What a terrible tragedy. What's the cause?

HJALMAR *sighs.* It's probably hereditary.

GREGERS *starts.* Hereditary?

GINA. Hjalmar's mother had weak eyes, too.

HJALMAR. So my father says. Of course, I can't remember.

GREGERS. Poor child. And how does she take it?

HJALMAR. Oh, you don't imagine we have the heart to tell

her? She suspects nothing. Carefree and gay, singing like a
little bird, she will fly into the night.

Overcome.

Oh, it will be the death of me, Gregers.

HEDVIG *brings a tray with beer and glasses, and sets it on
the table.* HJALMAR *strokes her head.*

Thank you, Hedvig.

She puts her arm round his neck and whispers in his ear.

No, no sandwiches now.

Glances at GREGERS.

Unless you'd like some, Gregers?

GREGERS. No, no, thank you.

HJALMAR, *still melancholy.* Well, you might bring a few in,
anyway. A crust will be enough for me. Put plenty of butter
on it, mind.

HEDVIG *nods happily and goes back into the kitchen.*

GREGERS *follows her with his eyes.* She looks quite strong and
healthy, apart from that, I think.

GINA. Yes, there's nothing else the matter with her, thank God.

GREGERS. She's going to look very like you, Mrs. Ekdal. How
old would she be now?

GINA. Almost exactly fourteen. It's her birthday the day after
tomorrow.

GREGERS. Quite big for her age.

GINA. Yes, she's certainly shot up this last year.

GREGERS. Seeing these young people grow up makes one realise
how old one's getting oneself. How long have you two been
married now?

GINA. We've been married—er—yes, nearly fifteen years.

GREGERS. Good Lord, is it as long as that?

GINA, *suddenly alert; looks at him.* Yes, that's right.

HJALMAR. It certainly is. Fifteen years, all but a few months.
Changes his tone.

They must have seemed long to you, those years up at the mill, Gregers.

GREGERS. They seemed long at the time. Looking back on them, I hardly know where they went.

OLD EKDAL *enters from his room, without his pipe but wearing his old army helmet. He walks a little unsteadily.*

EKDAL. Well, Hjalmar, now we can sit down and talk about that—er—. What was it we were going to talk about?

HJALMAR *goes over to him.* Father, we have a guest. Gregers Werle. I don't know if you remember him.

EKDAL *looks at* GREGERS, *who has got up.* Werle? The son? What does he want with me?

HJALMAR. Nothing. He's come to see me.

EKDAL. Oh. Nothing's wrong, then?

HJALMAR. No, of course not. Nothing at all.

EKDAL *waves an arm.* Mind you, I'm not afraid. It's just that—

GREGERS *goes over to him.* I only wanted to bring you a greeting from your old hunting grounds, Lieutenant Ekdal.

EKDAL. Hunting grounds?

GREGERS. Yes—up around Hoydal.

EKDAL. Oh, up there. Yes, I used to know that part well, in the old days.

GREGERS. You were a famous hunter then.

EKDAL. Oh, well. Maybe I was. I won't deny it. You're looking at my uniform. I don't ask anyone's permission to wear it in here. As long as I don't go out into the street in it—

HEDVIG *brings a plate of sandwiches and puts it on the table.*

HJALMAR. Sit down now, Father, and have a glass of beer. Gregers, please.

EKDAL *mumbles to himself and stumbles over to the sofa.* GREGERS *sits in the chair nearest to him,* HJALMAR *on the other side of* GREGERS. GINA *sits a little away from the table, sewing.* HEDVIG *stands beside her father.*

GREGERS. Do you remember, Lieutenant Ekdal, how Hjalmar

and I used to come up and visit you during the summer, and at Christmas?

EKDAL. Did you? No, no, no, I don't remember it. But though I say it myself, I was a first-rate shot. I've killed bears too, you know. Nine of them.

GREGERS *looks at him sympathetically.* And now your hunting days are over?

EKDAL. Oh, I wouldn't say that, my boy. Do a bit of hunting now and again. Not quite the way I used to. You see, the forest—the forest, you see, the forest—

Drinks.

How does the forest look up there now? Still good, eh?

GREGERS. Not as good as in your day. It's been thinned out a lot.

EKDAL. Thinned out? Chopped down?

More quietly, as though in fear.

That's dangerous. Bad things'll come of that. The forest'll have its revenge.

HJALMAR *fills his glass.* Have a little more, Father.

GREGERS. How can a man like you, a man who loves the open air as you do, bear to live in the middle of a stuffy town, boxed between four walls?

EKDAL *gives a short laugh and glances at* HJALMAR. Oh, it's not too bad here. Not bad at all.

GREGERS. But what about the cool, sweeping breezes, the free life in the forest, and up on the wide, open spaces among animals and birds? These things which had become part of you?

EKDAL *smiles.* Hjalmar, shall we show it to him?

HJALMAR, *quickly, a little embarrassed.* Oh, no, Father, no. Not tonight.

GREGERS. What does he want to show me?

HJALMAR. It's only something that—. You can see it another time.

GREGERS *continues speaking to* EKDAL. What I was going to

suggest, Lieutenant Ekdal, was that you should come with me back to the mill. I shall be returning there soon. I'm sure we could find you some copying to do up there, too. And there's nothing here to keep you cheerful and interested.

EKDAL *stares at him, amazed.* Nothing here—?

GREGERS. Of course you have Hjalmar; but then he has his own family. And a man like you, who has always been drawn to a life that is wild and free—

EKDAL *strikes the table.* Hjalmar, he *shall* see it!

HJALMAR. But, Father, what's the point of showing it to him now? It's dark.

EKDAL. Nonsense, there's the moonlight.

Gets up.

He shall see it, I tell you. Let me come through. Come and help me, Hjalmar.

HEDVIG. Oh, yes, do, Father!

HJALMAR *gets up.* Oh, very well.

GREGERS, *to* GINA. What are they talking about?

GINA. Oh, don't take any notice. It's nothing very much.

EKDAL and HJALMAR *go to the rear wall, and each of them pushes back one of the sliding doors.* HEDVIG *helps the old man.* GREGERS *remains standing by the sofa.* GINA *continues calmly with her sewing. Through the open doors can be seen a long and irregularly shaped loft, full of dark nooks and crannies, with a couple of brick chimney-pipes coming through the floor. Through small skylights bright moonlight shines on to various parts of the loft, while the rest lies in shadow.*

EKDAL, *to* GREGERS. You can come right in, if you like.

GREGERS *goes over to them.* What is it, exactly?

EKDAL. Have a look. Hm.

HJALMAR, *somewhat embarrassed.* This belongs to my father, you understand.

GREGERS, *in the doorway, peers into the. loft.* Why, you keep chickens, Lieutenant Ekdal.

EKDAL. I should think we do keep chickens! They've gone to roost now. But you should just see them by daylight!

HEDVIG. And then there's the—!

EKDAL. Ssh! Don't say anything yet.

GREGERS. And you've pigeons, too, I see.

EKDAL. Why, yes! Of course we've pigeons. They've got their roosting-boxes up there under the roof. Pigeons like to nest high, you know.

HJALMAR. They're not all ordinary pigeons.

EKDAL. Ordinary! No, I should say not! We've tumblers. And a pair of pouters, too. But come over here! Do you see that hutch over there against the wall?

GREGERS. Yes. What do you use that for?

EKDAL. The rabbits go there at night.

GREGERS. Oh, you have rabbits, too?

EKDAL. You're damn right we've got rabbits. You hear that, Hjalmar? He asks if we've got rabbits! Hm! But now I'll show you! This is really something. Move over, Hedvig. Stand here. That's right. Now look down there. Can you see a basket with straw in it?

GREGERS. Yes. And there's a bird lying in the straw.

EKDAL. Hm! A bird!

GREGERS. Isn't it a duck?

EKDAL, *hurt*. Of course it's a duck.

HJALMAR. Ah, but what *kind* of a duck?

HEDVIG. It's not just an ordinary duck—

EKDAL. Ssh!

GREGERS. It's not one of those Muscovy ducks, is it?

EKDAL. No, Mr. Werle, it's not a Muscovy duck. It's a wild duck.

GREGERS. Oh, is it really? A wild duck?

EKDAL. Yes, that's what it is. That "bird," as you called it— that's a wild duck, that is. That's our wild duck, my boy.

HEDVIG. My wild duck. I own it.

GREGERS. But can it live up here in this loft? Is it happy here?

EKDAL. Well, naturally she has a trough of water to splash about in.

HJALMAR. Fresh water every other day.

GINA *turns towards* HJALMAR. Hjalmar dear, it's getting icy cold up here.

EKDAL. Mm. Well, let's shut up, then. It's best not to disturb them when they're sleeping, anyway. Give me a hand, Hedvig.

HJALMAR *and* HEDVIG *slide the doors together.*

Some other time you must have a proper look at her.

Sits in the armchair by the stove.

Ah, they're strange creatures, you know, these wild ducks.

GREGERS. But how did you manage to catch it, Lieutenant Ekdal?

EKDAL. I didn't catch it. There's a certain gentleman in this town whom we have to thank for that.

GREGERS *starts slightly.* You don't mean my father, surely?

EKDAL. Indeed I do. Your father. Hm.

HJALMAR. How odd that you should guess that, Gregers.

GREGERS. You told me earlier that you were indebted to my father for so many things, so I thought perhaps—

GINA. Oh, we didn't get it from Mr. Werle himself—

EKDAL. All the same, it's Haakon Werle we have to thank for her, Gina.

To GREGERS.

He was out in his boat, you see, and he shot her. But his eyesight isn't very good. Hm. So he only winged her.

GREGERS. Oh, I see. She got a couple of pellets in her.

HJALMAR. Yes, two or three.

HEDVIG. She got them under her wing, so that she couldn't fly.

GREGERS. Oh, and so she dived to the bottom, I suppose?

EKDAL, *sleepily, in a thick voice.* Of course. Wild ducks always do that. Dive down to the bottom, as deep as they can go, and hold on with their beaks to the seaweed or whatever they can find down there. And they never come up again.

GREGERS. But your wild duck did come up again, Lieutenant Ekdal.

EKDAL. He had such a damned clever dog, your father. And that dog—he dived down after the duck, and brought her to the surface.

GREGERS *turns to* HJALMAR. And then you took her in here?

HJALMAR. Not at once. To begin with, they took her home to your father's house. But she didn't seem to thrive there. So Pettersen was told to wring her neck.

EKDAL, *half asleep.* Hm. Yes. Pettersen. Damn fool—

HJALMAR *speaks more softly.* That was how we got her, you see. Father knows Pettersen, and when he heard all this about the wild duck he got him to give it to us.

GREGERS. And now she's thriving in your loft.

HJALMAR. Yes, she's doing extraordinarily well. She's got fat. Well, she's been in there so long now that she's forgotten what it's like to live the life she was born for; that's the whole trick.

GREGERS. Yes, you're right there, Hjalmar. Just make sure she never gets a glimpse of the sky or the sea. But I mustn't stay longer. I think your father's fallen asleep.

HJALMAR. Oh, never mind about that.

GREGERS. By the bye, you said you had a room to let.

HJALMAR. Yes, why? Do you know anyone who—?

GREGERS. Could I have it?

HJALMAR. You?

GINA. No, but Mr. Werle, it isn't—

GREGERS. Can I have that room? I'd like to move in right away. Tomorrow morning.

HJALMAR. Why, yes, with the greatest pleasure—

GINA. Oh no, Mr. Werle, it's not at all the kind of room for you.

HJALMAR. Why, Gina, how can you say that?

GINA. Well, it's dark and poky.

GREGERS. That won't bother me, Mrs. Ekdal.

HJALMAR. Personally I think it's quite a nice room. Not too badly furnished, either.

GINA. Don't forget those two who live down below.

GREGERS. Who are they?

GINA. Oh, one of them used to be a tutor—

HJALMAR. A Mr. Molvik.

GINA. And the other's a doctor called Relling.

GREGERS. Relling? I know him slightly. He had a practice up at Hoydal once.

GINA. They're a real couple of good-for-nothings. They often go out on the spree and come home very late at night, and aren't always—

GREGERS. One soon gets accustomed to that sort of thing. I hope I shall manage to acclimatise myself like the wild duck.

GINA. Well, I think you ought to sleep on it first, all the same.

GREGERS. You evidently don't want to have me living here, Mrs. Ekdal.

GINA. For heaven's sake! How can you think that?

HJALMAR. You're really behaving very strangely, Gina.

To GREGERS.

But tell me, are you thinking of staying in town for a while?

GREGERS *puts on his overcoat.* Yes, now I'm staying.

HJALMAR. But not at home with your father? What do you intend to do?

GREGERS. Ah, if only I knew that, Hjalmar, it wouldn't be so bad. But when one has the misfortune to be called Gregers— with Werle on top of it—Hjalmar, have you ever heard anything so awful?

HJALMAR. Oh, I don't think it's awful at all.

GREGERS. Oh, nonsense. Ugh! I'd want to spit on anyone who had a name like that.

HJALMAR *laughs.* If you weren't Gregers Werle, what would you like to be?

GREGERS. If I could choose, I think most of all I'd like to be a clever dog.

GINA. A dog?

HEDVIG, *involuntarily.* Oh, no!

GREGERS. Oh, yes. A tremendously clever dog. The sort that dives down after wild ducks when they have plunged to the bottom and gripped themselves fast in the seaweed and the mud.

HJALMAR. Honestly, Gregers, I don't understand a word of all this.

GREGERS. Oh, well, it doesn't mean much really. I'll move in tomorrow morning, then.

To GINA.

I shan't cause you any trouble. I do everything for myself.

To HJALMAR.

We'll talk about everything else tomorrow. Good night, Mrs. Ekdal.

Nods to HEDVIG.

Good night.

GINA. Good night, Mr. Werle.

HEDVIG. Good night.

HJALMAR, *who has lit a candle.* Wait a moment. I'll have to light you down. It's very dark on the stairs.

GREGERS *and* HJALMAR *go out through the front door.*

GINA, *thoughtfully, her sewing in her lap.* Wasn't that a funny thing, saying he'd like to be a dog?

HEDVIG. You know, Mother—I think when he said that he meant something else.

GINA. What could he mean?

HEDVIG. I don't know. But I felt as though he meant something different from what he was saying all the time.

GINA. You think so? Yes, it certainly was strange.

HJALMAR *comes back.* The light was still on.

Snuffs the candle and puts it down.

Ah, now I can get a little food inside me at last.

Begins eating the sandwiches.

Well, there you are, Gina. If one only keeps one's eyes and ears open—

GINA. How do you mean?

HJALMAR. Well, it's jolly lucky we've managed to let that room at last, isn't it? And, what's more, to a man like Gregers. A dear old friend.

GINA. Well, I don't know what to say about it.

HEDVIG. Oh, Mother! You'll see—it'll be such fun!

HJALMAR. You're very awkward. You were aching to let the room, and now we've done it you're not happy.

GINA. Oh, yes I am, Hjalmar. I only wish it had been to someone else. But what do you suppose the old man will say?

HJALMAR. Old Werle? It's none of his business.

GINA. Can't you see? They must have quarrelled again if his son's walked out of the house. You know how things are between those two.

HJALMAR. That may well be, but—

GINA. Now perhaps Mr. Werle'll think you're behind it all.

HJALMAR. All right, let him think so, if he wants to! Old Werle's done a great deal for me, I admit it. But that doesn't make me his vassal for life.

GINA. But, dear Hjalmar, he might take it out of Grandfather. Maybe now he'll lose the little bit of money he gets through Graaberg.

HJALMAR. Good riddance—I've half a mind to say. Don't you think it's a little humiliating for a man like me to see his grey old father treated like a leper? But I've a feeling the time is getting ripe.

Takes another sandwich.

As sure as I have a mission in life, it shall be fulfilled.

HEDVIG. Oh, Father, yes! It must, it must!

GINA. Ssh! For heaven's sake, don't wake him.

HJALMAR, *more quietly.* It shall be accomplished. The day will come, I tell you—and that's why it's good we've let that room—it makes me more independent.

Over by the armchair, emotionally.

My poor old father! Bless his white hairs! Put your trust in your son. He has broad shoulders—well, strong shoulders, anyway. One fine day you will wake up—

To GINA.

Don't you believe it?

GINA *gets up.* Of course I believe it. But let's get him to bed first.

HJALMAR. Yes, let's.

They take hold of the old man gently.

ACT THREE

HJALMAR EKDAL's *studio. It is morning. The daylight is shining in through the large window in the sloping ceiling, from which the curtain is drawn back.*

HJALMAR *is seated at the table re-touching a photograph. Several others lie in front of him. After a few moments,* GINA *enters through the front door wearing a hat and coat. She has a lidded basket on her arm.*

HJALMAR. Back already, Gina?

GINA. Yes, I've no time to waste.

Puts the basket down on a chair and takes off her coat.

HJALMAR. Did you look in on Gregers?

GINA. I'll say I did. Lovely it looks. He's made it really nice and cosy for himself right from the start.

HJALMAR. Oh, how?

GINA. Manage for himself, he said he would. So he starts lighting the stove. Well, he shoved that damper in so far the whole room got full of smoke. Ugh! It stank like a—

HJALMAR. Oh dear, oh dear!

GINA. That's not all. Then he wants to put out the fire, so he throws all his washing water into the stove. That floor's swimming like a pigsty.

HJALMAR. Oh, I'm sorry about that.

GINA. I've got the caretaker's wife to clean up after him, the pig. But that room won't be fit to live in till this afternoon.

HJALMAR. What's he doing with himself meanwhile?

GINA. He said he'd go out for a bit.

HJALMAR. I went in there too for a moment. After you'd gone.

GINA. So I gathered. I hear you've invited him for lunch.

HJALMAR. Just a little snack, I thought. After all, it's his first day here—we can't very well not. You've got something, I suppose?

GINA. I'll have to find something, won't I?

HJALMAR. Don't skimp it too much. Relling and Molvik may be looking in, too, I think. I ran into Relling on the stairs just now, you see, so I couldn't very well—

GINA. Oh, we're having those two as well, are we?

HJALMAR. Good God, a couple more or less, what difference does that make?

OLD EKDAL *opens his door and looks out.* I say, Hjalmar—

Notices GINA.

Oh.

GINA. Do you want something, Grandfather?

OLD EKDAL. Oh, no. It doesn't matter. Hm!

Goes inside again.

GINA *picks up the basket.* Watch him. See he doesn't go out.

HJALMAR. All right, all right. I say, Gina, a little of that herring salad of yours mightn't be a bad idea. I think Relling and Molvik were out on the tiles again last night.

GINA. Well, as long as they don't come too soon—

HJALMAR. Of course, of course. You take your time.

GINA. Yes, well; and you can get a little work done in the meantime.

HJALMAR. I *am* working! I'm working as hard as I can!

GINA. I only meant, then you'll have it out of the way.

She goes out with her basket to the kitchen. HJALMAR *sits working at the photograph with a brush, slowly and listlessly.*

EKDAL *pokes his head in, looks around the room and says in a whisper.* Are you working?

HJALMAR. Yes, can't you see I'm struggling away at these pictures?

EKDAL. Oh. Well, never mind. If you're working so hard, I— Hm.

Goes out again. His door remains open.

HJALMAR *continues silently for a few moments, then puts down his brush and goes across to the door.* Are *you* working, Father?

EKDAL, *grumblingly, from the other room.* If you're working, I'm working, too. Hm!

HJALMAR. Yes, yes, of course.

Goes back to his work.

EKDAL, *after a moment, reappears in the doorway.* You know —I'm not working as hard as all that, Hjalmar.

HJALMAR. I thought you were writing.

EKDAL. Damn it, that Graaberg can wait a day or two. It's not a matter of life and death, is it?

HJALMAR. No. Anyway, you're not a slave, are you?

EKDAL. And then there's that thing in there—

HJALMAR. I was just thinking of that. Did you want to go in? Shall I open the door for you?

EKDAL. That's not a bad idea.

HJALMAR *gets up.* Then we'd have it out of the way.

EKDAL. That's what I was thinking. We've got to have it ready by tomorrow morning. It is tomorrow, isn't it? Eh?

HJALMAR. Yes, of course it's tomorrow.

HJALMAR *and* EKDAL *each slide back one of the doors. Within, the morning sun is shining in through the skylights. Some pigeons are flying back and forth, while others perch, cooing, on the rafters. Now and then the hens cackle further back in the loft.*

Well now. Get on with it, Father.

EKDAL *goes inside.* Aren't you going to help?

HJALMAR. You know, I think I—

Sees GINA *in the kitchen doorway.*

Me? No, I've no time. I've got to work. Oh—my con-
traption—

*He pulls a cord. A curtain falls in the attic; the lower sec-
tion of this consists of a strip of old sailcloth, the upper of a
piece of fishing net, stretched taut. The floor of the attic is
thus no longer visible.*

Goes over to the table.

Good. Now perhaps I can be allowed to work in peace for
a few minutes.

GINA. Is he messing around in there again?

HJALMAR. Would you rather he sneaked off down to Madame
Eriksen's?

Sits.

Did you want something? You were saying—

GINA. I only wanted to ask whether you think it'd be all right
if we eat in here.

HJALMAR. Yes, we haven't any early sittings today, have we?

GINA. Only those two young lovers who want to be taken together.

HJALMAR. Why the devil can't they be taken together some
other day?

GINA. It's all right, dear. I've fixed for them to come after
lunch, when you'll be having your nap.

HJALMAR. Oh, good. Very well, then, let's eat in here.

GINA. All right. But there's no hurry about laying the table
just yet. You can go on using it for a bit longer.

HJALMAR. Surely you can see I'm working as hard as I can!

GINA. I only meant, then you'll be free later.

She goes back into the kitchen. Short pause.

EKDAL *peers through the net in the loft.* Hjalmar!

HJALMAR. What is it?

EKDAL. Afraid we'll have to move that water trough after all.

HJALMAR. That's what I've said all along.

EKDAL. Hm—hm—hm.

Goes away from the door again.

HJALMAR *works for a few moments, then glances towards the attic and half rises.* HEDVIG *comes in from the kitchen.*

HJALMAR *sits quickly down.* What do you want?

HEDVIG. I only wanted to be with you, Father.

HJALMAR, *after a moment.* What are you nosing around for? Have you been told to keep an eye on me?

HEDVIG. No, of course not.

HJALMAR. What's your mother up to now?

HEDVIG. Oh, she's in the middle of the herring salad.

Goes over to the table.

Isn't there some little thing I could help you with, Father?

HJALMAR. Oh, no. I'd better cope with it alone. While I still can. All will be well, Hedvig. As long as your father's strength holds out—

HEDVIG. Oh, no, Father, you mustn't say such dreadful things.

She wanders around for a little, then stops by the open doorway and looks into the loft.

HJALMAR. What's he up to, Hedvig?

HEDVIG. I think he's making a new path up to the water trough.

HJALMAR. He'll never manage that by himself! And I'm forced to sit here—

HEDVIG *comes over to him.* Let me take the brush, Father. I know how to do it.

HJALMAR. Oh, no, you'll only ruin your eyes.

HEDVIG. Nonsense. Come on, give me the brush.

HJALMAR *gets up.* Yes, well, it won't take more than a minute or two.

HEDVIG. Oh, what does it matter?

Takes the brush.

There, now.

Sits.

Here's one I can start on.

HJALMAR. But listen—if you ruin your eyes, I won't take the responsibility. On your own head be it. You hear?

HEDVIG, *busy on the photograph.* Yes, yes, I know.

HJALMAR. You're a clever girl, Hedvig. It'll only take a couple of minutes—

He squeezes into the loft past the edge of the curtain. HEDVIG *sits working.* HJALMAR *and* EKDAL *can be heard arguing in the loft.*

HJALMAR *comes back through the curtain.*

Hedvig, get me those pliers from that shelf. And the chisel.

Turns round towards the loft.

Now you'll see, Father. Just let me show you.

HEDVIG *gets the tools from the bookcase and hands them to him.*

HJALMAR. Ah, thanks. Good thing I came, Hedvig.

He goes away from the doorway. They can be heard working and chatting inside. HEDVIG *stands watching them. After a moment, there is a knock on the front door. She does not hear it.*

GREGERS *enters bareheaded and without an overcoat. He pauses in the doorway.* Hm—

HEDVIG *turns and goes towards him.* Good morning. Please come in.

GREGERS. Thank you.

Looks towards the attic.

Have you got workmen in the house?

HEDVIG. No, that's only Father and Grandfather. I'll tell them you're here.

GREGERS. No, no, don't do that. I'd rather wait.

Sits on the sofa.

HEDVIG. It's so untidy in here.

Begins to clear away the photographs.

GREGERS. Oh, never mind that. Are those photographs that have to be—er—finished off?

HEDVIG. Yes, just a few I'm helping Father with.

GREGERS. Please don't let me disturb you.

HEDVIG. All right.

Arranges the things again and sits down to work. GREGERS *watches her in silence.*

GREGERS. Did the wild duck sleep well last night?

HEDVIG. Yes, thank you, I think so.

GREGERS *turns towards the loft.* It looks quite different in there by daylight.

HEDVIG. Oh, yes. It varies a lot. In the morning it looks quite different from what it does in the afternoon. And when it's raining it looks different from when it's fine.

GREGERS. You've noticed that, have you?

HEDVIG. Yes, you can't help seeing it.

GREGERS. Do you like being in there with the wild duck, too?

HEDVIG. Yes, when I'm able to—

GREGERS. But you haven't so much spare time, I dare say. You go to school, of course?

HEDVIG. No, not any longer. Father's afraid I shall ruin my eyes.

GREGERS. Oh. So he reads with you himself?

HEDVIG. Father's promised to read with me, but he hasn't found time for it yet.

GREGERS. But isn't there someone else who could help you a little?

HEDVIG. Yes, there's Mr. Molvik—he's a student who lives downstairs—but he isn't always—er—altogether quite—

GREGERS. Does he drink?

HEDVIG. I think he does.

GREGERS. Oh. Then you've time for all sorts of things. In there, it's like a different world, I suppose?

HEDVIG. Quite, quite different. And there are so many strange things in there.

GREGERS. Oh?

HEDVIG. Yes. There are big cupboards with books in them. And a lot of the books have got pictures.

GREGERS. Ah.

HEDVIG. And there's an old bureau with drawers and bits that slide out, and a big clock with figures that are meant to pop out. But the clock doesn't work any more.

GREGERS. So time has stopped in there with the wild duck.

HEDVIG. Yes. And there are old paintboxes and things like that. And all the books.

GREGERS. And you read books, I suppose?

HEDVIG. Oh yes, when I can get the chance. But most of them are in English, and I can't understand that. But I look at the pictures. There's a great big book called *Harrison's History of London*—I should think it must be a hundred years old—and that's got heaps and heaps of pictures in it. On the front there's a picture of death with an hourglass, and a girl. That's horrid, I think. But then there are lots of other pictures of churches and castles and streets and great ships sailing on the sea.

GREGERS. But tell me, where have all these wonderful things come from?

HEDVIG. Oh, there was an old sea captain who used to live here once, and he brought them home. They called him The Flying Dutchman. It's funny, because he wasn't a Dutchman.

GREGERS. Wasn't he?

HEDVIG. No. But in the end he got lost at sea and left all these things behind.

GREGERS. Tell me—as you sit in there and look at the pictures, don't you feel you want to get out and see the world as it really is?

HEDVIG. Oh, no! I want to stay at home always, and help Father and Mother.

GREGERS. Help them retouch photographs?

HEDVIG. No, not only that. Most of all I'd like to learn to engrave pictures like the ones in the English books.

GREGERS. Hm. What does your father say to that?

HEDVIG. I don't think Father likes the idea. He's so strange about anything like that. Imagine, he talks about my learning how to plait straw and make baskets! I don't think there can be any future in that.

GREGERS. No, neither do I.

HEDVIG. But Father's right when he says that if I'd learned basket-making I could have made the new basket for the wild duck.

GREGERS. Yes, so you could. It was your job really, wasn't it?

HEDVIG. Yes, because it's my wild duck.

GREGERS. Of course it is.

HEDVIG. Oh, yes. I own it. But Father and Grandfather are allowed to borrow it whenever they want.

GREGERS. Oh, and what do they do with it?

HEDVIG. Oh, they look after it and build things for it, and that kind of thing.

GREGERS. I should think so. The wild duck's the most important thing in there, isn't it?

HEDVIG. Oh, yes. She's a real wild bird, you see. That's why I feel so sorry for her. She's got no one to care for, poor thing.

GREGERS. No family like the rabbits.

HEDVIG. No. The hens have got friends they used to be chicks with; but she's been separated from all her family. And there's so much that's strange about the wild duck. No one knows her. And no one knows where she came from.

GREGERS. And she's been down to the bottom of the deep blue sea.

HEDVIG *glances quickly at him and represses a smile.* Why do you say "the deep blue sea"?

GREGERS. What should I have said?

HEDVIG. You could have said the "sea bed," or just the "bottom of the sea."

GREGERS. Oh, why can't I say "the deep blue sea"?

HEDVIG. Yes, but it always sounds so odd to me when other people talk about "the deep blue sea."

GREGERS. Why? Tell me.

HEDVIG. No, I won't. It's silly.

GREGERS. Not at all. Tell me now, why did you smile?

HEDVIG. It's because if I suddenly—without thinking—remember what's in there, I always think of it all as being "the deep blue sea." But that's just silly.

GREGERS. No, you mustn't say that.

HEDVIG. Well, it's only a loft.

GREGERS *looks hard at her.* Are you so sure?

HEDVIG, *astonished.* That it's only a loft?

GREGERS. Yes. You are quite certain about that?

HEDVIG *stares silently at him, open-mouthed.* GINA *comes from the kitchen with cutlery and tablecloth.*

GREGERS *gets up.*

I'm afraid I've come too early.

GINA. Oh, you've got to sit somewhere. Anyway, I'll be ready in a minute. Clear the table, Hedvig.

HEDVIG *clears the table. She and* GINA *lay the cloth, etc., during the following scene.* GREGERS *sits in an armchair and turns the pages of an album.*

GREGERS. I hear you know how to retouch photographs, Mrs. Ekdal.

GINA *gives him a quick glance.* Why—yes, I know how.

GREGERS. That was a lucky chance, wasn't it?

GINA. Why lucky?

GREGERS. Since Hjalmar was to become a photographer, I mean.

HEDVIG. Mother can take photographs, too.

GINA. Oh, yes, I've had to teach myself that.

GREGERS. Then it's really you who run the business?

GINA. Yes, when Hjalmar hasn't time himself, I—

GREGERS. His old father takes up a lot of his time, I dare say.

GINA. Yes. And anyway it's no real job for a man like Hjalmar to have to take the portraits of just anyone.

GREGERS. I quite agree. But after all, he has chosen this profession—

GINA. Hjalmar isn't just an ordinary photographer, you know, Mr. Werle.

GREGERS. I'm sure he isn't. But—

A shot is fired inside the loft.

GREGERS *jumps up.*

What's that?

GINA. Ugh, they're shooting again.

GREGERS. Do they shoot too?

HEDVIG. They go hunting.

GREGERS. What!

By the door of the loft.

Are you hunting, Hjalmar?

HJALMAR, *from beyond the curtain.* Are you here? Oh, I didn't know. I was so busy with—

To HEDVIG.

Why didn't you tell us?

Comes into the studio.

GREGERS. Do you go shooting in the loft?

HJALMAR *shows him a double-barrelled pistol.* Oh, only with this.

GINA. You and Grandfather'll do yourselves an injury one of these fine days with that popgun.

HJALMAR, *irritated.* This is a pistol, as I think I've told you before.

GINA. I don't see that that improves matters.

GREGERS. So you've turned hunter, too, Hjalmar?

HJALMAR. Oh, I just go out after rabbits now and then. Mostly for the old man's sake, you know.

GINA. Men are funny creatures. Always got to have something to diverge themselves with.

HJALMAR, *bad-temperedly.* Quite so. As Gina says, we've always got to have something to divert ourselves with.

GINA. Isn't that what I said?

HJALMAR. Hm. Well—.

To GREGERS.

Yes, you see, as luck would have it the loft's placed in such a way that no one can hear us when we shoot.

Puts down the pistol on the top shelf of the bookcase.

Don't touch that pistol, Hedvig. One of the barrels is loaded. Now don't forget.

GREGERS *peers in through the net.* You've a shotgun too, I see.

HJALMAR. That's Father's old gun. It's no use any longer, something's gone wrong with the lock. But it's quite fun to have it around. We can take it to pieces now and then and clean it and grease it and put it together again. Of course it's mostly Father who fiddles around like that.

HEDVIG, *to* GREGERS. Now you can see the wild duck properly.

GREGERS. Yes, I was just looking at her. She droops a little on one wing, doesn't she?

HJALMAR. No wonder. That's where she was shot.

GREGERS. And she trails one foot a little. Am I right?

HJALMAR. Perhaps just a little.

HEDVIG. Yes, that's where the dog bit her.

HJALMAR. But otherwise there's nothing wrong with her. It's really marvellous when you think she's had a charge of shot in her and has been between the teeth of a dog—

GREGERS *glances at* HEDVIG. And has been on the bottom of the deep blue sea for so long.

HEDVIG *smiles.* Yes.

GINA, *laying the table.* Oh, that blessed wild duck. You make too much of a song and dance about her.

HJALMAR. Hm. Are you nearly ready with that?

GINA. Yes, I shan't be a minute. Hedvig, come and give me a hand.

GINA *and* HEDVIG *go out into the kitchen.*

HJALMAR, *in a low voice.* I think you'd better not stand there watching Father. He doesn't like it.

GREGERS *comes away from the loft door.*

HJALMAR. I'd better close up before the others arrive.

Claps his hands to frighten the birds.

Shoo, shoo! Get away with you!

Pulls up the curtain and closes the doors as he speaks.

I invented these gadgets myself. It's really rather fun to have something like this to fiddle with, and fix when it goes wrong. We've got to have it, because Gina doesn't like rabbits and hens in here.

GREGERS. No, no. It's your wife who runs the studio, I suppose?

HJALMAR. I generally leave the details of the business to her. Then I can lock myself away in the parlour and think about more important things.

GREGERS. What kind of things, Hjalmar?

HJALMAR. I wonder you haven't asked me that before. But perhaps you haven't heard about my invention?

GREGERS. Your invention? No.

HJALMAR. Really? Haven't you? Oh no, I suppose being cut off up there in those forests—

GREGERS. So you've invented something?

HJALMAR. It's not quite finished yet. But I'm working on it. As you can imagine, when I decided to give up my life to the service of photography it wasn't because I wanted to take portraits of the *bourgeoisie.*

GREGERS. No, that's what your wife said just now.

HJALMAR. I made a vow that if I was going to dedicate my powers to this craft, I would exalt it to the level of both an art and a science. And so I decided to make this astonishing invention.

GREGERS. But what *is* this invention? What's the idea behind it?

HJALMAR. Oh, my dear fellow, you mustn't ask me about details yet. It takes time, you know. And you mustn't think it's vanity that's inspiring me to do this. It isn't for myself that I'm doing it. Oh, no. I have a mission in life that I can never forget.

GREGERS. What kind of mission?

HJALMAR. Have you forgotten that old man with the silver hair?

GREGERS. Your poor father. Yes, but there isn't very much you can do for him, is there?

HJALMAR. I can rekindle his self-respect by restoring to the name of Ekdal the honour and dignity which it once had.

GREGERS. And that's your mission?

HJALMAR. I want to save that shipwrecked soul, yes. Right from the moment the storm broke over him, he was a wreck. And during those terrible investigations he was no longer himself. That pistol over there, Gregers—the one we use for shooting rabbits—has played its part in the tragedy of the House of Ekdal.

GREGERS. Really? That pistol?

HJALMAR. When sentence had been pronounced and he was about to be taken to prison—he had the pistol in his hand—

GREGERS. You mean—?

HJALMAR. Yes. But he didn't dare. He was a coward. His spirit had been broken. Can you understand it? He, a soldier, who had killed nine bears, and was descended from two lieutenant colonels—one after the other, of course— Can you understand it, Gregers?

GREGERS. Yes, I understand it very well.

HJALMAR. I can't. But that wasn't the last time that pistol played a part in the history of our family. When he was in his grey garb, under lock and key—oh, it was a terrible time for me, believe me. I kept the blinds drawn over both my windows. When I peeped out I saw that the sun still shone. I couldn't understand it. I saw people in the street, laughing and chatting, about trivial things. I couldn't understand it. I thought the whole world ought to stand still, as though in eclipse.

GREGERS. That is how I felt when my mother died.

HJALMAR. At such a moment, Hjalmar Ekdal held the pistol pointed at his own breast.

GREGERS. You mean you, too, thought of—?

HJALMAR. Yes.

GREGERS. But you didn't fire?

HJALMAR. No. At the critical moment, I triumphed over myself. I decided to remain alive. But I can tell you, Gregers, it takes courage under such circumstances to choose life.

GREGERS. Yes, well—that depends on how one—

HJALMAR. Believe me, Gregers, I am right. Anyway, it was better so. Now I shall make my invention; and then, Dr. Relling agrees with me, Father may be allowed to wear his uniform again. I shall demand it as my sole reward.

GREGERS. So it's the uniform he—?

HJALMAR. Yes, that's what he longs for most. You can't imagine how my heart bleeds for him. Every time we have any little family celebration—for example, Gina's and my wedding anniversary, or whatever it may be—the old man appears as the lieutenant he used to be in happier days. But if there's a knock on the door he scampers back to his room as fast as his old legs will carry him, because he daren't show himself to strangers. Oh, it's heart-rending for a son to have to witness such things, Gregers.

GREGERS. How soon do you expect this invention to be ready?

HJALMAR. Good heavens, you can't expect me to work to a

schedule. An invention is something that even the inventor himself isn't completely master of. It depends largely on intuition—on inspiration—and it's almost impossible to predict when that's going to come.

GREGERS. But you're making progress?

HJALMAR. Of course I am. I think about it every day. It's always with me. Every afternoon, after I've eaten, I shut myself up in the parlour where I can meditate in peace. But I mustn't be rushed. That won't help at all. Relling says so too.

GREGERS. And you don't think that all that business in the loft distracts you too much, and dissipates your energies?

HJALMAR. No, no, no—quite the contrary. I can't spend all my time brooding over the same exhausting problem. I must have some distraction while I wait for the inspiration to come. Inspiration, you see, comes when it comes.

GREGERS. My dear Hjalmar, I really believe there is something of the wild duck in you.

HJALMAR. The wild duck? How do you mean?

GREGERS. You've plunged to the bottom and are holding on to the seaweed.

HJALMAR. Are you referring to that stroke of fate which crippled Father—and me as well?

GREGERS. Not that so much. I wouldn't say you've been crippled. You've wandered into a poisonous swamp, Hjalmar. You've got a creeping disease in your body, and you've sunk to the bottom to die in the dark.

HJALMAR. Me? Die in the dark? Now really, Gregers, you must stop that talk.

GREGERS. Don't worry. I shall get you up again. I've found a mission in life, too, you see. I found it yesterday.

HJALMAR. I dare say, but please leave me out of it. I can assure you that—apart from a certain melancholy, which is easily explained—I'm as contented with life as anyone could wish to be.

GREGERS. That's another effect of the poison.

HJALMAR. Oh, my dear Gregers, do stop talking about diseases and poisons. I'm not used to this kind of conversation. In my house we don't talk about disagreeable matters.

GREGERS. No, I can well believe that.

HJALMAR. Yes—it's not good for me, you see. And you won't find any poisonous fumes here, as you insinuate. In the poor photographer's home the roof is low, I know that well. And the circumstances are narrow. But I am an inventor, Gregers —the breadwinner for my family—and that lifts me above the poverty of my surroundings. Ah, lunch!

GINA *and* HEDVIG *bring in bottles of beer, a decanter of aquavit, glasses, etc. . . . At the same time* RELLING *and* MOLVIK *enter from the passage. Neither has a hat or overcoat.* MOLVIK *is dressed in black.*

GINA, *putting the things on the table.* Trust those two to come on time!

RELLING. Molvik thought he could smell herring salad, so there was no holding him. Good morning again, Ekdal.

HJALMAR. Gregers, may I present Mr. Molvik? Dr.—but of course you know Relling.

GREGERS. Yes, we have met.

RELLING. Oh, it's Mr. Werle Junior. Yes, we two have clashed before, up at Hoydal. You moved in here?

GREGERS. I moved in this morning.

RELLING. Molvik and I live underneath, so you haven't far to go for a doctor or a priest, if you should ever need either of them.

GREGERS. Thank you, I well may. Yesterday we were thirteen at table.

HJALMAR. Oh, don't start that awful business again.

RELLING. Take it easy, Ekdal. You were one of the twelve.

HJALMAR. I hope so, for my family's sake. But now let's sit down, and eat and drink and be merry.

GREGERS. Oughtn't we to wait for your father?

HJALMAR. No, he wants his taken in to him later. Come along now, everybody!

The men sit down at the table, and start eating and drinking. GINA *and* HEDVIG *come and go, waiting on them.*

RELLING. Molvik was as tight as a drum again last night, Mrs. Ekdal.

GINA. Oh? Last night again?

RELLING. Didn't you hear him when I brought him home?

GINA. No, I can't say I did.

RELLING. That's as well. Molvik was *awful* last night.

GINA. Is this true, Molvik?

MOLVIK. Let us draw a veil over the events of last night. It was not a manifestation of my better self.

RELLING, *to* GREGERS. It comes on him like an inspiration. And then I have to go out and paint the town with him. Molvik's daemonic, you see.

GREGERS. Daemonic?

RELLING. Yes, daemonic.

GREGERS. Hm.

RELLING. And people who are born daemonic can't keep a straight course through life. They have to go off the rails now and then. Well, so you're still sticking it out at that ugly black mill, are you?

GREGERS. I have stuck it out until now.

RELLING. And did you manage to enforce that claim you went round pestering everyone with?

GREGERS. Claim?

Understands him.

I see.

HJALMAR. Have you been acting as a debt collector, Gregers?

GREGERS. Oh, nonsense.

RELLING. Oh yes, he has. He went round all the workmen's cottages, shoving something in their faces which he called the "claim of the ideal."

GREGERS. I was young then.

RELLING. You're right there. You were very young. And as for that claim of the ideal—you never got anyone to honour it before I left.

GREGERS. Nor since, either.

RELLING. Then I hope you've grown wise enough to reduce your demands a little.

GREGERS. Not when I stand face to face with a man.

HJALMAR. Well, that sounds reasonable enough. A little butter, Gina.

RELLING. And a slice of pork for Molvik.

MOLVIK. Oh no, not pork!

There is a knock on the door of the loft.

HJALMAR. Open the door, Hedvig. Father wants to come out.

HEDVIG *goes across and opens the door a little.* OLD EKDAL *comes out with a fresh rabbit skin. She closes the door behind him.*

EKDAL. Morning, gentlemen. Good hunting today. I've shot a big one.

HJALMAR. Why did you have to skin it before I came?

EKDAL. Salted it, too. It's good, tender meat, rabbit meat. Sweet, too. Tastes like sugar. Enjoy your dinner, gentlemen! *Goes into his room.*

MOLVIK *gets up.* Excuse me—I can't—I must—quickly—

RELLING. Drink some soda water, man!

MOLVIK *hurries out.* Ah—ah! *Goes out through the front door.*

RELLING, *to* HJALMAR. Let's drink to the old huntsman.

HJALMAR *clinks glasses with him.* A great sportsman at the end of the road.

RELLING. His hair tempered with grey— *Drinks.*

By the way, tell me, is his hair grey or white?

HJALMAR. Oh—somewhere between the two. Actually, he hasn't very many hairs left on his head.

RELLING. Well, one can get through the world with a wig, as one can with a mask. You're a lucky man, Ekdal. A beautiful mission to fight for—

HJALMAR. And I do fight for it, believe me.

RELLING. And a clever wife, jogging quietly in and out in her felt slippers, rocking her hips and making everything nice and comfortable for you.

HJALMAR. Yes, Gina.

Nods to her.

You are a good companion to have on life's journey.

GINA. Oh, get along with you!

RELLING. And then you have your little Hedvig.

HJALMAR, *moved.* My child, yes. Above all, my child. Hedvig, come to me.

Strokes her hair.

What day is it tomorrow, Hedvig?

HEDVIG *shakes him.* Oh no, Father, you mustn't tell them!

HJALMAR. It wounds me like a knife through the heart when I think how poor it must be. Just a little party in the attic—

HEDVIG. But Father, that's just what's so wonderful!

RELLING. And just you wait till your father's ready with his great invention, Hedvig.

HJALMAR. Yes, then you'll see! Hedvig, I have resolved to secure your future. You shall never want. I shall make it a condition that you get—er—something or other. That shall be the poor inventor's sole reward.

HEDVIG *whispers, her arm round his neck.* Oh, dear, kind Father!

RELLING, *to* GREGERS. Well, don't you find it pleasant for a change to sit down to a good meal surrounded by a happy family?

HJALMAR. Yes, I think I appreciate these hours at the table more than anything.

GREGERS. Personally I don't like poisonous fumes.

RELLING. Poisonous fumes!

HJALMAR. Oh, for heaven's sake, don't start that again.

GINA. By God, you'll find no fumes in here, Mr. Werle. I give the whole place a good airing every day.

GREGERS, *leaving the table.* You can't drive out the stench I mean by opening the windows.

HJALMAR. Stench!

GINA. How do you like that, Hjalmar!

RELLING. I beg your pardon—you couldn't possibly have brought the stench in yourself from those pits up there?

GREGERS. Yes, it's like you to call what I bring with me a stench.

RELLING *goes over to him.* Listen, Mr. Werle Junior. I've a strong suspicion you're still carrying that "claim of the ideal" unabridged in your back pocket.

GREGERS. I carry it in my heart.

RELLING. Well, wherever you have the bloody thing I'm damned if I'll let you blackmail anyone with it as long as I'm in this house.

GREGERS. And if I choose to ignore your warning?

RELLING. Then you'll go headfirst down those stairs. Now you know.

HJALMAR *gets up.* But—but, Relling—

GREGERS. All right, throw me out.

GINA *goes between them.* Relling, you can't do that. But I must say, Mr. Werle, after the mess you made with your stove you're in no position to come and complain to me about fumes.

There is a knock on the front door.

HEDVIG. Mother, someone's knocking.

HJALMAR. Oh, now that's going to start.

GINA. Let me take care of it.

Goes over, opens the door and steps back in surprise.

Oh! Oh, no!

HAAKON WERLE, *in a fur-lined coat with a fur collar, takes a step into the room.*

WERLE. I beg your pardon, but I believe my son is living in this house.

GINA *swallows.* Yes.

HJALMAR *goes towards him.* Wouldn't you do us the honour, sir, to—?

WERLE. Thank you, I only want to speak to my son.

GREGERS. Well? I'm here. What is it?

WERLE. I want to speak to you in your room.

GREGERS. Oh? In my room?

Moves towards the door.

GINA. No, for heaven's sake, that's in no state—

WERLE. Out in the passage, then. I want to speak with you alone.

HJALMAR. You can do that here, sir. Relling, come into the parlour.

HJALMAR *and* RELLING *go out to the right.* GINA *takes* HEDVIG *into the kitchen.*

GREGERS, *after a short pause.* Well. Now we're alone.

WERLE. You let drop a few remarks last night about— And since you've now come to lodge with the Ekdals I can only assume that you intend some action directed against me.

GREGERS. I intend to open the eyes of Hjalmar Ekdal. He must see his situation as it really is. That is all.

WERLE. And that is the mission in life you spoke of yesterday?

GREGERS. Yes. It's the only one you have left me.

WERLE. So it's I who have soured your mind, Gregers?

GREGERS. You have soured my whole life. Oh, I'm not just thinking of what happened to my mother. But it's you I have to thank for the fact that I'm continually haunted by a guilty conscience.

WERLE. Oh, so it's your conscience that's queasy, is it?

GREGERS. I ought to have stood up to you when those traps were laid for Lieutenant Ekdal. I ought to have warned him. I knew in my mind what was going on.

WERLE. Then you ought to have spoken out.

GREGERS. I was frightened. I was a coward. I was so miserably afraid of you then. And long afterwards.

WERLE. You seem to have got over that very well now.

GREGERS. Yes, thank God, I have. The crimes that have been committed against old Ekdal, by me and by—others—can never be undone. But at least I can free Hjalmar from the conspiracy of silence and deceit which is killing him here.

WERLE. And you think that'd be doing him a service?

GREGERS. I have no doubt of it.

WERLE. You think this photographer is the kind of man who would thank you for such a proof of friendship?

GREGERS. Yes. He is that kind of man.

WERLE. Well. We shall see.

GREGERS. And besides—if I am to go on living, I must try to find some cure for my sick conscience.

WERLE. Your conscience has been sickly ever since you were a child. There's no cure for it. That's an heirloom from your mother, Gregers. The only thing she left you.

GREGERS, *with a scornful smile.* Haven't you got over your disappointment yet? You miscalculated badly, didn't you, when you thought you'd get rich through her.

WERLE. Don't try to distract me with irrelevancies. Are you still resolved to carry out your intention of guiding Ekdal on to what you suppose to be the right path?

GREGERS. Yes. I am resolved.

WERLE. In that case I might have saved myself the trouble of climbing the stairs. I don't suppose it's any use now asking if you'll come back home?

GREGERS. No.

WERLE. And you won't enter the firm either, I suppose?

GREGERS. No.

WERLE. Very good. But since I am intending to enter into a new marriage, I will arrange for the estate to be divided between us.

GREGERS, *quickly*. No, I don't want that.

WERLE. You don't want it?

GREGERS. No. My conscience won't allow me.

WERLE, *after a moment*. Are you going back to the mill?

GREGERS. No. I have left your service.

WERLE. But what will you do?

GREGERS. I shall simply fulfil my mission. That is all.

WERLE. But afterwards? How will you live?

GREGERS. I have saved a little out of my salary.

WERLE. Yes, but how long will that last?

GREGERS. I think it will see me through.

WERLE. What does that mean?

GREGERS. I think you've asked me enough questions.

WERLE. Good-bye, then, Gregers.

GREGERS. Good-bye.

> HAAKON WERLE *goes out.*

HJALMAR *looks in.* Has he gone?

GREGERS. Yes.

> HJALMAR *and* RELLING *come in.* GINA *and* HEDVIG *enter from the kitchen.*

RELLING. Well, that's the end of our lunch.

GREGERS. Get your coat, Hjalmar. You and I must take a long walk together.

HJALMAR. Yes, let's. What did your father want? Was it anything to do with me?

GREGERS. Come along. We must have a little talk. I'll go and fetch my coat.

> *Goes out through the front door.*

GINA. I don't like you going out with him, Hjalmar.

RELLING. She's right. Stay here with us.

HJALMAR *takes his hat and overcoat.* What! When an old schoolfellow feels the need to pour out his heart to me—?

RELLING. But, for Christ's sake—don't you see the fellow's mad, twisted, out of his mind?

GINA. There you are! Well, what do you expect? His mother had weird fits like that too, sometimes.

HJALMAR. All the more need for someone to keep a friendly eye on him, then.

To GINA.

Make sure dinner's ready in good time. Good-bye for now. *Goes out through the front door.*

RELLING. What a pity that fellow didn't fall into one of his own mines and drop right down to Hell!

GINA. Mercy on us! Why do you say that?

RELLING *mutters.* Oh, I have my reasons.

GINA. Do you think young Mr. Werle's really mad?

RELLING. No, worse luck. He's no madder than most people. He's sick all right, though.

GINA. What do you think's wrong with him?

RELLING. I'll tell you, Mrs. Ekdal. He's suffering from a surfeit of self-righteousness.

GINA. Surfeit of self-righteousness?

HEDVIG. Is that a disease?

RELLING. Yes. It's a national disease. But it only very seldom becomes acute.

Nods to GINA.

Thanks for the lunch.

Goes out through the front door.

GINA *walks round uneasily.* Ugh! That Gregers Werle. He always was a queer fish.

HEDVIG *stands by the table and looks searchingly at her.* I think this is all very strange.

ACT FOUR

HJALMAR EKDAL's *studio. A photograph has just been taken; a camera with a cloth over it, a stand, two or three chairs, a folding table, etc., stand round the room. Afternoon light; the sun is just going down; a little later it begins to grow dark.* GINA *is standing in the open doorway with a small box and a wet glass plate in her hand, talking to someone outside.*

GINA. Yes, definitely. When I make a promise I always keep it. I'll have the first dozen ready by Monday. Good-bye, good-bye.

The other person goes downstairs. GINA *closes the door, puts the glass plate in the box and places the latter in the covered camera.*

HEDVIG *comes in from the kitchen.* Have they gone?

GINA, *tidying up.* Yes, thank God, I got rid of them at last.

HEDVIG. Why do you suppose Father hasn't come home yet?

GINA. Are you sure he's not down with Relling?

HEDVIG. No, he's not there. I've just run down the back stairs to ask.

GINA. And his dinner's getting cold too, I suppose?

HEDVIG. It's funny—Father's always on time for dinner.

GINA. Oh, he'll be here soon. You'll see.

HEDVIG. I wish he'd come. Everything seems so strange suddenly.

GINA *cries out.* Here he is!

HJALMAR EKDAL *comes in through the front door.*

HEDVIG *runs towards him.* Oh, Father! Oh, we've waited and waited for you!

GINA *gives him a glance.* You've been a long time, Hjalmar.

HJALMAR, *without looking at her.* Yes, I have rather, haven't I?

He takes off his overcoat. GINA *and* HEDVIG *try to help him, but he gestures them away.*

GINA. Have you eaten with Werle?

HJALMAR *hangs up his coat.* No.

GINA *goes towards the kitchen door.* I'll bring in your food, then.

HJALMAR. No, never mind the food. I don't want any.

HEDVIG *goes closer.* Aren't you well, Father?

HJALMAR. Well? Oh yes, tolerably. We had rather a tiring walk, Gregers and I.

GINA. You shouldn't do that, Hjalmar. You're not used to it.

HJALMAR. But there are a lot of things in life a man's got to get used to.

Wanders round a little.

Anyone been here while I was out?

GINA. Only those two sweethearts.

HJALMAR. No new orders?

GINA. No, not today.

HEDVIG. There'll be some tomorrow, Father. You'll see.

HJALMAR. Let's hope so. Because tomorrow I intend to start working in real earnest.

HEDVIG. Tomorrow? But don't you remember what day it is tomorrow?

HJALMAR. Ah, that's true. Well, the day after tomorrow, then. From now on I'm going to do everything myself. I'm going to manage the whole business on my own.

GINA. But why should you do that, Hjalmar? It'll only make

you miserable. No, I'll take care of the photography, and you can go on puzzling with your invention.

HEDVIG. And think of the wild duck, Father. And all the hens and rabbits, and—

HJALMAR. Don't talk to me about all that nonsense. From now on I shall never set foot in that loft again.

HEDVIG. But Father, you promised tomorrow we'd have a party—

HJALMAR. Hm, that's true. Well, from the day after tomorrow, then. I'd like to wring the neck of that damned wild duck.

HEDVIG *screams.* The wild duck!

GINA. I never heard such nonsense!

HEDVIG, *shaking him.* But Father! It's my wild duck!

HJALMAR. That's why I won't do it. I haven't the heart to—I haven't the heart—because of you, Hedvig. But I know in my heart that I ought to do it. I ought not to allow any creature to live under my roof which has been in *his* hands.

GINA. For heaven's sake! Just because Grandfather got it from that wretched Pettersen—

HJALMAR, *wandering around.* There are certain demands—demands a man makes of himself—how shall I put it?—a striving for perfection—one might say the demands of an ideal—which a man may not ignore without danger to his soul.

HEDVIG *goes after him.* But Father, the wild duck! The poor wild duck!

HJALMAR *stops.* I've told you I shall spare it. For your sake. I shall not touch a hair of its—well, as I told you, I shall spare it. I have more important tasks than that to get down to. But you'd better go and take your walk now, Hedvig. It's getting dark—the light won't hurt your eyes now.

HEDVIG. No, I won't bother to go out today.

HJALMAR. Yes, you must. You screw up your eyes so; all these fumes in here are bad for you. The air under this roof is unclean.

HEDVIG. All right, all right. I'll run down the back stairs and go for a little walk. My coat and hat? Oh, they're in my room. Father, you won't hurt the wild duck while I'm out?

HJALMAR. Not a feather of its head shall be touched.

Presses her to him.

You and I, Hedvig—we two—! Well, run along.

HEDVIG *nods to her parents and goes out through the kitchen.*

HJALMAR *walks around without looking up.* Gina.

GINA. Yes?

HJALMAR. From tomorrow—or let's say the day after tomorrow—I'd like to keep the household accounts myself.

GINA. You want to look after the household accounts too now?

HJALMAR. Yes. I want to find out where the money comes from.

GINA. Well, heaven knows that won't take you long.

HJALMAR. One would imagine it would. You seem to make it go a remarkably long way.

Stops and looks at her.

How do you do it?

GINA. It's because Hedvig and I need so little.

HJALMAR. Is it true that Father gets paid very generously for the copying he does for Mr. Werle?

GINA. I don't know if it's so very generous. But then I don't know what that kind of work is worth.

HJALMAR. Well, roughly how much does he get? Come on, tell me!

GINA. It varies. On an average about what it costs us to keep him, and a bit of pocket money over.

HJALMAR. What it costs us to keep him! And you never told me!

GINA. How could I? You were so happy because you thought he got everything from you.

HJALMAR. And all the time he gets it from Mr. Werle!

GINA. Oh, there's more where that comes from.

HJALMAR. I suppose we'd better light that lamp.

GINA *lights it.* Of course, we don't know if it's the old man himself. It might easily be Graaberg—

HJALMAR. Why drag in Graaberg?

GINA. No, I don't know. I just thought—

HJALMAR. Hm!

GINA. I didn't get this work for Grandfather. It was Berta— when she came to live there.

HJALMAR. Your voice has gone funny.

GINA *puts the shade on the lamp.* My voice?

HJALMAR. And your hands are trembling. Do you deny it?

GINA, *firmly.* Don't beat about the bush, Hjalmar. What's he been telling you about me?

HJALMAR. Is it true—can it be true—that there was a kind of relationship between you and Mr. Werle when you were in his service?

GINA. No, it's not true. Not at that time. Oh, he was after me, all right. And Mrs. Werle thought there was something do- ing; she created a great hullaballoo, and pulled my hair, she did, so I gave my notice and went.

HJALMAR. But it happened afterwards!

GINA. Yes, well I went home. And Mother—she wasn't such a simple soul as you thought, Hjalmar. She kept talking to me about one thing and another. Well, the old man was a widower by then, you see—

HJALMAR. Go on!

GINA. Well, I suppose you'd better know. He wouldn't give in till he'd had his way.

HJALMAR. And this is the mother of my child! How could you keep such a thing from me?

GINA. Yes, it was very wrong. I ought to have told you about it long ago.

HJALMAR. You ought to have told me at once. Then I'd have known what kind of woman you were.

GINA. If I had, would you have married me?

HJALMAR. What do you think?

GINA. Yes, well, that's why I didn't dare to say anything to you at the time. You know how fond I'd grown of you. How could I throw away my whole life?

HJALMAR, *walking about.* And this is the mother of my Hedvig! And to know that everything I see around me—

Kicks a chair.

—my entire home—I owe to a predecessor in your favours! Oh, that seductive old Werle!

GINA. Do you regret the fifteen years we have lived together?

HJALMAR *stops in front of her.* Have you not every day, every moment, regretted the web of concealment and deceit that you've spun around me like a spider? Answer me that! Do you mean to tell me that all this time you haven't been living in anguish and remorse?

GINA. Oh, my dear Hjalmar, I've had enough to think about trying to run the house without—

HJALMAR. Then you never probe your past with a questioning eye?

GINA. You know, I'd almost forgotten the whole dirty business.

HJALMAR. Oh, this soulless, unfeeling complacency! It always fills me with moral indignation. And what is more, you don't even regret it!

GINA. Yes, but tell me, Hjalmar. What would have become of you if you hadn't had a wife like me?

HJALMAR. Like you?

GINA. Yes; I've always been a little more down-to-earth and practical than you. Well, it's natural, I suppose, I'm just that much older.

HJALMAR. What would have become of me!

GINA. Yes. You'd gone a bit off the rails when you met me. You surely won't deny that.

HJALMAR. You call that going off the rails? Oh, you don't understand what it's like when a man is full of sorrow and despair. Particularly a man of my fiery temperament.

GINA. No, no. Perhaps I don't. Anyway, I'm not complaining; you became such a good man once you'd got a house and home of your own. And now it was getting to be so homely and nice here; and Hedvig and I were just thinking we might be able to spend a little on food and clothes.

HJALMAR. Yes, in this swamp of deceit.

GINA. Oh, why did that repulsive little man have to come to our house?

HJALMAR. I too used to think this was a good home. It was a delusion. Where shall I now find the strength I need to transfer my invention into terms of reality? Perhaps it will die with me. And it will be your past, Gina, which will have killed it.

GINA, *on the verge of tears.* No, you mustn't say things like that, Hjalmar. All our married life I've never thought of anyone but you.

HJALMAR. I ask you—what will become of the breadwinner's dream now? As I lay in there on the sofa brooding over the invention I had a feeling that it would devour my energies to the last drop. I sensed that the day on which I held the patent in my hands—that day would spell my release. And it was my dream that you should live on as the late inventor's prosperous widow.

GINA, *drying her tears.* Now you mustn't talk like that, Hjalmar. May the good Lord never let me live to see myself a widow.

HJALMAR. Oh, what does it matter? It's all finished now. Everything!

GREGERS WERLE *cautiously opens the front door and looks in.*

GREGERS. May one come in?

HJALMAR. Yes, come in.

GREGERS *comes forward with a radiant, gratified expression and holds out his hands to them.* Well, my dear friends! *Looks from one to the other and whispers to* HJALMAR.

Hasn't it happened yet?

HJALMAR. Oh, it has happened.

GREGERS. It has!

HJALMAR. I have just lived through the bitterest moment of my life.

GREGERS. But also, surely, the most sublime.

HJALMAR. Well, we've put that behind us. For the time being, anyway.

GINA. May God forgive you, Mr. Werle.

GREGERS, *greatly amazed*. But what I don't see is—

HJALMAR. What don't you see?

GREGERS. From such a crisis there must spring a mutual understanding on which a whole new life can be founded—a partnership built on truth, without concealment.

HJALMAR. Yes, I know, Gregers. I know.

GREGERS. I felt so sure, that when I walked through that door you would be standing there transfigured, and that my eyes would be dazzled by the light. And instead I see nothing but this dull heaviness and misery—

GINA. Oh, I see.

Takes the shade off the lamp.

GREGERS. You don't want to understand me, Mrs. Ekdal. Ah, well. I suppose you need a bit more time. But you, Hjalmar, you? Surely you must have gained a higher understanding now that the crisis is over?

HJALMAR. Yes, of course I have. That is—in a kind of way.

GREGERS. For there is nothing in the world that can compare with the joy of forgiving someone who has sinned, and raising her to one's heart in love.

HJALMAR. Do you think that a man can so easily digest the bitter draught that I have just drained?

GREGERS. Not an ordinary man, perhaps. But a man like you—

HJALMAR. Oh yes, I know, I know. But you mustn't rush me, Gregers. It takes time, you see.

GREGERS. There's a lot of the wild duck in you, Hjalmar.

RELLING *has entered through the front door.*

RELLING. So the wild duck's in the air again?

HJALMAR. Yes. Mr. Werle's winged victim.

RELLING. Mr. Werle? Are you talking about him?

HJALMAR. About him and—the rest of us.

RELLING, *aside, to* GREGERS. You bloody fool, why don't you go to Hell?

HJALMAR. What did you say?

RELLING. I was expressing my heartfelt desire to see this quack doctor back where he belongs. If he stays here he's quite capable of messing up both your lives.

GREGERS. You needn't fear for these two, Dr. Relling. I shan't speak about Hjalmar. We both know him. But in her too, deep in her heart, there is something of honesty and truthfulness.

GINA, *near to tears.* Then you ought to have let me stay as I was.

RELLING. Would it be impertinent to ask exactly what it is you're trying to do in this house?

GREGERS. I want to lay the foundations of a true marriage.

RELLING. Then you don't think their marriage is good enough as it stands?

GREGERS. It's probably as good a marriage as most others, I'm afraid. But it is not yet a true marriage.

HJALMAR. You've never had much faith in ideals, Dr. Relling.

RELLING. Rubbish, my boy! May I ask, Mr. Werle—how many true marriages have you seen in your life? Just roughly.

GREGERS. I hardly think I've seen a single one.

RELLING. Neither have I.

GREGERS. But I've seen so many, many marriages of the opposite kind. And I've had the opportunity to study one at sufficiently close quarters to realise how it can demoralise two human beings.

HJALMAR. The whole moral foundation of a man's life can crumble under his feet. That's the terrible thing.

RELLING. Yes, well, I've never been what you'd call married, so

I wouldn't presume to judge. But I do know this, that children are as much a part of any marriage as their parents. So you leave that child alone.

HJALMAR. Ah! Hedvig! My poor Hedvig!

RELLING. Yes, I'll thank you to keep Hedvig out of this. You two are adults; muck about with your own lives if you enjoy it. But I'm warning you, be gentle with Hedvig, or you may do her irreparable harm.

HJALMAR. Harm?

RELLING. Yes, or she may come to do herself harm—and perhaps others too.

GINA. What would you know about that, Relling?

HJALMAR. There isn't any immediate danger to her eyes, is there?

RELLING. This has nothing to do with her eyes. Hedvig's at a difficult age just now. She's capable of getting up to anything.

GINA. Yes, that's true—I've noticed it already. She's started fooling around with the kitchen stove. She calls it playing with fire. I'm often afraid she'll burn down the house.

RELLING. There you are. You see. I thought as much.

GREGERS, *to* RELLING. But how would you explain that kind of behaviour?

RELLING, *quietly.* My boy. Her voice is breaking.

HJALMAR. As long as the child has me— As long as my head is above the ground—

There is a knock on the door.

GINA. Quiet, Hjalmar. There's someone on the landing.

Calls.

Come in.

MRS. SOERBY *enters, in an overcoat.*

MRS. SOERBY. Good evening.

GINA *goes to greet her.* Berta, is it you?

MRS. SOERBY. Yes, it's me. But perhaps I've come at an inconvenient moment?

HJALMAR. Of course not. Any messenger from that house is always—

MRS. SOERBY, *to* GINA. To be honest, I hoped I might find you alone at this hour of the evening, so I looked in to have a chat and to say good-bye.

GINA. Oh? Are you going away?

MRS. SOERBY. Yes. Tomorrow morning. Up to Hoydal. Mr. Werle left this afternoon.

Casually, to GREGERS.

He asked to be remembered to you.

GINA. Well, fancy that!

HJALMAR. So Mr. Werle has gone away. And you're going after him?

MRS. SOERBY. Yes. What have you got to say about that, Ekdal?

HJALMAR. I say: take care!

GREGERS. I'd better explain. My father is marrying Mrs. Soerby.

HJALMAR. Going to *marry* her?

GINA. Berta! So it's happened at last!

RELLING, *with a slight tremor in his voice.* This isn't true, surely?

MRS. SOERBY. Yes, dear Relling, it's perfectly true.

RELLING. You want to get married again?

MRS. SOERBY. Yes, I've decided I do. Mr. Werle has obtained a special licence, and we're going to get married quite quietly up at Hoydal.

GREGERS. Well, in that case nothing remains but to wish you happiness, as a dutiful stepson.

MRS. SOERBY. Thank you; if you really mean it. I certainly hope it will bring happiness to Mr. Werle and to me.

RELLING. Oh, I'm sure it will. Mr. Werle never gets drunk—as far as I know—and I don't think he's in the habit of beating up his wives, as the late lamented horse-doctor used to.

MRS. SOERBY. Oh, let Soerby rest in peace. He had his good points.

RELLING. But Mr. Werle, we gather, has better ones.

MRS. SOERBY. At least he hasn't wasted all that was best in him. Men who do that must accept the consequences.

RELLING. I'm going out with Molvik tonight.

MRS. SOERBY. Don't do that, Relling. Please, for my sake.

RELLING. What else do you suggest?

To HJALMAR.

Care to join us?

GINA. No, thank you. Hjalmar doesn't go on that kind of spree.

HJALMAR, *aside, irritated.* Oh, be quiet.

RELLING. Good-bye, Mrs.—Werle.

Goes out through front door.

GREGERS, *to* MRS. SOERBY. It seems that you and Dr. Relling know each other pretty well.

MRS. SOERBY. Yes, we've known each other for many years. At one time it even seemed as though our friendship might lead to something more permanent.

GREGERS. Lucky for you it didn't.

MRS. SOERBY. I know. But I've always been wary of acting on impulse. A woman can't just throw herself away, can she?

GREGERS. Aren't you afraid I might tell my father about this old friendship?

MRS. SOERBY. You don't imagine I haven't told him myself?

GREGERS. Oh?

MRS. SOERBY. Anything anyone could truthfully say about me I have already told him. It was the first thing I did when I gathered his intentions.

GREGERS. In that case you've been uncommonly frank.

MRS. SOERBY. I've always been frank. It's by far the best policy for a woman.

HJALMAR. What do you say to that, Gina?

GINA. Oh, we women are so different. We can't all be like Berta.

MRS. SOERBY. Well, Gina, I really believe I did the only sensible thing. Mr. Werle hasn't hidden anything from me, either. And perhaps that's what binds us so closely. Now he can talk to me as freely as a child. He's never been able to do that with anyone before. Fancy a strong and vigorous man like him having to spend all his youth and the best years of his life listening to sermons—very often occasioned by quite imaginary offences, from what I've heard.

GINA. Yes, that's true enough.

GREGERS. If you ladies are going to discuss that subject, I had better go.

MRS. SOERBY. Don't bother. I've had my say. I haven't lied to him or kept anything from him. I dare say you think I've done very well for myself. Well, perhaps I have. But I don't think I'm taking more than I shall be able to give him. I shall never fail him. I shall serve him and look after him better than anyone, now that he's growing helpless.

HJALMAR. He? Growing helpless?

GREGERS, to MRS. SOERBY. Look, I'd rather we didn't discuss that.

MRS. SOERBY. It's no use trying to hide it any longer, though I know he wants to. He's going blind.

HJALMAR starts. Going blind? That's strange. Is he going blind, too?

GINA. It happens to lots of people.

MRS. SOERBY. It's not hard to imagine what that must mean to a man like him. Well, I shall try to make my eyes serve for the two of us as best I can. But I mustn't stay any longer, I've so much to do just now. Oh, what I wanted to tell you, Ekdal, was that if there's anything Mr. Werle can ever do for you, just go and speak to Graaberg.

GREGERS. I hardly think Hjalmar Ekdal will want to accept that offer.

MRS. SOERBY. Oh? I haven't noticed in the past that he—

GINA. Yes, Berta. Hjalmar doesn't need to take anything from Mr. Werle any longer.

HJALMAR, *slowly and emphatically*. Will you present my compliments to your future husband and tell him that I intend at the earliest opportunity to visit Mr. Graaberg—

GREGERS. Hjalmar!

HJALMAR. I repeat, to visit Mr. Graaberg and demand from him an account of the sum I owe his employer. I shall repay this debt of honour—
Laughs.
—debt of honour! But enough of that. I shall repay it to the last penny, with five per cent interest.

GINA. But my dear Hjalmar, we haven't the money to do that.

HJALMAR. Will you please tell your fiancé that I am working indefatigably at my invention. Will you tell him that my spirit is sustained throughout this exhausting struggle by the desire to be rid of the embarrassing burden of this debt. That is why I have become an inventor. The entire profits shall be used to free me from the money of which your prospective husband has seen fit to disgorge himself.

MRS. SOERBY. What's been going on in this house?

HJALMAR. Never mind.

MRS. SOERBY. Well, good-bye. There was something else I wanted to talk to you about, Gina; but it'll have to wait till another time. Good-bye.

HJALMAR *and* GREGERS *bow silently.* GINA *accompanies* MRS. SOERBY *to the door.*

HJALMAR. Not beyond the threshold, Gina.

MRS. SOERBY *goes.* GINA *closes the door behind her.*

There, Gregers. Thank God I've managed to get that debt off my conscience.

GREGERS. Well, you will soon, anyway.

HJALMAR. I think I can claim I behaved correctly.

GREGERS. You behaved exactly as I always knew you would.

HJALMAR. A time comes when a man can no longer ignore the command of his ideals. As the family breadwinner I am continually tormented by this command. I tell you,

Gregers, it isn't easy for a man of small means to repay an old debt on which, as one might say, there has settled the dust of oblivion. But there's no other way. I must do what is right.

GREGERS *puts his hand on* HJALMAR's *shoulders.* My dear Hjalmar. Aren't you glad I came?

HJALMAR. Yes.

GREGERS. Aren't you glad to see yourself as you really are?

HJALMAR, *a little impatiently.* Of course I'm glad. But there's one thing which troubles my sense of justice. Well, but I don't know whether I should speak so bluntly about your father.

GREGERS. Say what you like. I don't mind.

HJALMAR. Well, then—it offends me to think that it is he, and not I, who is going to make a true marriage.

GREGERS. What are you saying!

HJALMAR. But it's true. Your father and Mrs. Soerby are entering upon a marriage founded on absolute trust, with complete frankness on both sides. They are keeping nothing from each other. They have confessed their sins, if I may so put it, and have forgiven each other.

GREGERS. Well, what of it?

HJALMAR. But that's the whole point. You just said yourself that it's only by overcoming all that that you can found a true marriage.

GREGERS. But that's quite different, Hjalmar. You surely don't compare yourself or her with these two—? Well, you know what I mean.

HJALMAR. I can't get away from the fact that there's something here which wounds and offends my sense of justice. Well, it looks as though there's no just power ruling this world.

GINA. Oh, Hjalmar, really! You mustn't speak like that!

GREGERS. Hm—let's not get on to that subject!

HJALMAR. But on the other hand I seem to see the finger of fate at work restoring the balance. He is going blind.

GINA. Oh, we don't know for sure about that.

HJALMAR. Can we doubt it? At least, we ought not to; for there lie justice and retribution. He has blinded a loyal and trusting friend—

GREGERS. I'm afraid he has blinded many.

HJALMAR. And now comes the inexorable, the unfathomable, and demands his own eyes.

GINA. Oh, how can you say such a horrible thing? You make me feel quite frightened.

HJALMAR. It is useful to face up to the darker aspects of existence now and then.

HEDVIG, *in her hat and coat, enters happy and breathless through the front door.*

GINA. Are you back already?

HEDVIG. Yes, I didn't want to walk any more. And a good thing too, for I met someone coming out of the front door.

HJALMAR. That Mrs. Soerby, I suppose.

HEDVIG. Yes.

HJALMAR, *walking up and down.* I hope you have seen her for the last time.

Silence. HEDVIG *looks timidly from one to the other as though to find out what is the matter.*

HEDVIG *goes nearer him; wooingly.* Father.

HJALMAR. Well, what is it, Hedvig?

HEDVIG. Mrs. Soerby brought something for me.

HJALMAR *stops.* For you?

HEDVIG. Yes. Something for tomorrow.

GINA. Berta always brings something for your birthday.

HJALMAR. What is it?

HEDVIG. No, you mustn't know yet. Mother's going to bring it to me in bed tomorrow morning.

HJALMAR. Oh, this conspiracy to keep me out of everything!

HEDVIG, *quickly.* No, of course you can see it. It's a big letter. *Takes the letter from her coat pocket.*

HJALMAR. A letter too?

HEDVIG. Only a letter. The present'll come later, I suppose.
But fancy—a letter! I've never had a letter before. And
there's "Miss" written on the outside!

Reads.

"Miss Hedvig Ekdal." That's me!

HJALMAR. Let me see that letter.

HEDVIG *holds it out to him.* Here—look!

HJALMAR. This is Mr. Werle's writing.

GINA. Are you sure, Hjalmar?

HJALMAR. Look for yourself.

GINA. How should I know?

HJALMAR. Hedvig, may I open this letter and read it?

HEDVIG. Yes, certainly, if you want to.

GINA. No, Hjalmar, not tonight. It's for tomorrow.

HEDVIG, *quietly.* Oh, do let him read it, please! It's sure to be
something nice, and then Father'll be happy, and it'll be
nice here again.

HJALMAR. I may open it, then?

HEDVIG. Yes, do, Father. It'll be fun to know what's in it.

HJALMAR. Right.

*Opens the letter, takes out a sheet of paper, reads it and
looks bewildered.*

What on earth—?

GINA. What does it say?

HEDVIG. Oh yes, Father! Do tell us!

HJALMAR. Be quiet!

Reads it through again. Then, pale but controlled, he says.

It's a deed of gift, Hedvig.

HEDVIG. I say! What do I get?

HJALMAR. See for yourself.

HEDVIG *goes over to the lamp and reads the letter under it.*

HJALMAR *softly, clenching his fists.*

The eyes! The eyes! And this letter!

HEDVIG *looks up from her reading.* But I think Grandfather ought to have it.

HJALMAR *takes the letter from her.* Gina, can you make any sense of this?

GINA. You know I don't understand anything. Tell me what it's about.

HJALMAR. Mr. Werle writes to Hedvig that her old grandfather need no longer trouble to copy letters but that he can henceforth draw from the office the sum of one hundred crowns per month—

GINA. Really?

HEDVIG. A hundred crowns, Mother! That's what it says!

GINA. Well, that'll be nice for Grandfather.

HJALMAR. One hundred crowns, for as long as he needs it. That means, of course, for as long as he lives.

GINA. Well, at least he's provided for then, poor old man.

HJALMAR. But there's something else. You didn't read this part, Hedvig. Afterwards, this money is to be paid to you.

HEDVIG. To me? All of it?

HJALMAR. "You are assured of this sum for the rest of your life," he writes. Did you hear that, Gina?

GINA. Yes, I heard.

HEDVIG. Imagine all the money I'm going to have!
Shakes him.

Oh, Father, Father, aren't you happy—?

HJALMAR *avoids her.* Happy!
Walks about.

Oh, what vistas, what perspectives begin to unroll before my eyes! It's Hedvig! She's the one he remembers so generously!

GINA. Yes—well, it's Hedvig's birthday.

HEDVIG. But you shall have it all, Father! I want to give all the money to you and Mother!

HJALMAR. Yes, to Mother! There we have it!

GREGERS. Hjalmar, this is a trap which has been laid for you.

HJALMAR. You think this is another trap?

GREGERS. When he was here this morning, he said to me: "Hjalmar Ekdal is not the man you think he is."

HJALMAR. Not the man—!

GREGERS. "You'll see," he said.

HJALMAR. Meaning that I would let myself be fobbed off with money!

HEDVIG. Mother, what are they talking about?

GINA. Go in there and take your coat off.

HEDVIG *goes out through the kitchen door, almost in tears.*

GREGERS. Well, Hjalmar, now we shall see which of us is right. He or I.

HJALMAR *slowly tears the letter in two and puts the pieces on the table.* There is my reply.

GREGERS. I knew it would be.

HJALMAR *goes over to* GINA *who is standing by the stove and says in a low voice.* And now let's have the truth. If it was all over between you and him when you—began to grow fond of me, as you put it—why did he make it possible for us to get married?

GINA. I suppose he thought he could have a key.

HJALMAR. Was that all? Wasn't he afraid of a certain possibility?

GINA. I don't know what you mean.

HJALMAR. I want to know if—your child has the right to live beneath my roof.

GINA *draws herself up; her eyes flash.* You ask me that?

HJALMAR. Answer me! Is Hedvig mine or—? Well?

GINA *looks at him in cold defiance.* I don't know.

HJALMAR *trembles slightly.* You don't know!

GINA. How could I? You know yourself what I'm like.

HJALMAR, *quietly, turning away from her.* Then I have no further business in this house.

GREGERS. Consider, Hjalmar!

HJALMAR *puts on his overcoat.* There's nothing for a man like me to consider.

GREGERS. You're wrong. There's a great deal to consider. You three must stay together if you are to win the forgiveness that comes with self-sacrifice.

HJALMAR. I don't want to win it! Never, never! My hat!

Takes his hat.

My home has crashed in ruins about me!

Bursts into tears.

Gregers, I have no child!

HEDVIG, *who has opened the kitchen door.* What are you saying!

Runs over to him.

Daddy, daddy!

GINA. There, you see!

HJALMAR. Don't come near me, Hedvig! Go—go far away! I can't bear to look at you! Ah—those eyes! Good-bye!

Goes towards the door.

HEDVIG *clings tightly to him and screams.* No! No! Don't leave me!

GINA *cries.* Look at the child, Hjalmar! Look at the child!

HJALMAR. I won't! I can't! I must get away! Away from all this!

Tears himself free from HEDVIG *and goes out through the front door.*

HEDVIG, *with despair in her eyes.* He's leaving us, Mother! He's leaving us! He'll never come back again!

GINA. Don't cry, Hedvig. Daddy will come back.

HEDVIG *throws herself sobbing on the sofa.* No, no. He'll never come back to us again.

GREGERS. Will you believe that I meant it all for your good, Mrs. Ekdal?

GINA. Yes, I believe it. But God forgive you.

HEDVIG, *lying on the sofa.* Oh, I shall die, I shall die! What have I done to him? Mother, you must make him come back home!

GINA. Yes, yes, yes, all right. Calm yourself, and I'll go out and and look for him.

Puts on her overcoat.

Perhaps he's just gone down to Relling. But you mustn't lie there and cry. Promise me?

HEDVIG, *sobbing convulsively.* Yes, I'll stop. When Father comes back.

GREGERS, *to* GINA, *as she is about to go.* Wouldn't it be better to let him fight his bitter battle to the end?

GINA. Oh, that'll have to wait. Now we must think of the child.

Goes out through the front door.

HEDVIG *sits up and dries her tears.* I want to know what all this means. Why won't Father look at me any more?

GREGERS. You mustn't ask that till you're grown up.

HEDVIG *catches her breath.* But I can't go on being unhappy like this all the time till I'm grown up. I know what it is. I'm not really Daddy's child.

GREGERS, *uneasily.* How on earth could that be?

HEDVIG. Mummy might have found me. And perhaps Father's got to know about it. I've read of things like that.

GREGERS. Well, but even if it were true—

HEDVIG. Yes, I think he should love me just the same. Or even more. After all, we got the wild duck sent to us as a present, but I love it very much.

GREGERS, *changing the conversation.* Yes, that's true. Let's talk for a moment about the wild duck, Hedvig.

HEDVIG. The poor wild duck. He can't bear to look at her any longer, either. Do you know, he wants to wring her neck!

GREGERS. Oh, I'm sure he won't do that.

HEDVIG. No, but he said it. And I think it was such a horrid thing for Father to say. I say a prayer for the wild duck every evening. I pray that she may be delivered from death and from all evil.

GREGERS *looks at her*. Do you always say your prayers at night?

HEDVIG. Oh, yes.

GREGERS. Who taught you to do that?

HEDVIG. I taught myself. Once when Father was very ill, and had leeches on his neck. He said death was staring him in the face.

GREGERS. Yes?

HEDVIG. So I said a prayer for him after I'd gone to bed. And since then I've kept it up.

GREGERS. And now you pray for the wild duck, too?

HEDVIG. I thought I'd better include her, because she was so ill when she first came to us.

GREGERS. Do you say your prayers in the morning, too?

HEDVIG. Oh, no. Of course not.

GREGERS. Well, why not in the morning?

HEDVIG. In the morning it's light, and then there's nothing to be afraid of any more.

GREGERS. And your father wanted to wring the neck of the wild duck, which you love so much?

HEDVIG. No, he said he ought to, but he'd spare her for my sake. That was kind of him, wasn't it?

GREGERS, *a little closer*. Yes, but what if you now gave up the wild duck for his sake?

HEDVIG *rises*. The wild duck?

GREGERS. Yes. Suppose you sacrificed for him the most precious of your possessions—the thing you love most dearly?

HEDVIG. Do you think that would help?

GREGERS. Try it, Hedvig.

HEDVIG, *quietly, her eyes aglow*. Yes, I will try it.

GREGERS. Do you think you have the strength to do it?

HEDVIG. I'll ask Grandfather to shoot the wild duck for me.

GREGERS. Yes, do that. But not a word to your mother about this!

HEDVIG. Why not?

GREGERS. She doesn't understand us.

HEDVIG. The wild duck! I'll do it tomorrow morning.

GINA *comes in through the front door.*

HEDVIG *goes to meet her.*

Did you find him, Mother?

GINA. No. But I heard he'd called in to see Relling and they'd gone off together.

GREGERS. Are you sure?

GINA. Yes, the caretaker told me. Molvik went with them too, she said.

GREGERS. Now, when he needs to wrestle with his soul alone!

GINA *takes off her coat.* Well, men are difficult creatures. God knows where Relling's dragged him off to. I ran over to Mrs. Eriksen's, but they weren't there.

HEDVIG, *trying not to cry.* Oh, suppose he never comes back!

GREGERS. He'll come back. I shall tell him the news tomorrow, and then you'll see how quickly he will come. Don't worry, Hedvig. You can sleep in peace. Good night.

Goes out through the front door.

HEDVIG *throws her arms, sobbing, round* GINA's *neck.* Mummy, mummy!

GINA *pats her on the back and sighs.* Oh, yes, Relling was right. This is what happens when people go round preaching about the commands of the ideal.

ACT FIVE

HJALMAR EKDAL's *studio. A cold, grey morning light. Wet snow lies on the large panes of glass in the roof.* GINA, *wearing an apron, enters from the kitchen with a brush and duster and goes towards the parlour door. At the same moment,* HEDVIG *runs in from the passage.*

GINA *stops.* Well?

HEDVIG. Yes, Mother, I think he's down with Relling—

GINA. There you are!

HEDVIG. The caretaker said Relling had two people with him when he came back last night.

GINA. I thought as much.

HEDVIG. But that's no good, if he won't come up and see us.

GINA. You leave it to me. I'll go down and have a word with him.

OLD EKDAL, *in a dressing gown and slippers and with a lighted pipe, appears in the doorway of his room.*

EKDAL. Hjalmar, I! Isn't Hjalmar at home?

GINA. No, he seems to have gone out.

EKDAL. What, already? And in this blizzard? Oh, well. Let him. I can go for a walk by myself.

He pushes aside the door of the loft. HEDVIG *helps him. He goes in, and she closes the door behind him.*

HEDVIG, *softly.* Poor Grandfather! What will he say when he hears Father's leaving us?

GINA. Don't be silly, Grandfather mustn't be told about that. Thank God he wasn't here yesterday when all the hullaballoo was going on.

HEDVIG. Yes, but—

GREGERS *enters through the front door.*

GREGERS. Well? Have you found where he is?

GINA. They say he's downstairs with Relling.

GREGERS. With Relling! Has he really been out with those people?

GINA. So it seems.

GREGERS. But he needed so much to be alone, and to collect his thoughts—

GINA. Yes, you may well say that.

RELLING *enters from the passage.*

HEDVIG *goes towards him.* Is Father with you?

GINA, *simultaneously.* Is he there?

RELLING. He certainly is.

HEDVIG. And you didn't tell us!

RELLING. Yes, I'm a beast. But I had to put the other beast to bed first—I refer of course to our daemonic friend—and then I fell asleep—

GINA. What has Hjalmar got to say today?

RELLING. Nothing.

HEDVIG. Doesn't he say anything?

RELLING. Not a damn thing.

GREGERS. No, no. I can understand that so well.

GINA. But what's he doing, then?

RELLING. He's on the sofa, snoring.

GINA. Is he? Yes, Hjalmar's a terrible snorer.

HEDVIG. You mean he's asleep?

RELLING. It certainly sounds like it.

GREGERS. It's quite understandable. After the spiritual conflict that's been rending him—

GINA. And he's not used to wandering around outside at night.

HEDVIG. Perhaps it's a good thing he's getting some sleep, Mother.

GINA. Yes, I was just thinking that. We'd better not wake him up too soon. Thanks, Relling. I must just clean the place up a bit, and then I'll— Come and give me a hand, Hedvig.

GINA *and* HEDVIG *go into the parlour.*

GREGERS *turns to* RELLING. Can you explain this spiritual turmoil in Hjalmar Ekdal?

RELLING. Can't say I've ever noticed any spiritual turmoil in him.

GREGERS. What! At such a crisis, when his whole life has been given a new moral foundation—! How do you suppose a man of Hjalmar's personality—?

RELLING. Personality—*him*? If he ever had any tendency to the kind of abnormalities you call personality, they were nipped out of him, root and branch, before his voice broke. You take my word for it.

GREGERS. That's surprising, considering the love and care with which he was brought up.

RELLING. By those two twisted, hysterical maiden aunts, you mean?

GREGERS. At least they were idealists—but I suppose you'll laugh at me again for saying that.

RELLING. No, I'm not in the mood for that. I know all about it. I've had to endure vomits of rhetoric about his "two spiritual mothers." But I don't think he's got much to be grateful to them for. Hjalmar's tragedy is that all his life he's been regarded by everyone around him as a genius—

GREGERS. Well, isn't he? Deep down inside?

RELLING. I've never noticed any evidence of it. Oh, his father thought so, but—well, *he's* been a bloody fool all his life.

GREGERS. No, he has kept the innocence of a child all his life. That's something you can't understand.

RELLING. All right, have it your way. But when dear little

Hjalmar somehow got to university, he was at once hailed
as the great white hope there too. Well, he was handsome
of course—that helps—you know, peaches and cream, the
shopgirl's dream—and with his romantic temperament and
throbbing voice and talent for declaiming other people's
poetry and ideas—

GREGERS, *indignantly.* Are you talking about Hjalmar Ekdal?

RELLING. Yes. With your permission, that's what this idol you
grovel to really looks like when you take him apart.

GREGERS. Well, I don't think I'm completely blind.

RELLING. You're not far off. You're a sick man too, you know.

GREGERS. Yes, you're right there.

RELLING. Oh, yes. Yours is a complicated case. To begin with,
you've this tiresome rash of righteousness; and what's worse,
you live in a perpetual delirium of hero-worship. You've always got to have something outside yourself that you can
idolise.

GREGERS. That's true. I have to seek it outside myself.

RELLING. It's pathetic the way you make a fool of yourself
over these supermen you imagine you see all around you.
This is just another of those workmen's cottages where you
started hawking your ideals. We're all insolvent here.

GREGERS. If that's your opinion of Hjalmar Ekdal, how can
you spend so much time with him?

RELLING. I'm meant to be a doctor of sorts, God forgive me.
I've got to do something for these wretched cripples I share
a roof with.

GREGERS. I see. So Hjalmar Ekdal is sick too?

RELLING. Well, who isn't?

GREGERS. And what medicine are you giving him?

RELLING. My usual one. I feed the life-lie in him.

GREGERS. Life-*lie*, did you say?

RELLING. Yes, that's right. The universal stimulant.

GREGERS. And what is the life-lie with which Hjalmar Ekdal
is infected, if I may ask?

RELLING. You may not. I don't betray professional secrets to quacks. I wouldn't put it past you to make an even worse mess of him. But my remedy's infallible. I've used it on Molvik for years. I've made him daemonic. That's the serum I've injected into his skull.

GREGERS. Isn't he daemonic, then?

RELLING. What the hell does it mean, daemonic? It's just a bit of claptrap I thought up to keep him alive. If I hadn't done it the poor swine would have succumbed to self-contempt and despair years ago. And what about the old lieutenant? Well, he found the cure himself.

GREGERS. Lieutenant Ekdal? How do you mean?

RELLING. What about that? The great bear hunter going into that musty old loft to chase rabbits? There isn't a happier sportsman in the world than that old man when they let him potter around in there among all that junk. Those four or five withered Christmas trees smell the same to him as the great forests of Hoydal; the chickens are the wild game in the pine tops; and the rabbits that flop across the floor are bears to challenge the strength and skill of the mighty hunter.

GREGERS. Poor Lieutenant Ekdal! Yes, he's had to abandon his youthful ideals.

RELLING. While I remember it, Mr. Werle Junior, forget that foreign word "ideals." Why not use that good old Norwegian word: "lies"?

GREGERS. Do you suggest the two are related?

RELLING. About as closely as typhus and putrid fever.

GREGERS. Dr. Relling, I will not give up until I have rescued Hjalmar Ekdal from your clutches.

RELLING. So much the worse for him. Deprive the average human being of his life-lie, and you rob him of his happiness.

To HEDVIG, *as she enters from the parlour.*

Well, little wild-duck-mother, I'm off downstairs to see if your father's still pondering his great invention on my sofa.

Goes out through front door.

GREGERS *goes closer to* HEDVIG. I can see it, Hedvig. You haven't done it.

HEDVIG. What? Oh, that thing about the wild duck. No.

GREGERS. Your strength of purpose failed you when the moment for action came, I suppose.

HEDVIG. No, it wasn't that. It was just that when I woke this morning and remembered what we'd been talking about, I thought it all seemed so strange.

GREGERS. Strange?

HEDVIG. I don't know. Yesterday evening, when you first mentioned it, I thought there was something so beautiful in the idea; but when I'd slept on it and thought about it again, it didn't seem so good.

GREGERS. Oh, no. Of course you can't have grown up in this house without some rot setting in.

HEDVIG. I don't care about that. If only Father would come back, I'd—

GREGERS. Oh, if only your eyes could be opened to whát really matters in life! If only you had the courage to make your sacrifice truly and joyfully, you'd see—he'd come back to you! But I still believe in you, Hedvig. I believe in you.

He goes out through the front door.

HEDVIG *walks around for a little; then she is about to go into the kitchen when there is a knock on the door of the loft.* HEDVIG *goes over and opens it slightly.* OLD EKDAL *comes out. She closes the door again.*

EKDAL. Hm! It's not much fun having to take my exercise alone.

HEDVIG. Didn't you feel like hunting today, Grandfather?

EKDAL. It's bad weather for hunting today. Dark. You can hardly see your hand in front of your face.

HEDVIG. Don't you ever feel you'd like to shoot something else besides rabbits?

EKDAL. What's wrong with rabbits? Aren't they good enough?

HEDVIG. Yes, but what about—well, the wild duck?

EKDAL *laughs.* Oh, so you're afraid I'll shoot your wild duck, are you? Don't you worry, my child. I'd never do that.

HEDVIG. No, of course, you couldn't. I've heard it's very difficult to shoot wild ducks.

EKDAL. Couldn't? What do you mean? Of course I could.

HEDVIG. How would you go about it, Grandfather? I don't mean with my wild duck, but with other ones?

EKDAL. I'd shoot them under the breast, Hedvig. That's the safest place. And you've got to shoot against the feathers, mind, not with them.

HEDVIG. Do they die then, Grandfather?

EKDAL. You bet they die, if you shoot them properly. Well, I must go in and—hm—clean myself up. You understand—hm?

He goes into his room. HEDVIG *waits a few moments, glances towards the door of the parlour, goes over to the bookcase, reaches up on tiptoe, takes down the double-barrelled pistol from the shelf and looks at it.* GINA *enters from the parlour with her duster and brush.* HEDVIG *quickly puts down the pistol, unnoticed.*

GINA. Don't stand there messing about with your father's things, Hedvig.

HEDVIG *leaves the bookcase.* I only wanted to tidy up a little.

GINA. Go into the kitchen and see if the coffee's still hot. I'll take the tray when I go down.

HEDVIG goes out. GINA *begins to sweep and clean the studio. After a few moments, the front door is cautiously opened and* HJALMAR *looks in. He is wearing his overcoat but is hatless and unwashed. His hair is tousled and his eyes are dull and tired.*

GINA *stands with the brush in her hand and looks at him.* Oh. Hullo, Hjalmar. You've come.

HJALMAR *walks in and answers in a flat voice.* I've come—but only to go at once.

GINA. Yes, yes, of course. But, my goodness, look at you!

HJALMAR. At me?

GINA. And your nice winter coat! Well, that's done for.

HEDVIG, *in the kitchen doorway.* Mother, hadn't I better—?

Sees HJALMAR, *gives a cry of joy and runs towards him.*

Oh, Father, Father!

HJALMAR *turns away with a gesture of rejection.* Get away, get away, get away!

To GINA.

Get her away from me!

GINA, *softly.* Go into the parlour, Hedvig.

HEDVIG *goes silently out.*

HJALMAR *feverishly pulls out the drawer of the table.* I must take my books with me. Where are my books?

GINA. What books?

HJALMAR. My scientific books, of course. The technical maga-zines I need for my invention.

GINA *looks in the bookcase.* Are these the ones, without any covers?

HJALMAR. Of course they are.

GINA *puts a heap of magazines on the table.* Shall I get Hedvig to cut the pages for you?

HJALMAR. I don't want them cut.

Short silence.

GINA. So you're really leaving us, Hjalmar?

HJALMAR, *rummaging among the books.* Have I any choice?

GINA. No, no.

HJALMAR, *vehemently.* I can't go on being pierced to the heart every hour of every day!

GINA. May God forgive you for thinking so vilely of me!

HJALMAR. Give me proof—!

GINA. I think you're the one who needs to do the proving.

HJALMAR. With your past! There are certain things a man has a right to demand—one might be tempted to call them de-mands of the ideal—

GINA. What about Grandfather? What's going to become of him, poor old man?

HJALMAR. I know my duty. That helpless old man leaves with me. I shall go into town and make arrangements. Hm—

Unwillingly.

Has anyone seen my hat on the stairs?

GINA. No. Have you lost your hat?

HJALMAR. I had it on when I came back last night. Naturally. There can be no doubt about that. But I haven't been able to find it today.

GINA. For 'mercy's sake, where on earth did you get to with those two scallywags?

HJALMAR. Don't bother me with trivialities. Do you suppose I'm in a mood to recall details?

GINA. Well, I only hope you haven't caught cold, Hjalmar.

Goes out into the kitchen.

HJALMAR *mutters to himself, half audibly and furiously as he empties the drawer beneath the table.* You're a scoundrel, Relling! A cad, that's what you are! Oh, you vile seducer! I wish I could hire someone to stick a knife in your back!

He puts some old letters on one side, finds the letter he tore up yesterday, picks it up and looks at the pieces, then puts it quickly down again as GINA *returns.*

GINA *puts a tray with coffee, etc., on the table.* I've brought you a cup of something warm, in case you feel inclined. And some bread and butter and a bit of cold fish.

HJALMAR *glances at the tray.* Cold fish? Under this roof? Never! I've had no solid food for nearly twenty-four hours, but no matter. My notes! The first chapter of my memoirs! Where's my diary? Where are all my important papers?

Opens the parlour door, but shrinks back.

There she is again!

GINA. But for heaven's sake, the child's got to be somewhere.

HJALMAR. Come out.

He moves aside to make way for her. HEDVIG *enters, frightened.*

HJALMAR, *with his hand on the door handle, says to* GINA. During my last minutes in what *was* my home, I wish to be spared the presence of outsiders.

Goes out into the parlour.

HEDVIG *runs to her mother and asks softly, trembling.* Does he mean me?

GINA. Stay in the kitchen, Hedvig. No, you'd better go to your room.

To HJALMAR, *as she goes in to him.*

Stop rummaging in those drawers. I know where everything is.

HEDVIG *stands motionless for a moment, anguished and bewildered, biting her lips to keep back her tears. Then she clenches her fists convulsively and says quietly.* The wild duck!

She steals over and takes the pistol from the shelf, opens the loft door a few inches, creeps in and pulls it shut behind her. In the parlour offstage, HJALMAR *and* GINA *begin to argue.*

HJALMAR *comes out with some notebooks and old loose papers, which he puts down on the table.* Oh, that old bag's no use. There are hundreds of things I've got to lug away.

GINA *comes after him with the bag.* Well, just take a shirt and a pair of pants with you. You can come back for the rest later.

HJALMAR. Phew! It's so exhausting, all this packing!

Tears off his overcoat and throws it on the sofa.

GINA. And now your coffee's getting cold, too.

HJALMAR. Hm.

Automatically takes a mouthful; then another.

GINA, *dusting the backs of the chairs.* The big difficulty'll be to find another big loft like this for the rabbits.

HJALMAR. What! Do you expect me to drag all those rabbits along too?

GINA. Well, you know Grandfather can't live without his rabbits.

HJALMAR. Well, he'll have to learn. I'm giving up more important things than rabbits.

GINA, *dusting the bookshelves.* Shall I pack the flute?

HJALMAR. No. No flute for me. Give me the pistol, though.

GINA. Are you going to take the pistol?

HJALMAR. Yes. My loaded pistol.

GINA *looks for it.* It's gone. He must have taken it with him.

HJALMAR. Is he in the loft?

GINA. Yes, of course he's in the loft.

HJALMAR. Hm. The lonely old man!

Takes a piece of bread and butter, eats it and empties his cup.

GINA. If only we hadn't let that room, you could have moved in there.

HJALMAR. What! Live under the same roof as—? Never! Never!

GINA. Couldn't you manage in the parlour for a day or two? You'd be alone there.

HJALMAR. Within these walls? Never!

GINA. Well, how about downstairs with Relling and Molvik?

HJALMAR. Don't mention their names to me! The mere thought of them makes me lose my appetite. No, I must go out into the wind and snow, wandering from door to door seeking shelter for myself and my old father.

GINA. But you've no hat, Hjalmar. You've lost your hat.

HJALMAR. Scum! Vice-ridden scum, that's what they are! We must find a hat.

Takes another piece of bread and butter.

Something must be done. I don't intend to die of exposure.

GINA. What are you looking for?

HJALMAR. Butter.

GINA. Coming up right away.

Goes out into the kitchen.

HJALMAR *shouts after her.* Oh, it doesn't matter. I can eat dry bread.

GINA *comes back with a butter-dish.* Here, this is meant to be fresh.

She pours him another cup of coffee. He sits on the sofa, spreads more butter on his bread, and eats and drinks for a few moments in silence.

HJALMAR. Would I really not be bothered by anyone if I stayed a couple of days in that room? Anyone at all?

GINA. No, of course not. Why don't you?

HJALMAR. I can't see any hope of getting all Father's things moved out all at once.

GINA. And don't forget you've got to break the news to him about your not wanting to live with us any longer.

HJALMAR *pushes away his coffee cup.* Yes, there's that too. I've got to dig up all those complications again. I must think things over. I must give myself breathing-space. I can't cope with so many different burdens in one day.

GINA. No, of course not. Especially with the weather what it is.

HJALMAR *touches* WERLE's *letter.* I see that letter's still lying around.

GINA. Yes, I haven't touched it.

HJALMAR. Of course, it's nothing to do with me—

GINA. Well, I certainly don't want to make anything out of it.

HJALMAR. Still, there's no point in letting it get lost. In the confusion of my moving, it might easily—

GINA. I'll see it doesn't.

HJALMAR. Of course, this deed of gift really belongs to Father. It's up to him to decide whether it's to be used or not.

GINA *sighs.* Yes, poor old Father!

HJALMAR. Perhaps for safety's sake—where can I find some glue?

GINA *goes over to the bookcase.* The pot's here.

HJALMAR. And a brush.

GINA. The brush is here, too.

Brings them to him.

HJALMAR *takes a pair of scissors.* Just a strip of paper along the back—

Cuts and glues.

Far be it from me to deprive other people of what belongs to them. Least of all a destitute old man. Or—any other person. There, now! Let that stand for a few minutes. And when it's dry, take it away. I never want to see the thing again. Never!

GREGERS WERLE *enters from the passage.*

GREGERS, *a little surprised.* Oh! Are you here, Hjalmar?

HJALMAR *gets up quickly.* I was overcome by fatigue.

GREGERS. I see you've had breakfast, however.

HJALMAR. The body makes its demands too, you know.

GREGERS. Well, what have you decided?

HJALMAR. For a man like me, there is no choice. I'm just getting my most important belongings together. But that takes time, you know.

GINA, *a little impatiently.* Well, shall I make the room ready or shall I pack your bag?

HJALMAR *gives an annoyed glance at* GREGERS. Pack. *And* make it ready.

GINA *takes the bag.* Well, well. I'll put in a shirt and p— and the other thing.

Goes into the parlour and closes the door behind her.

GREGERS, *after a short silence.* I'd never envisaged it ending like this. Must you really leave your home?

HJALMAR *wanders around restlessly.* Well, what do you want me to do? I wasn't cut out to suffer, Gregers. I must have peace and calm and comfort around me.

GREGERS. Well, why not? Try! It seems to me that now you

have firm ground to build on. Start afresh! And remember, you have your invention to live for too.

HJALMAR. Oh, don't talk about the invention. That may be further off than you think.

GREGERS. Oh?

HJALMAR. Well, dammit, what *is* there for me to invent? Other people have invented almost everything already. It's becoming more and more difficult every day—

GREGERS. But you've put so much work into it.

HJALMAR. It was that drunkard Relling who started me off on it.

GREGERS. Relling?

HJALMAR. Yes. It was he who first made me conscious that I had the talent to make some invention that would revolutionise photography.

GREGERS. I see. So it was Relling.

HJALMAR. Oh, it's made me so happy thinking about it! Not so much for the sake of the invention itself, but because Hedvig believed in it—believed in it as passionately and trustingly as only a child can believe in a thing. What I mean to say is—I was fool enough to delude myself into thinking she believed in it.

GREGERS. Do you seriously believe that Hedvig hasn't been sincere?

HJALMAR. I can believe anything now. Hedvig's the one who stands in my way. Her shadow is going to shut the sunlight out of my life.

GREGERS. Hedvig? Are you talking about Hedvig?

HJALMAR. I loved that child beyond words. I felt so incredibly happy every time I came back to this humble home and she ran to greet me with those sweet eyes peering at me. Oh, what a credulous fool I was! I loved her so, I loved her so. And I dreamed, I deluded myself into believing that she loved me too.

GREGERS. You call that a delusion?

HJALMAR. How can I know? I can't get anything out of Gina—and anyway, she's so totally insensitive to the idealistic aspect of all these complicated— But to you, Gregers, I feel impelled to open my heart. There's this dreadful doubt in my mind that perhaps Hedvig has never really and truly loved me.

GREGERS. Perhaps you may be given proof that she does.

Listens.

What was that? I think I can hear the wild duck crying.

HJALMAR. Yes, that's her quacking. Father's there in the loft.

GREGERS. Is he?

His eyes shine with joy.

I tell you, you may perhaps be given proof that your poor, misjudged Hedvig does love you.

HJALMAR. Oh, what proof can she give me? I couldn't believe anything from those lips.

GREGERS. Hedvig is incapable of deceit.

HJALMAR. Oh, Gregers, that's just what I can't be sure of. Who knows what Gina and that Mrs. Soerby may not have said when they were gossiping up here? And that child keeps her ears open. That deed of gift may not have come as such a surprise to her as she made out. I thought I noticed something odd in her manner.

GREGERS. What on earth has come over you?

HJALMAR. I've had my eyes opened. Just you wait—you'll see. That deed of gift is only the beginning. Mrs. Soerby's always had a soft spot for Hedvig, and now she's in a position to do anything she likes for the child. They can take her from me any moment they want.

GREGERS. Hedvig will never leave you.

HJALMAR. I wouldn't be too sure of that. If they stand there beckoning to her with their hands full of—and I, who loved her so much, so much! I couldn't imagine any greater happiness than to take her gently by the hand and lead her as a man leads a child who is afraid of the dark through a large, empty room. I can see it now so clearly—the poor photographer in his attic has never really meant very much to her. She was just cunning enough to keep on good terms with him until the time was ripe.

GREGERS. Oh, Hjalmar, you don't believe that.

HJALMAR. The tragedy is that I don't know what to believe—and that I never will know. Oh, you're too much of an idealist, my dear Gregers. If they came to her with their hands full of gold and cried to the child: "Leave him! We can offer you life!"—

GREGERS, *swiftly.* Yes? What do you think she would reply?

HJALMAR. If I were to ask her: "Hedvig, will you sacrifice your life for me?"—

He laughs scornfully.

Oh, yes! You'd hear what answer she'd give me!

A pistol shot is heard from the loft.

GREGERS *cries joyfully.* Hjalmar!

HJALMAR, *enviously.* Oh, now he's started hunting.

GINA *enters, worried.* Oh, Hjalmar, Grandfather's banging away in there on his own.

HJALMAR. I'll go and have a look.

GREGERS, *alive, excited.* Wait! Do you know what that was?

HJALMAR. Of course I do.

GREGERS. No, you don't. But I know. It was the proof you wanted.

HJALMAR. What proof?

GREGERS. A child's sacrifice. She has got your father to shoot the wild duck.

HJALMAR. Shoot the wild duck?

GINA. What an idea!

HJALMAR. But why?

GREGERS. She wanted to sacrifice for you the most precious of her possessions, because she thought that then you would have to love her again.

HJALMAR, *gently, emotionally*. Oh, child, child!

GINA. The things she gets up to!

GREGERS. She only wanted you to love her again, Hjalmar. She couldn't live without it.

GINA, *almost in tears*. There, Hjalmar, you see.

HJALMAR. Where is she, Gina?

GINA *sniffs*. Sitting outside in the kitchen, I suppose, poor child.

HJALMAR *walks across and flings open the kitchen door*. Hedvig, come here. Come and talk to me.

Looks round.

No, she isn't here.

GINA. She must be in her room, then.

HJALMAR, *outside*. No, she isn't there, either.

Comes back.

She must have gone out.

GINA. Well, you didn't want to have her in the house.

HJALMAR. Oh, I wish she'd come home again soon, so that I can tell her! Now everything will be all right, Gregers. Now I think we can start life afresh.

GREGERS, *quietly*. I knew it. Through the child will come resurrection.

OLD EKDAL *appears in the doorway of his room. He is in full uniform, and is busy buckling on his sword.*

HJALMAR, *amazed*. Father! Have you been in there?

GINA. Have you been shooting in your room?

EKDAL, *indignantly, comes closer*. So you go hunting alone now, do you, Hjalmar?

HJALMAR, *confused*. Then it wasn't you who fired that shot in the loft?

EKDAL. Wasn't me? Hm!

GREGERS *cries to* HJALMAR. Hjalmar! She has shot the wild duck herself!

HJALMAR. What's going on round here?

Runs over to the door of the loft, pulls it open, looks in and cries.

Hedvig!

GINA *runs over to the door.* Oh, God! What is it?

HJALMAR *goes inside.* She's lying on the floor.

GREGERS. Lying on the floor? Hedvig?

Joins HJALMAR *inside.*

GINA, *simultaneously.* Hedvig!

Goes into the loft.

Oh, no, no, no!

EKDAL *laughs.* Now she's started hunting too!

HJALMAR, GINA *and* GREGERS *drag* HEDVIG *into the studio. Her right hand is hanging down with the pistol tightly clasped between her fingers.*

HJALMAR, *distraught.* The pistol's gone off! She's shot herself! Call for help! Help!

GINA *runs out into the passage and calls down.* Relling! Relling! Dr. Relling! Come upstairs! As quick as you can!

HJALMAR *and* GREGERS *lay* HEDVIG *on the sofa.*

EKDAL, *quietly.* The forest has taken its revenge.

HJALMAR, *on his knees beside her.* She's coming round now! She'll be all right!

GINA *comes back.* Where's the wound? I can't see anything—

RELLING *hurries in.* MOLVIK *follows, with no waistcoat or tie, and with his coat hanging open.*

RELLING. What's happened?

GINA. They say Hedvig's shot herself.

HJALMAR. Come here and help us.

RELLING. Shot herself!

Pushes the table aside and begins to examine her.

HJALMAR, *lying on the floor, gazes up at him in anguish.* It can't be dangerous? Can it, Relling? She's hardly bleeding at all. It can't be dangerous, can it?

RELLING. How did it happen?

HJALMAR. Oh, how do I know?

GINA. She was going to shoot the wild duck.

RELLING. The wild duck?

HJALMAR. The pistol must have gone off.

RELLING. Hm. I see.

EKDAL. The forest has taken its revenge. But I'm not afraid of it. *Goes into the loft and closes the door behind him.*

HJALMAR. Well, Relling, why don't you say something?

RELLING. The bullet has entered her breast.

HJALMAR. But she'll be all right?

RELLING. Surely you can see that Hedvig is dead.

GINA *bursts into tears.* Oh, my child, my child!

GREGERS, *hoarsely.* The deep blue sea—!

HJALMAR *jumps up.* Yes, yes, she must live! Oh, God bless you, Relling, only for a moment! Only long enough for me to tell her how much I loved her—always—always!

RELLING. The bullet entered her heart. Internal haemorrhage. She died instantaneously.

HJALMAR. And I drove her from me like an animal! And she crept into the loft in terror, and died there—because she loved me!

Sobs.

I can never atone for this—never tell her—!

Clasps his hands and cries upwards.

Oh—You up there—if You exist! Why have You done this to me?

GINA. Hush, hush, don't carry on like that. We had no right to keep her—I suppose—

MOLVIK. The child is not dead, but sleepeth.

RELLING. Rubbish!

HJALMAR *becomes calm, goes across to the sofa and looks down at* HEDVIG, *with folded hands.* How stiff and still she lies!

RELLING *tries to free the pistol from her fingers.* She's holding on to it so tightly. So tightly.

GINA. No, no, Relling, don't break her fingers. Let the pistol stay there.

HJALMAR. Let her keep it.

GINA. Yes, let her. But the child mustn't lie here like a show. We'll take her into her own room. Help me, Hjalmar.

HJALMAR *and* GINA *pick* HEDVIG *up.*

HJALMAR, *as they carry her out.* Oh, Gina, Gina! How shall we live after this?

GINA. We must help each other. Now she belongs to both of us, you know.

MOLVIK *stretches out his arms and mumbles.* Praised be the Lord! To dust thou shalt return! To dust thou shalt return!

RELLING *whispers.* Shut up, man. You're drunk.

HJALMAR *and* GINA *carry the body out through the kitchen door.* RELLING *shuts it behind them.* MOLVIK *slinks out into the passage.*

RELLING *goes over to* GREGERS *and says.* No one's ever going to make me believe that this was an accident.

GREGERS, *who has stood overcome by horror, shaking convulsively.* No one will ever know how this dreadful thing happened.

RELLING. The powder had burned her dress. She must have pressed the pistol against her breast before she fired.

GREGERS. Hedvig has not died in vain. Did you see how grief set free all that is most noble in him?

RELLING. Most men are noble when they stand by a death-bed. But how long do you think this nobility will last?

GREGERS. For as long as he lives. And it will grow, and grow.

RELLING. In nine months, little Hedvig will be nothing more to him than a theme for a recitation.

GREGERS. You dare to say that about Hjalmar Ekdall

RELLING. Let's talk about it again when the first grasses have withered on her grave. Then you'll hear him gulping about "the child untimely ripped from her father's bosom." You'll see him stewing in emotion and self-admiration and self-pity. Just you wait.

GREGERS. If you are right and I am wrong, life is not worth living.

RELLING. Oh, life would be all right if we didn't have to put up with these damned creditors who keep pestering us with the demands of their ideals.

GREGERS *stares ahead of him.* In that case, I am glad that my destiny is what it is.

RELLING. And what, if I may ask, is your destiny?

GREGERS, *as he goes towards the door.* To be the thirteenth at table.

RELLING *laughs and spits.*

Hedda Gabler

INTRODUCTION

HEDDA GABLER occupies a curious, almost anachronistic position in the Ibsen cycle. He wrote it in 1890, between *The Lady from the Sea* and *The Master Builder*, but if one had to date it from internal evidence one would be tempted to place it ten years earlier, as a companion piece to *A Doll's House*, *Ghosts* and *An Enemy of the People*. Like them, it is written very simply and directly; we feel, as in those plays, that he is working within an illuminated circle and not, as in the plays of his final period from *The Lady from the Sea* onwards, that he is exploring the darkness outside that circle. At first sight, again, it appears to differ from these final plays in not being an exercise in self-analysis. This, however, is an illusion, for if we examine HEDDA GABLER closely we find that it contains one of the most revealing self-portraits he ever painted. The play might, indeed, be subtitled *Portrait of the Dramatist as a Young Woman*.

The circumstances under which he wrote HEDDA GABLER were as follows. In the summer of 1889, while holidaying at Gossensass in the Tyrol, Ibsen, then aged sixty-one, had become violently infatuated with an eighteen-year-old Viennese girl named Emilie Bardach. After his return to Munich in September, they wrote to each other continuously for four months; then Ibsen broke off the correspondence, and apart from two brief letters towards the end of the year and a third seven years later in acknowledgment of a telegram of congratulations, he did not contact her again. Two years later he was to use this relationship of mutual infatuation as the basis for *The*

Master Builder, but the change it wrought on Ibsen was immediate. For years he had deliberately suppressed his own emotional life, an undersized and ugly man resigned to a loveless marriage; but his encounter with Emilie had awoken him to the realisation that, as Mr. Graham Greene has recently remarked, fame is a powerful aphrodisiac, and he now entered on a series of romantic relationships with women thirty to forty years his junior. (Indeed, the second of these, with the artist Helene Raff, began while he was still corresponding with Emilie.)

It is unlikely, however, that any of these relationships ever resulted in a physical affair, and this meant that, while immensely enriching his work, they also introduced into it a strong undertone of pessimism. In 1887, in a speech in Stockholm, he had startled his audience by describing himself as an "optimist," and *The Lady from the Sea,* written in 1888, had reflected this optimism. "After so many tragedies," Edmund Gosse had written on its appearance, "this is a comedy . . . the tone is quite unusually sunny, and without a tinge of pessimism. It is in some respects the reverse of *Rosmersholm,* the bitterness of restrained and balked individuality, which ends in death, being contrasted with the sweetness of emancipated and gratified individuality, which leads to health and peace." But none of his five subsequent plays could by any possible stretch of the imagination be described as comedies. The theme of HEDDA GABLER, *The Master Builder, Little Eyolf, John Gabriel Borkman,* and *When We Dead Awaken* is, like that of *Rosmersholm,* "restrained and balked individuality," and I do not think there can be much doubt that this stems from the realisation that for various reasons (fear of scandal, sense of duty towards his wife, consciousness of old age, perhaps the consciousness or fear of physical impotence), he, who had suppressed his emotional life for so long, now had the opportunities to fulfil it but was unable to take advantage of them. As a result of his meeting with Emilie Bardach a new glory, but also a new darkness, entered into his work.

He began to plan a new play immediately on his return from Gossensass. Only a week after arriving in Munich, on

October 7, 1889, he wrote to Emilie: "A new poem begins to dawn in me. I want to work on it this winter, transmuting into it the glowing inspiration of the summer. But the end may be disappointment. I feel it. It is my way." A week later, on October 15, he wrote to her: "My imagination is ragingly at work, but always straying to where in working hours it should not. I cannot keep down the memories of this summer, nor do I want to. The things we have lived through I live again and again—and still again. To make of them a poem is for the time being impossible. For the time being? Shall I ever succeed in the future? And do I really wish that I could and would so succeed? For the moment, at any rate, I cannot." However, on November 19 he wrote more cheerfully: "I am greatly occupied with the preparations for my new work. Sit tight at my desk the whole day. Go out only towards evening. I dream and remember and write."

Unfortunately, we do not know whether the play he was working on at this time was in fact HEDDA GABLER. Ibsen left eight sets of rough notes dating from around this period; most of them obviously refer to HEDDA GABLER, but some seem to point towards *The Master Builder* and others towards a third play which he never ultimately wrote, and since these notes are undated we cannot be sure to which of the three projects he was referring in his letters to Emilie. Some scholars think he did not begin to plan HEDDA until April 1890; others believe he had already conceived it as early as February 1889. At any rate, by the spring of 1890 Ibsen's plans for HEDDA were sufficiently advanced for him to express the hope that he would have his first draft ready by midsummer, so that he would be able to work on it during his summer holiday in (again) Gossensass. But on June 29, 1890, he wrote to Carl Snoilsky, the Swedish poet (generally assumed to be the original of Rosmer), that the play had not worked out and that he was staying in Munich until he could get the first draft finished. Perhaps he feared Gossensass might awake disturbing memories.

As things turned out, he did not complete the first draft of even Act 1 until August 10. On August 13 he began Act 2, but early in September he scrapped this, and on September 6 he began a new draft of this act. Things now went better, for by October 7 he had completed the draft not only of Act 2 but also of Acts 3 and 4. The play was at this stage entitled simply HEDDA, and the draft in which it exists bears all the appearance of having been made as a fair copy to send to the printer. But he was not satisfied, and rewrote the play thoroughly, introducing into it for the first time many of its most striking and famous features. This revisionary work occupied him until November 18, and HEDDA GABLER, as he now entitled it, to underline the fact that she was her father's daughter rather than her husband's wife, was published by Gyldendals of Copenhagen on December 16, 1890, only just in time for the Christmas sales—always an important consideration with Ibsen, who depended on book sales in Scandinavia for a large proportion of his income.*

As with every play he wrote after *A Doll's House* in 1879, excepting only the comparatively light and simple *Enemy of the People,* the public reaction was one of utter bewilderment. Halvdan Koht, in his introduction (1934) to the play in the centenary edition of Ibsen's works, has described how Norway received it. "Its only message seemed to be despair. No meaning nor purpose, simply a suicide ending an absolutely pointless life . . . In contemporary criticisms the most common word used to describe the main character is 'puzzling,' 'improbable' or 'incredible.' Readers got the impression that in the concluding line of the play—'But, good God! People don't do such things!'—Ibsen was making fun of them; for it reminded them that too many of them had said just that about Nora's final action in *A Doll's House.* There were things in HEDDA GABLER that seemed almost intended to parody *A Doll's House*—for example, Hedda's lie about having destroyed the manuscript to help her husband, or the curious form of 'comradeship' between man and woman portrayed here." Bredo Morgenstierna wrote in *Aftenposten* of "the obscurity, the eccentric and abnormal psychology, the empty and deso-

---

* His plays, though widely staged, were usually put on for a few performances only. For example, it was not until 1925 that any English production achieved a run of 50 performances.

late impression which the whole picture leaves," while Alfred
Sinding-Larsen in *Morgenbladet* described Hedda herself as "a
horrid miscarriage of the imagination, a monster in female form
to whom no parallel can be found in real life."

Nor, as with some of his plays (e.g., *Ghosts*), were people
much enlightened when HEDDA GABLER was performed. At
the première on January 31, 1891, at the Residenztheater,
Munich, the public whistled. Ibsen was present and was much
displeased at the declamatory manner of the actress who
played Hedda. On February 10 there was a rather better performance at the Lessing Theater in Berlin, but even here
neither the public nor the critics seem to have understood the
play. Nor was it a success in Stockholm three days later, while
in Copenhagen on February 25 it was a complete fiasco, being
greeted by hissing, whistling and laughter. The following evening it was given in Christiania, also inadequately. The first
respectable performance of HEDDA GABLER was, improbably,
in London (April 20, 1891), where, although it called forth
the usual stream of abuse* from the popular newspapers, intelligent opinion was considerably impressed. William Archer,
who was often critical of early Ibsen productions in England,
described this one as "admirable," and wrote of Elizabeth
Robins's Hedda:

* "It was like a visit to the Morgue . . . There they all lay on
their copper couches, fronting us, and waiting to be owned . . .
There they all were, false men, wicked women, deceitful friends,
sensualists, egotists, piled up in a heap behind the screen of glass,
which we were thankful for . . . What a horrible story! What a
hideous play!" (Clement Scott in the *Daily Telegraph*)

"Hideous nightmare of pessimism . . . the play is simply a bad
escape of moral sewage gas . . . Hedda's soul is a-crawl with the
foulest passions of humanity." (*Pictorial World*)

"Tedious turmoil of knaves and fools." (*People*)

"Mean and sordid philosophy . . . Insidious nastiness of photographic studies of vice and morbidity." (*Saturday Review*)

"Funereal clown [i.e., Ibsen] . . . For sheer unadulterated stupidity, for inherent meanness and vulgarity, for pretentious trivial-
ity . . . no Bostonian novel nor London penny novelette has sur-
passed *Hedda Gabler*." (Robert Buchanan in *Illustrated London
News*)

"I do not hesitate to call her performance in the last act the finest piece of modern tragedy within my recollection. Sarah Bernhardt could not have done this scene better; and it is long since Sarah attempted a scene so well worth doing. . . . From what I hear of representations of *Hedda Gabler* on the Continent, I very much doubt whether it has anywhere been played to such perfection as at the Vaudeville."

Henry James, who had been puzzled by the play on reading it, found the performance gratifyingly illuminating. "The play on perusal," he wrote (*On the Occasion of Hedda Gabler*, 1891), "left one comparatively muddled and mystified, fascinated but—in one's intellectual sympathy—snubbed. Acted, it leads that sympathy over the straightest of roads with all the exhilaration of a superior pace." But he added a gentle rider. "Much more, I confess, one doesn't get from it; but an hour of refreshing exercise is a reward in itself . . . Ibsen is various, and *Hedda Gabler* is probably an ironical pleasantry, the artistic exercise of a mind saturated with the vision of human infirmities; saturated, above all, with a sense of the infinitude, for all its mortal savour, of *character*, finding that an endless romance and a perpetual challenge. Can there have been at the source of such a production a mere refinement of conscious power, an enjoyment of difficulty and a preconceived victory over it?"

There are many people who share James's view of HEDDA GABLER as a brilliant but, for Ibsen, curiously detached, objective, almost brutal "exercise"—a view which has been greatly fostered by the tendency of actresses to portray Hedda as an evil genius, a kind of suburban Lady Macbeth. The opposite view, that it is one of Ibsen's most "committed" plays, has been brilliantly argued by Dr. Arne Duve in his wayward but stimulating book *Symbolikken i Henrik Ibsens Skuespill* (Nasjonalforlaget, Oslo, 1945). Dr. Duve suggests that Hedda represents Ibsen's repressed and crippled emotional life. As a young man, he reminds us, Ibsen had been wildly emotional; at sixteen he had fathered an illegitimate child, and at least once during those early years he became a near-alcoholic and is thought to have attempted suicide. Loevborg and Tesman,

Dr. Duve argues, are aspects of Ibsen's own self; Loevborg is an idealised portrait of himself as he had been in the wild years of his youth, Tesman a *reductio ad absurdum* of what he had chosen to become. Loevborg stands for Ibsen's emotional self, Tesman for his intellectual self. Ibsen was haunted throughout the latter half of his life by the feeling that he had stifled his emotional self and that only his bourgeois and slightly ludicrous intellectual self had lived on. He had persuaded himself to accept this state of affairs, but the encounter with Emilie Bardach seems to have brought all his old feelings of guilt rushing to the surface. Hedda longs to be like Loevborg but lacks the courage; she is repelled by the reality of sex (as Ibsen himself was?) and prefers to experience it vicariously by encouraging Loevborg to describe his experiences to her. Two emotions are dominant in her, the fear of scandal and the fear of ridicule, and Ibsen himself, though always willing to trail his coat in print, seems also to have been privately dominated by these emotions.

But if HEDDA GABLER is in fact a self-portrait, it is certainly an unconscious one—not that that makes it any the less truthful or valuable; rather the reverse. Ibsen's rough preliminary jottings referred to above make it clear that he *intended* the play as a tragedy of the purposelessness of life, and in particular of the purposelessness imposed on women of his time both by their upbringing and by the social conventions which limited their activities. The following extracts will serve as examples:

"1. They aren't all created to be mothers.

2. They all have a leaning towards sensuality, but are afraid of the scandal.

3. They realize that life holds a purpose for them, but they cannot find that purpose."

"Women have no influence on public affairs. So they want to influence individuals spiritually."

"The great tragedy of life is that so many people have nothing to do but yearn for happiness without ever being able to find it."

"Men and women don't belong to the same century."

"There are very few true parents in the world. Most people are brought up by uncles or aunts—neglected or misunderstood or spoiled."

"The play is to be about 'the insuperable'—the longing and striving to defy convention, to defy what people accept (including Hedda)."

"Hedda is typical of women in her position and with her character. One marries Tesman but one titillates one's imagination with Eilert Loevborg. One leans back in one's chair, closes one's eyes and pictures to oneself his adventure. The enormous difference: Mrs. Elvsted 'works to improve him morally,' while for Hedda he is merely a subject for cowardly and tantalising dreams. She lacks the courage to partake actively in such goings-on. Then her confession as to how she really feels. Tied! Don't understand— But to be an object of ridicule! Of ridicule!"

"The daemon in Hedda is that she wants to influence another human being, but once that has happened, she despises him."

"Loevborg has leanings towards Bohemianism. Hedda is also attracted to it, but dares not take the jump."

"It's really a man's life she wants to lead. In all respects. But then scruples intervene. Some inherited—some implanted."

"Remember I was born the child of an old man. And not merely old. Played-out—or anyway, decrepit. Perhaps that's left its mark."

"It is a great delusion that one only loves one person."

"Tesman represents propriety. Hedda represents *ennui*. Mrs. R. [i.e., Mrs. Elvsted] modern nervousness and hysteria. Brack the representative of bourgeois society."

"H.L. [i.e., Loevborg]'s despair arises from the fact that he wants to control the world but cannot control himself."

"Life for Hedda is a farce which isn't worth seeing through to the end."

As usual with Ibsen's plays, certain elements in HEDDA GABLER can be traced to incidents in the lives of people whom he knew personally or had heard or read about. For example, when he visited Norway in 1885 he must have heard of the marriage the previous winter between a famous beauty named Sophie Magelssen and the philologist Peter Groth. Groth had married her on a research grant which he had won in competition with one Hjalmar Falk, whom many thought the better scholar of the two (and who gets a kind of consolatory mention in the play as the dead Cabinet Minister who had previously owned the Tesmans' villa). Neither Tesman nor Loevborg, however, was modelled on either of these two. Ibsen told his son Sigurd that he had based Tesman on Julius Elias, a young German student of literature whom he had got to know in Munich. Elias's great passion was for "putting other people's papers in order"; later he became a distinguished man of letters, and ironically enough it fell to him to put Ibsen's own papers in order when he shared with Halvdan Koht the task of editing the dramatist's literary remains.* Loevborg was closely modelled on a Dane named Julius Hoffory, who was Professor of Scandinavian Philology and Phonetics in Berlin. Hoffory was a gifted but unbalanced man who mixed freely with women of low repute and had once lost the manuscript of a book during a nocturnal orgy. He recognised himself delightedly when HEDDA GABLER appeared, and thereafter adopted Loevborg as his pseudonym. A few years later he became mentally disordered and never fully recovered his sanity.

Miss Tesman, George's aunt, was based on an old lady from Trondhjem named Elise Hokk. Ibsen had met her a number of times during the early seventies in Dresden, where she tended a sick sister for three years until the latter died. He wrote a charming poem in tribute to her in 1874. She is the only character in the play, as far as is known, who was based

---

* In fairness to Elias, it should be stated that Tesman is a much less ridiculous character in the early draft of the play than Ibsen subsequently made him. His maddening repetition of genteel phrases such as "Fancy that!" was added during revision.

on a Norwegian original, and this may have influenced early
critics who wrote that HEDDA GABLER was the least Norwegian
of Ibsen's plays and that the town (unnamed as usual) in
which the action takes place was less suggestive of Christiania
than of a Continental capital. William Archer, however, who
knew Christiania well, felt sure that Ibsen had that city in
mind, and added the interesting comment that Ibsen, although
writing in 1890, seemed to have set the play some thirty years
earlier. "The electric cars, telephones and other conspicuous
factors in the life of a modern capital," he wrote in his introduction (1907) to the English translation by himself and Edmund Gosse, "are notably absent from the play. There is no
electric light in Secretary Falk's villa. It is still the habit for
ladies to return on foot from evening parties, with gallant
swains escorting them. This 'suburbanism' which so distressed
the London critics of 1891 was characteristic of the Christiania
Ibsen himself had known in the eighteen-sixties—the Christiania of *Love's Comedy*—rather than of the greatly extended
and modernised city of the end of the century."

Three further incidents which came to Ibsen's notice found
their way into the play. While he was actually working on it,
a young married couple came to seek his advice; their happiness, they said, had been ruined because the husband had
been hypnotised by another woman. Then there was the unfortunate case of the Norwegian composer Johan Svendsen,
whose wife, Sally, in a fit of rage at discovering a letter from
another woman hidden in a bouquet of flowers, had burned
the score of a symphony which he had just composed. Finally,
Ibsen heard of the even more unfortunate incident of the Norwegian lady whose husband had cured himself of drink and
had resolved never to touch it again. To see how much power
she had over him, she rolled a keg of brandy into his room as
a birthday present, and before the day was over he was dead
drunk. All these episodes are reflected in HEDDA GABLER.

The original of Hedda herself is not known. She has been
rather glibly assumed by some critics to be a portrait of
Emilie, on the grounds that both were beautiful and aristocratic and did not know what to do with their lives, and that

Ibsen's description of Hedda (aristocratic face, fine complexion, veiled expression in the eyes, etc.) corresponds to early photographs of Emilie. The same characteristics could, however, be found in the photograph of almost any well-born young lady of the period; the description would apply equally to Queen Alexandra; and few women of Ibsen's time, let alone girls of eighteen, knew what to do with their lives. In any case, the idea of creating such a character had been at the back of Ibsen's mind long before he met Emilie, for his rough notes for *Rosmersholm* (1886) contain a sketch of a girl, intended as Rosmer's elder daughter though he finally decided not to include her in the play, who "is in danger of succumbing to inactivity and loneliness. She has rich talents which are lying unused." On the other hand, Emilie must certainly have been at the back of his mind when he was writing HEDDA GABLER, and it is possible that Hedda may be a portrait, conscious or unconscious, of what Emilie might become in ten years if she did not marry the right man or find a fixed purpose in life. If so, it was a prophecy that came uncomfortably near the truth, for Emilie, though she lived to be eighty-three—she died as late as November 1, 1955—accomplished nothing and never married.

The differences between Ibsen's first draft and his final version as we know it are, as has already been remarked, numerous and revealing. Apart from changing Tesman from an ordinary bourgeois husband into a ninny spoiled (like Hjalmar Ekdal) by loving aunts, he improved him morally, for in the first draft it is Tesman who suggests hiding the manuscript to give Loevborg a fright, and so is partly responsible for the latter's death. Miss Tesman's important account to Bertha in Act 1 of Hedda's life with her father was an afterthought; so were Mademoiselle Danielle, Mrs. Elvsted's abundant hair and Hedda's jealousy of it, the image of the vine-leaves, and Hedda's threat (before the play opens) to shoot Loevborg. Act 1 ends much more feebly in the draft, with no mention of the pistols; and Tesman and Mrs. Elvsted both know of Hedda's former close relationship with Loevborg. Miss Tesman's role is much less

rich than in the final version; she does not realise in Act 1 that
Hedda is going to have a baby, and has a far less effective
scene with Hedda in Act 4. The conversation between Hedda,
Loevborg and Tesman over the photograph album about the
honeymoon contains a direct reference to Gossensass, subsequently deleted. And Brack, in a passage one is rather sorry
to lose, describes sadly to Hedda how three "triangles" of
which he was a part have been broken up during the past six
months—not, as Hedda guesses, by other bachelors but by in-
truders far more destructive to extramarital relationships—
children. Finally, one may note two remarks which Ibsen
originally put into Hedda's mouth but subsequently deleted:
(1) "I can't understand how anyone could fall in love with a
man who isn't married—or engaged—or at least in love with
someone else." (2) "To take someone from someone else—I
think that must be so wonderful!" He saved these lines for a
character, already created in miniature in *The Lady from the
Sea*, to whom he was to allot the principal female role in his
next play two years later—Hilde Wangel in *The Master Builder*.

The repeated references to the "vine-leaves" continues to
puzzle critics, even though William Archer cleared the problem
up fifty years ago. "Surely," he wrote, "this is a very obvious
image or symbol of the beautiful, the ideal aspect of bacchic
elation and revelry . . . Professor Dietrichson relates that
among the young artists whose society Ibsen frequented during his first years in Rome it was customary, at their little
festivals, for the revellers to deck themselves in this fashion.
But the image is so obvious that there is no need to trace it to
any personal experience. The attempt to place Hedda's vine-
leaves among Ibsen's obscurities is an example of the firm reso-
lution not to understand which animated the criticism of the
nineties." Not, alas, only of the nineties. The picture which the
vine-leaves are intended to evoke is that of the young god,
"burning and unashamed," in Hedda's words; as Archer noted,
it was an image Ibsen had used previously in both *Peer Gynt*
and *Emperor and Galilean*.

A point that is sometimes missed in productions of HEDDA
GABLER is the importance of correct casting for Bertha, the

Tesmans' maid. Ibsen never created a role, however tiny, that was not both integral to the play and rewarding to the player, and his servants are no exceptions—one thinks of the two butlers, the superior Pettersen and the inferior Jensen, in *The Wild Duck*, the housekeeper Mrs. Helseth in *Rosmersholm*, and Malene, the sour maid in *John Gabriel Borkman*. Ibsen underlined Bertha's importance in a letter which he wrote to Kristine Steen on January 14, 1891, concerning the casting of the play for Christiania. "Mrs. Wolf," he wrote, "wishes to be released from playing the maid Bertha in my new play, since she is of opinion that this role could be adequately filled by any other member of the company. She is mistaken. There is no one else at the theatre who can perform Bertha as I wish her to be performed. Only Mrs. Wolf can do it. She has evidently not taken the trouble to read the play carefully, or she could hardly fail to appreciate this. George Tesman, his old aunts and Bertha together create a picture of completeness and unity. They have common thoughts, common memories, a common attitude towards life. To Hedda they represent a force foreign and hostile to her and to everything she stands for. The harmony that exists between them must be apparent on the stage. And this can be achieved if Mrs. Wolf plays the part. But only if she does. My respect for Mrs. Wolf's soundness of judgment is too great for me seriously to believe that she regards it as artistically beneath her to create a servant. I did not regard it as artistically beneath me to create this honest, artless old creature. Here in Munich this unpretentious character is to be created by one of the Hoftheater's leading actresses, and she has embraced the task with love and interest. Besides being an actress, she is also an artist. By this I mean that she regards it as a matter of honour not merely to 'give a performance' but to turn a created character into a thing of flesh and blood."

Despite its early failures on the stages of Europe, HEDDA GABLER has come to be accepted as one of the most popular of Ibsen's plays. London has seen no less than eighteen separate productions, a number exceeded only, among Ibsen's other plays, by *A Doll's House* and *Ghosts*. Among the actresses who have played it there are Elizabeth Robins, Eleonora Duse, Mrs. Patrick Campbell, Lydia Yavorska, Jean Forbes Robertson and Peggy Ashcroft. Probably the finest English Hedda, however, was Pamela Brown, who in 1941 at the age of twenty-two gave a performance at the Oxford Playhouse which led James Agate to compare her seriously with the young Sarah Bernhardt. America first saw the play on March 30, 1898, when Elizabeth Robins presented a single performance at the Fifth Avenue Theatre in New York. *The Critic* wrote of this production that "it was, on the whole, the most satisfactory representation of an Ibsen play ever given in this city," and described Miss Robins's performance as "in every way a remarkable achievement." Unfortunately, according to Norman Hapgood in *The Stage in America, 1897–1900*, "it failed to interest the public enough to continue contemplated Ibsen experiments." Blanche Bates played it for a single matinée in Washington in 1900; then in 1903 Minnie Fiske presented it in New York for a whole week to crowded houses, and brought it back to the Manhattan Theatre in November 1904, when it achieved the, by the standard of those days, considerable number of twenty-six performances. The cast included George Arliss as Judge Brack. In 1905 Alla Nazimova played it at the Russian Theatre, New York, in Russian, and the following year she performed it in English, creating a tremendous impression. Subsequent Heddas in New York have included Emily Stevens, Eva Le Gallienne and, in 1960, Anne Meacham, in a production for which this translation was specially commissioned.

M. M.

CHARACTERS

GEORGE TESMAN, research graduate, in cultural history
HEDDA, his wife
MISS JULIANA TESMAN, his aunt
MRS. ELVSTED
JUDGE BRACK
EILERT LOEVBORG
BERTHA, a maid

The action takes place in TESMAN's *villa in the fashionable quarter of town.*

This translation was commissioned by David Ross and was presented by him at the Fourth Street Theatre, New York, on November 9, 1960, with the following cast:

GEORGE TESMAN	Lester Rawlings
HEDDA	Anne Meacham
MISS JULIANA TESMAN	Lois Holmes
MRS. ELVSTED	Lori March
JUDGE BRACK	Frederick Rolf
EILERT LOEVBORG	Mark Lenard
BERTHA	Elizabeth Colquhoun

Directed by David Ross

ACT ONE

A large drawing room, handsomely and tastefully furnished;
decorated in dark colours. In the rear wall is a broad open
doorway, with curtains drawn back to either side. It leads
to a smaller room, decorated in the same style as the draw-
ing room. In the right-hand wall of the drawing room, a
folding door leads out to the hall. The opposite wall, on the
left, contains french windows, also with curtains drawn back
on either side. Through the glass we can see part of a ve-
randah, and trees in autumn colours. Downstage stands an
oval table, covered by a cloth and surrounded by chairs.
Downstage right, against the wall, is a broad stove tiled with
dark porcelain; in front of it stand a high-backed armchair,
a cushioned footrest, and two footstools. Upstage right, in
an alcove, is a corner sofa, with a small, round table. Down-
stage left, a little away from the wall, is another sofa. Up-
stage of the french windows, a piano. On either side of the
open doorway in the rear wall stand what-nots holding
ornaments of terra cotta and majolica. Against the rear wall
of the smaller room can be seen a sofa, a table, and a couple
of chairs. Above this sofa hangs the portrait of a handsome
old man in general's uniform. Above the table a lamp hangs
from the ceiling, with a shade of opalescent, milky glass.
All round the drawing room bunches of flowers stand in
vases and glasses. More bunches lie on the tables. The floors
of both rooms are covered with thick carpets. Morning light.
The sun shines in through the french windows.

MISS JULIANA TESMAN, *wearing a hat and carrying a parasol, enters from the hall, followed by* BERTHA, *who is carrying a bunch of flowers wrapped in paper.* MISS TESMAN *is about sixty-five, of pleasant and kindly appearance. She is neatly but simply dressed in grey outdoor clothes.* BERTHA, *the maid, is rather simple and rustic-looking. She is getting on in years.*

MISS TESMAN *stops just inside the door, listens, and says in a hushed voice.* No, bless my soul! They're not up yet.

BERTHA, *also in hushed tones.* What did I tell you, miss? The boat didn't get in till midnight. And when they did turn up —Jesus, miss, you should have seen all the things Madam made me unpack before she'd go to bed!

MISS TESMAN. Ah, well. Let them have a good lie in. But let's have some nice fresh air waiting for them when they do come down.

Goes to the french windows and throws them wide open.

BERTHA, *bewildered at the table, the bunch of flowers in her hand.* I'm blessed if there's a square inch left to put anything. I'll have to let it lie here, miss.

Puts it on the piano.

MISS TESMAN. Well, Bertha dear, so now you have a new mistress. Heaven knows it nearly broke my heart to have to part with you.

BERTHA *snivels.* What about me, Miss Juju? How do you suppose I felt? After all the happy years I've spent with you and Miss Rena?

MISS TESMAN. We must accept it bravely, Bertha. It was the only way. George needs you to take care of him. He could never manage without you. You've looked after him ever since he was a tiny boy.

BERTHA. Oh, but, Miss Juju, I can't help thinking about Miss Rena, lying there all helpless, poor dear. And that new girl! She'll never learn the proper way to handle an invalid.

MISS TESMAN. Oh, I'll manage to train her. I'll do most of the work myself, you know. You needn't worry about my poor sister, Bertha dear.

BERTHA. But Miss Juju, there's another thing. I'm frightened Madam may not find me suitable.

MISS TESMAN. Oh, nonsense, Bertha. There may be one or two little things to begin with—

BERTHA. She's a real lady. Wants everything just so.

MISS TESMAN. But of course she does! General Gabler's daughter! Think of what she was accustomed to when the General was alive. You remember how we used to see her out riding with her father? In that long black skirt? With the feather in her hat?

BERTHA. Oh, yes, miss. As if I could forget! But, Lord! I never dreamed I'd live to see a match between her and Master Georgie.

MISS TESMAN. Neither did I. By the way, Bertha, from now on you must stop calling him Master Georgie. You must say: Dr. Tesman.

BERTHA. Yes, Madam said something about that too. Last night —the moment they'd set foot inside the door. Is it true, then, miss?

MISS TESMAN. Indeed it is. Just imagine, Bertha, some foreigners have made him a doctor. It happened while they were away. I had no idea till he told me when they got off the boat.

BERTHA. Well, I suppose there's no limit to what he won't become. He's that clever. I never thought he'd go in for hospital work, though.

MISS TESMAN. No, he's not that kind of doctor.

Nods impressively.

In any case, you may soon have to address him by an even grander title.

BERTHA. You don't say! What might that be, miss?

MISS TESMAN *smiles.* Ah! If you only knew!

Moved.

Dear God, if only poor dear Joachim could rise out of his grave and see what his little son has grown into!

Looks round.

But Bertha, why have you done this? Taken the chintz covers off all the furniture!

BERTHA. Madam said I was to. Can't stand chintz covers on chairs, she said.

MISS TESMAN. But surely they're not going to use this room as a parlour?

BERTHA. So I gathered, miss. From what Madam said. He didn't say anything. The Doctor.

GEORGE TESMAN *comes into the rear room, from the right, humming, with an open, empty travelling bag in his hand. He is about thirty-three, of medium height and youthful appearance, rather plump, with an open, round, contented face, and fair hair and beard. He wears spectacles, and is dressed in comfortable, indoor clothes.*

MISS TESMAN. Good morning! Good morning, George!

TESMAN, *in open doorway.* Auntie Juju! Dear Auntie Juju!

Comes forward and shakes her hand.

You've come all the way out here! And so early! What?

MISS TESMAN. Well, I had to make sure you'd settled in comfortably.

TESMAN. But you can't have had a proper night's sleep.

MISS TESMAN. Oh, never mind that.

TESMAN. We were so sorry we couldn't give you a lift. But you saw how it was—Hedda had so much luggage—and she insisted on having it all with her.

MISS TESMAN. Yes, I've never seen so much luggage.

BERTHA, *to* TESMAN. Shall I go and ask Madam if there's anything I can lend her a hand with?

TESMAN. Er—thank you, Bertha; no, you needn't bother. She says if she wants you for anything she'll ring.

BERTHA, *over to right.* Oh. Very good.

TESMAN. Oh, Bertha—take this bag, will you?

BERTHA *takes it.* I'll put it in the attic.

Goes out into the hall.

TESMAN. Just fancy, Auntie Juju, I filled that whole bag with notes for my book. You know, it's really incredible what I've managed to find rooting through those archives. By Jove! Wonderful old things no one even knew existed—

MISS TESMAN. I'm sure you didn't waste a single moment of your honeymoon, George dear.

TESMAN. No, I think I can truthfully claim that. But, Auntie Juju, do take your hat off. Here. Let me untie it for you. What?

MISS TESMAN, *as he does so.* Oh dear, oh dear! It's just as if you were still living at home with us.

TESMAN *turns the hat in his hand and looks at it.* I say! What a splendid new hat!

MISS TESMAN. I bought it for Hedda's sake.

TESMAN. For Hedda's sake? What?

MISS TESMAN. So that Hedda needn't be ashamed of me, in case we ever go for a walk together.

TESMAN *pats her cheek.* You still think of everything, don't you, Auntie Juju?

Puts the hat down on a chair by the table.

Come on, let's sit down here on the sofa. And have a little chat while we wait for Hedda.

They sit. She puts her parasol in the corner of the sofa.

MISS TESMAN *clasps both his hands and looks at him.* Oh, George, it's so wonderful to have you back, and be able to see you with my own eyes again! Poor dear Joachim's own son!

TESMAN. What about me! It's wonderful for me to see you again, Auntie Juju. You've been a mother to me. And a father, too.

MISS TESMAN. You'll always keep a soft spot in your heart for your old aunties, won't you, George dear?

TESMAN. I suppose Auntie Rena's no better? What?

MISS TESMAN. Alas, no. I'm afraid she'll never get better, poor
dear. She's lying there just as she has for all these years.
Please God I may be allowed to keep her for a little longer.
If I lost her I don't know what I'd do. Especially now I
haven't you to look after.

TESMAN *pats her on the back.* There, there, there!

MISS TESMAN, *with a sudden change of mood.* Oh but George,
fancy you being a married man! And to think it's you who've
won Hedda Gabler! The beautiful Hedda Gabler! Fancy!
She was always so surrounded by admirers.

TESMAN *hums a little and smiles contentedly.* Yes, I suppose
there are quite a few people in this town who wouldn't
mind being in my shoes. What?

MISS TESMAN. And what a honeymoon! Five months! Nearly
six.

TESMAN. Well, I've done a lot of work, you know. All those
archives to go through. And I've had to read lots of books.

MISS TESMAN. Yes, dear, of course.
Lowers her voice confidentially.
But tell me, George—haven't you any—any extra little piece
of news to give me?

TESMAN. You mean, arising out of the honeymoon?

MISS TESMAN. Yes.

TESMAN. No, I don't think there's anything I didn't tell you in
my letters. My doctorate, of course—but I told you about
that last night, didn't I?

MISS TESMAN. Yes, yes, I didn't mean that kind of thing. I was
just wondering—are you—are you expecting—?

TESMAN. Expecting what?

MISS TESMAN. Oh, come on George, I'm your old aunt!

TESMAN. Well actually—yes, I am expecting something.

MISS TESMAN. I knew it!

TESMAN. You'll be happy to hear that before very long I expect
to become a professor.

MISS TESMAN. Professor?

TESMAN. I think I may say that the matter has been decided. But, Auntie Juju, you know about this.

MISS TESMAN *gives a little laugh.* Yes, of course. I'd forgotten. *Changes her tone.*

But we were talking about your honeymoon. It must have cost a dreadful amount of money, George?

TESMAN. Oh well, you know, that big research grant I got helped a good deal.

MISS TESMAN. But how on earth did you manage to make it do for two?

TESMAN. Well, to tell the truth it was a bit tricky. What?

MISS TESMAN. Especially when one's travelling with a lady. A little bird tells me that makes things very much more expensive.

TESMAN. Well, yes, of course it does make things a little more expensive. But Hedda has to do things in style, Auntie Juju. I mean, she has to. Anything less grand wouldn't have suited her.

MISS TESMAN. No, no, I suppose not. A honeymoon abroad seems to be the vogue nowadays. But tell me, have you had time to look round the house?

TESMAN. You bet. I've been up since the crack of dawn.

MISS TESMAN. Well, what do you think of it?

TESMAN. Splendid. Absolutely splendid. I'm only wondering what we're going to do with those two empty rooms between that little one and Hedda's bedroom.

MISS TESMAN *laughs slyly.* Ah, George dear, I'm sure you'll manage to find some use for them—in time.

TESMAN. Yes, of course, Auntie Juju, how stupid of me. You're thinking of my books. What?

MISS TESMAN. Yes, yes, dear boy. I was thinking of your books.

TESMAN. You know, I'm so happy for Hedda's sake that we've managed to get this house. Before we became engaged she often used to say this was the only house in town she felt she could really bear to live in. It used to belong to Mrs. Falk—you know, the Prime Minister's widow.

MISS TESMAN. Fancy that! And what a stroke of luck it happened to come into the market. Just as you'd left on your honeymoon.

TESMAN. Yes, Auntie Juju, we've certainly had all the luck with us. What?

MISS TESMAN. But, George dear, the expense! It's going to make a dreadful hole in your pocket, all this.

TESMAN, *a little downcast.* Yes, I—I suppose it will, won't it?

MISS TESMAN. Oh, George, really!

TESMAN. How much do you think it'll cost? Roughly, I mean? What?

MISS TESMAN. I can't possibly say till I see the bills.

TESMAN. Well, luckily Judge Brack's managed to get it on very favourable terms. He wrote and told Hedda so.

MISS TESMAN. Don't you worry, George dear. Anyway I've stood security for all the furniture and carpets.

TESMAN. Security? But dear, sweet Auntie Juju, how could you possibly stand security?

MISS TESMAN. I've arranged a mortgage on our annuity.

TESMAN *jumps up.* What? On your annuity? And—Auntie Rena's?

MISS TESMAN. Yes. Well, I couldn't think of any other way.

TESMAN *stands in front of her.* Auntie Juju, have you gone completely out of your mind? That annuity's all you and Auntie Rena have.

MISS TESMAN. All right, there's no need to get so excited about it. It's a pure formality, you know. Judge Brack told me so. He was so kind as to arrange it all for me. A pure formality; those were his very words.

TESMAN. I dare say. All the same—

MISS TESMAN. Anyway, you'll have a salary of your own now. And, good heavens, even if we did have to fork out a little

—tighten our belts for a week or two—why, we'd be happy to do so for your sake.

TESMAN. Oh, Auntie Juju! Will you never stop sacrificing yourself for me?

MISS TESMAN *gets up and puts her hands on his shoulders.* What else have I to live for but to smooth your road a little, my dear boy? You've never had any mother or father to turn to. And now at last we've achieved our goal. I won't deny we've had our little difficulties now and then. But now, thank the good Lord, George dear, all your worries are past.

TESMAN. Yes, it's wonderful really how everything's gone just right for me.

MISS TESMAN. Yes! And the enemies who tried to bar your way have been struck down. They have been made to bite the dust. The man who was your most dangerous rival has had the mightiest fall. And now he's lying there in the pit he dug for himself, poor misguided creature.

TESMAN. Have you heard any news of Eilert? Since I went away?

MISS TESMAN. Only that he's said to have published a new book.

TESMAN. What! Eilert Loevborg? You mean—just recently? What?

MISS TESMAN. So they say. I don't imagine it can be of any value, do you? When your new book comes out, that'll be another story. What's it going to be about?

TESMAN. The domestic industries of Brabant in the Middle Ages.

MISS TESMAN. Oh, George! The things you know about!

TESMAN. Mind you, it may be some time before I actually get down to writing it. I've made these very extensive notes, and I've got to file and index them first.

MISS TESMAN. Ah, yes! Making notes; filing and indexing; you've always been wonderful at that. Poor dear Joachim was just the same.

TESMAN. I'm looking forward so much to getting down to that. Especially now I've a home of my own to work in.

MISS TESMAN. And above all, now that you have the girl you set your heart on, George dear.

TESMAN *embraces her.* Oh, yes, Auntie Juju, yes! Hedda's the loveliest thing of all!

Looks towards the doorway.

I think I hear her coming. What?

HEDDA *enters the rear room from the left, and comes into the drawing room. She is a woman of twenty-nine. Distinguished, aristocratic face and figure. Her complexion is pale and opalescent. Her eyes are steel-grey, with an expression of cold, calm serenity. Her hair is of a handsome auburn colour, but is not especially abundant. She is dressed in an elegant, somewhat loose-fitting morning gown.*

MISS TESMAN *goes to greet her.* Good morning, Hedda dear! Good morning!

HEDDA *holds out her hand.* Good morning, dear Miss Tesman. What an early hour to call. So kind of you.

MISS TESMAN *seems somewhat embarrassed.* And has the young bride slept well in her new home?

HEDDA. Oh—thank you, yes. Passably well.

TESMAN *laughs.* Passably. I say, Hedda, that's good! When I jumped out of bed, you were sleeping like a top.

HEDDA. Yes. Fortunately. One has to accustom oneself to anything new, Miss Tesman. It takes time.

Looks left.

Oh, that maid's left the french windows open. This room's flooded with sun.

MISS TESMAN *goes towards the windows.* Oh—let me close them.

HEDDA. No, no, don't do that. Tesman dear, draw the curtains. This light's blinding me.

TESMAN, *at the windows.* Yes, yes, dear. There, Hedda, now you've got shade and fresh air.

HEDDA. This room needs fresh air. All these flowers— But my dear Miss Tesman, won't you take a seat?

MISS TESMAN. No, really not, thank you. I just wanted to make sure you have everything you need. I must see about getting back home. My poor dear sister will be waiting for me.

TESMAN. Be sure to give her my love, won't you? Tell her I'll run over and see her later today.

MISS TESMAN. Oh yes, I'll tell her that. Oh, George—

Fumbles in the pocket of her skirt.

I almost forgot. I've brought something for you.

TESMAN. What's that, Auntie Juju? What?

MISS TESMAN *pulls out a flat package wrapped in newspaper and gives it to him.* Open and see, dear boy.

TESMAN *opens the package.* Good heavens! Auntie Juju, you've kept them! Hedda, this is really very touching. What?

HEDDA, *by the what-nots, on the right.* What is it, Tesman?

TESMAN. My old shoes! My slippers, Hedda!

HEDDA. Oh, them. I remember you kept talking about them on our honeymoon.

TESMAN. Yes, I missed them dreadfully.

Goes over to her.

Here, Hedda, take a look.

HEDDA *goes away towards the stove.* Thanks, I won't bother.

TESMAN *follows her.* Fancy, Hedda, Auntie Rena's embroidered them for me. Despite her being so ill. Oh, you can't imagine what memories they have for me.

HEDDA, *by the table.* Not for me.

MISS TESMAN. No, Hedda's right there, George.

TESMAN. Yes, but I thought since she's one of the family now—

HEDDA *interrupts.* Tesman, we really can't go on keeping this maid.

MISS TESMAN. Not keep Bertha?

TESMAN. What makes you say that, dear? What?

HEDDA *points.* Look at that! She's left her old hat lying on the chair.

TESMAN, *appalled, drops his slippers on the floor.* But, Hedda—!

HEDDA. Suppose someone came in and saw it?

TESMAN. But Hedda—that's Auntie Juju's hat.

HEDDA. Oh?

MISS TESMAN *picks up the hat.* Indeed it's mine. And it doesn't happen to be old, Hedda dear.

HEDDA. I didn't look at it very closely, Miss Tesman.

MISS TESMAN, *tying on the hat.* As a matter of fact, it's the first time I've worn it. As the good Lord is my witness.

TESMAN. It's very pretty, too. Really smart.

MISS TESMAN. Oh, I'm afraid it's nothing much really.

Looks round.

My parasol? Ah, here it is.

Takes it.

This is mine, too.

Murmurs.

Not Bertha's.

TESMAN. A new hat and a new parasol! I say, Hedda, fancy that!

HEDDA. Very pretty and charming.

TESMAN. Yes, isn't it? What? But Auntie Juju, take a good look at Hedda before you go. Isn't she pretty and charming?

MISS TESMAN. Dear boy, there's nothing new in that. Hedda's been a beauty ever since the day she was born.

Nods and goes right.

TESMAN *follows her.* Yes, but have you noticed how strong and healthy she's looking? And how she's filled out since we went away?

MISS TESMAN *stops and turns.* Filled out?

HEDDA *walks across the room.* Oh, can't we forget it?

TESMAN. Yes, Auntie Juju—you can't see it so clearly with that dress on. But I've good reason to know—

HEDDA, *by the french windows, impatiently.* You haven't good reason to know anything.

TESMAN. It must have been the mountain air up there in the Tyrol—

HEDDA, *curtly, interrupts him.* I'm exactly the same as when I went away.

TESMAN. You keep on saying so. But you're not. I'm right, aren't I, Auntie Juju?

MISS TESMAN *has folded her hands and is gazing at her.* She's beautiful—beautiful. Hedda is beautiful.

Goes over to HEDDA, *takes her head between her hands, draws it down and kisses her hair.*

God bless and keep you, Hedda Tesman. For George's sake.

HEDDA *frees herself politely.* Oh—let me go, please.

MISS TESMAN, *quietly, emotionally.* I shall come and see you both every day.

TESMAN. Yes, Auntie Juju, please do. What?

MISS TESMAN. Good-bye! Good-bye!

She goes out into the hall. TESMAN *follows her. The door remains open.* TESMAN *is heard sending his love to* AUNT RENA *and thanking* MISS TESMAN *for his slippers. Meanwhile* HEDDA *walks up and down the room raising her arms and clenching her fists as though in desperation. Then she throws aside the curtains from the french windows and stands there, looking out. A few moments later,* TESMAN *returns and closes the door behind him.*

TESMAN *picks up his slippers from the floor.* What are you looking at, Hedda?

HEDDA, *calm and controlled again.* Only the leaves. They're so golden. And withered.

TESMAN *wraps up the slippers and lays them on the table.* Well, we're in September now.

HEDDA, *restless again.* Yes. We're already into September.

TESMAN. Auntie Juju was behaving rather oddly, I thought,

didn't you? Almost as though she was in church or something. I wonder what came over her. Any idea?

HEDDA. I hardly know her. Does she often act like that?

TESMAN. Not to the extent she did today.

HEDDA *goes away from the french windows.* Do you think she was hurt by what I said about the hat?

TESMAN. Oh, I don't think so. A little at first, perhaps—

HEDDA. But what a thing to do, throw her hat down in someone's drawing room. People don't do such things.

TESMAN. I'm sure Auntie Juju doesn't do it very often.

HEDDA. Oh well, I'll make it up with her.

TESMAN. Oh Hedda, would you?

HEDDA. When you see them this afternoon invite her to come out here this evening.

TESMAN. You bet I will! I say, there's another thing which would please her enormously.

HEDDA. Oh?

TESMAN. If you could bring yourself to call her Auntie Juju. For my sake, Hedda? What?

HEDDA. Oh no, really Tesman, you mustn't ask me to do that. I've told you so once before. I'll try to call her Aunt Juliana. That's as far as I'll go.

TESMAN, *after a moment.* I say, Hedda, is anything wrong? What?

HEDDA. I'm just looking at my old piano. It doesn't really go with all this.

TESMAN. As soon as I start getting my salary we'll see about changing it.

HEDDA. No, no, don't let's change it. I don't want to part with it. We can move it into that little room and get another one to put in here.

TESMAN, *a little downcast.* Yes, we—might do that.

HEDDA *picks up the bunch of flowers from the piano.* These flowers weren't here when we arrived last night.

TESMAN. I expect Auntie Juju brought them.

HEDDA. Here's a card.

Takes it out and reads.

"Will come back later today." Guess who it's from?

TESMAN. No idea. Who? What?

HEDDA. It says: "Mrs. Elvsted."

TESMAN. No, really? Mrs. Elvsted! She used to be Miss Rysing, didn't she?

HEDDA. Yes. She was the one with that irritating hair she was always showing off. I hear she used to be an old flame of yours.

TESMAN *laughs.* That didn't last long. Anyway, that was before I got to know you, Hedda. By Jove, fancy her being in town!

HEDDA. Strange she should call. I only knew her at school.

TESMAN. Yes, I haven't seen her for—oh, heaven knows how long. I don't know how she manages to stick it out up there in the north. What?

HEDDA *thinks for a moment, then says suddenly.* Tell me, Tesman, doesn't he live somewhere up in those parts? You know —Eilert Loevborg?

TESMAN. Yes, that's right. So he does.

BERTHA *enters from the hall.*

BERTHA. She's here again, madam. The lady who came and left the flowers.

Points.

The ones you're holding.

HEDDA. Oh, is she? Well, show her in.

BERTHA *opens the door for* MRS. ELVSTED *and goes out.* MRS. ELVSTED *is a delicately built woman with gentle, attractive features. Her eyes are light blue, large, and somewhat prominent, with a frightened, questioning expression. Her hair is extremely fair, almost flaxen, and is exceptionally wavy and abundant. She is two or three years younger than* HEDDA. *She is wearing a dark visiting dress, in good taste but not quite in the latest fashion.*

HEDDA *goes cordially to greet her.* Dear Mrs. Elvsted, good morning. How delightful to see you again after all this time.

MRS. ELVSTED, *nervously, trying to control herself.* Yes, it's many years since we met.

TESMAN. And since *we* met. What?

HEDDA. Thank you for your lovely flowers.

MRS. ELVSTED. Oh, please—I wanted to come yesterday afternoon. But they told me you were away—

TESMAN. You've only just arrived in town, then? What?

MRS. ELVSTED. I got here yesterday, around midday. Oh, I became almost desperate when I heard you weren't here.

HEDDA. Desperate? Why?

TESMAN. My dear Mrs. Rysing—Elvsted—

HEDDA. There's nothing wrong, I hope?

MRS. ELVSTED. Yes, there is. And I don't know anyone else here whom I can turn to.

HEDDA *puts the flowers down on the table.* Come and sit with me on the sofa—

MRS. ELVSTED. Oh, I feel too restless to sit down.

HEDDA. You must. Come along, now.

She pulls MRS. ELVSTED *down on to the sofa and sits beside her.*

TESMAN. Well? Tell us, Mrs.—er—

HEDDA. Has something happened at home?

MRS. ELVSTED. Yes—that is, yes and no. Oh, I do hope you won't misunderstand me—

HEDDA. Then you'd better tell us the whole story, Mrs. Elvsted.

TESMAN. That's why you've come. What?

MRS. ELVSTED. Yes—yes, it is. Well, then—in case you don't already know—Eilert Loevborg is in town.

HEDDA. Loevborg here?

TESMAN. Eilert back in town? By Jove, Hedda, did you hear that?

HEDDA. Yes, of course I heard.

MRS. ELVSTED. He's been here a week. A whole week! In this city. Alone. With all those dreadful people—

HEDDA. But my dear Mrs. Elvsted, what concern is he of yours?

MRS. ELVSTED *gives her a frightened look and says quickly.* He's been tutoring the children.

HEDDA. Your children?

MRS. ELVSTED. My husband's. I have none.

HEDDA. Oh, you mean your stepchildren.

MRS. ELVSTED. Yes.

TESMAN, *gropingly.* But was he sufficiently—I don't know how to put it—sufficiently regular in his habits to be suited to such a post? What?

MRS. ELVSTED. For the past two to three years he has been living irreproachably.

TESMAN. You don't say! By Jove, Hedda, hear that?

HEDDA. I hear.

MRS. ELVSTED. Quite irreproachably, I assure you. In every respect. All the same—in this big city—with money in his pockets—I'm so dreadfully frightened something may happen to him.

TESMAN. But why didn't he stay up there with you and your husband?

MRS. ELVSTED. Once his book had come out, he became restless.

TESMAN. Oh, yes—Auntie Juju said he'd brought out a new book.

MRS. ELVSTED. Yes, a big new book about the history of civilisation. A kind of general survey. It came out a fortnight ago. Everyone's been buying it and reading it—it's created a tremendous stir—

TESMAN. Has it really? It must be something he's dug up, then.

MRS. ELVSTED. You mean from the old days?

TESMAN. Yes.

MRS. ELVSTED. No, he's written it all since he came to live with us.

TESMAN. Well, that's splendid news, Hedda. Fancy that!

MRS. ELVSTED. Oh, yes! If only he can go on like this!

HEDDA. Have you met him since you came here?

MRS. ELVSTED. No, not yet. I had such dreadful difficulty finding his address. But this morning I managed to track him down at last.

HEDDA *looks searchingly at her.* I must say I find it a little strange that your husband—hm—

MRS. ELVSTED *starts nervously.* My husband! What do you mean?

HEDDA. That he should send you all the way here on an errand of this kind. I'm surprised he didn't come himself to keep an eye on his friend.

MRS. ELVSTED. Oh, no, no—my husband hasn't the time. Besides, I—er—wanted to do some shopping here.

HEDDA, *with a slight smile.* Ah. Well, that's different.

MRS. ELVSTED *gets up quickly, restlessly.* Please, Mr. Tesman, I beg you—be kind to Eilert Loevborg if he comes here. I'm sure he will. I mean, you used to be such good friends in the old days. And you're both studying the same subject, as far as I can understand. You're in the same field, aren't you?

TESMAN. Well, we used to be, anyway.

MRS. ELVSTED. Yes—so I beg you earnestly, do please, please, keep an eye on him. Oh, Mr. Tesman, do promise me you will.

TESMAN. I shall be only too happy to do so, Mrs. Rysing.

HEDDA. Elvsted.

TESMAN. I'll do everything for Eilert that lies in my power. You can rely on that.

MRS. ELVSTED. Oh, how good and kind you are!

Presses his hands.

Thank you, thank you, thank you.

Frightened.

My husband's so fond of him, you see.

HEDDA *gets up.* You'd better send him a note, Tesman. He may not come to you of his own accord.

TESMAN. Yes, that'd probably be the best plan, Hedda. What?

HEDDA. The sooner the better. Why not do it now?

MRS. ELVSTED, *pleadingly.* Oh yes, if only you would!

TESMAN. I'll do it this very moment. Do you have his address, Mrs.—er—Elvsted?

MRS. ELVSTED. Yes.

Takes a small piece of paper from her pocket and gives it to him.

TESMAN. Good, good. Right, well I'll go inside and—

Looks round.

Where are my slippers? Oh yes, here.

Picks up the package and is about to go.

HEDDA. Try to sound friendly. Make it a nice long letter.

TESMAN. Right, I will.

MRS. ELVSTED. Please don't say anything about my having seen you.

TESMAN. Good heavens no, of course not. What?

Goes out through the rear room to the right.

HEDDA *goes over to* MRS. ELVSTED, *smiles, and says softly.* Well! Now we've killed two birds with one stone.

MRS. ELVSTED. What do you mean?

HEDDA. Didn't you realise I wanted to get him out of the room?

MRS. ELVSTED. So that he could write the letter?

HEDDA. And so that I could talk to you alone.

MRS. ELVSTED, *confused.* About this?

HEDDA. Yes, about this.

MRS. ELVSTED, *in alarm.* But there's nothing more to tell, Mrs. Tesman. Really there isn't.

HEDDA. Oh, yes there is. There's a lot more. I can see that. Come along, let's sit down and have a little chat.

She pushes MRS. ELVSTED *down into the armchair by the stove and seats herself on one of the footstools.*

MRS. ELVSTED *looks anxiously at her watch.* Really, Mrs. Tesman, I think I ought to be going now.

HEDDA. There's no hurry. Well? How are things at home?

MRS. ELVSTED. I'd rather not speak about that.

HEDDA. But my dear, you can tell me. Good heavens, we were at school together.

MRS. ELVSTED. Yes, but you were a year senior to me. Oh, I used to be terribly frightened of you in those days.

HEDDA. Frightened of me?

MRS. ELVSTED. Yes, terribly frightened. Whenever you met me on the staircase you used to pull my hair.

HEDDA. No, did I?

MRS. ELVSTED. Yes. And once you said you'd burn it all off.

HEDDA. Oh, that was only in fun.

MRS. ELVSTED. Yes, but I was so silly in those days. And then afterwards—I mean, we've drifted so far apart. Our backgrounds were so different.

HEDDA. Well, now we must try to drift together again. Now listen. When we were at school we used to call each other by our Christian names—

MRS. ELVSTED. No, I'm sure you're mistaken.

HEDDA. I'm sure I'm not. I remember it quite clearly. Let's tell each other our secrets, as we used to in the old days.

Moves closer on her footstool.

There, now.

Kisses her on the cheek.

You must call me Hedda.

MRS. ELVSTED *squeezes her hands and pats them.* Oh, you're so kind. I'm not used to people being so nice to me.

HEDDA. Now, now, now. And I shall call you Tora, the way I used to.

MRS. ELVSTED. My name is Thea.

HEDDA. Yes, of course. Of course. I meant Thea.

Looks at her sympathetically.

So you're not used to kindness, Thea? In your own home?

MRS. ELVSTED. Oh, if only I had a home! But I haven't. I've never had one.

HEDDA *looks at her for a moment.* I thought that was it.

MRS. ELVSTED *stares blankly and helplessly.* Yes—yes—yes.

HEDDA. I can't remember exactly now, but didn't you first go to Mr. Elvsted as a housekeeper?

MRS. ELVSTED. Governess, actually. But his wife—at the time, I mean—she was an invalid, and had to spend most of her time in bed. So I had to look after the house too.

HEDDA. But in the end, you became mistress of the house.

MRS. ELVSTED, *sadly.* Yes, I did.

HEDDA. Let me see. Roughly how long ago was that?

MRS. ELVSTED. When I got married, you mean?

HEDDA. Yes.

MRS. ELVSTED. About five years.

HEDDA. Yes; it must be about that.

MRS. ELVSTED. Oh, those five years! Especially the last two or three. Oh, Mrs. Tesman, if you only knew—!

HEDDA *slaps her hand gently.* Mrs. Tesman? Oh, Thea!

MRS. ELVSTED. I'm sorry, I'll try to remember. Yes—if you had any idea—

HEDDA, *casually.* Eilert Loevborg's been up there too, for about three years, hasn't he?

MRS. ELVSTED *looks at her uncertainly.* Eilert Loevborg? Yes, he has.

HEDDA. Did you know him before? When you were here?

MRS. ELVSTED. No, not really. That is—I knew him by name, of course.

HEDDA. But up there, he used to visit you?

MRS. ELVSTED. Yes, he used to come and see us every day. To give the children lessons. I found I couldn't do that as well as manage the house.

HEDDA. I'm sure you couldn't. And your husband—? I suppose

being a magistrate he has to be away from home a good deal?

MRS. ELVSTED. Yes. You see, Mrs.—you see, Hedda, he has to cover the whole district.

HEDDA *leans against the arm of* MRS. ELVSTED's *chair.* Poor, pretty little Thea! Now you must tell me the whole story. From beginning to end.

MRS. ELVSTED. Well—what do you want to know?

HEDDA. What kind of a man is your husband, Thea? I mean, as a person. Is he kind to you?

MRS. ELVSTED, *evasively.* I'm sure he does his best to be.

HEDDA. I only wonder if he isn't too old for you. There's more than twenty years between you, isn't there?

MRS. ELVSTED, *irritably.* Yes, there's that too. Oh, there are so many things. We're different in every way. We've nothing in common. Nothing whatever.

HEDDA. But he loves you, surely? In his own way?

MRS. ELVSTED. Oh, I don't know. I think he just finds me useful. And then I don't cost much to keep. I'm cheap.

HEDDA. Now you're being stupid.

MRS. ELVSTED *shakes her head.* It can't be any different. With him. He doesn't love anyone except himself. And perhaps the children—a little.

HEDDA. He must be fond of Eilert Loevborg, Thea.

MRS. ELVSTED *looks at her.* Eilert Loevborg? What makes you think that?

HEDDA. Well, if he sends you all the way down here to look for him—

Smiles almost imperceptibly.

Besides, you said so yourself to Tesman.

MRS. ELVSTED, *with a nervous twitch.* Did I? Oh yes, I suppose I did.

Impulsively, but keeping her voice low.

Well, I might as well tell you the whole story. It's bound to come out sooner or later.

HEDDA. But my dear Thea—?

MRS. ELVSTED. My husband had no idea I was coming here.

HEDDA. What? Your husband didn't know?

MRS. ELVSTED. No, of course not. As a matter of fact, he wasn't even there. He was away at the assizes. Oh, I couldn't stand it any longer, Hedda! I just couldn't. I'd be so dreadfully lonely up there now.

HEDDA. Go on.

MRS. ELVSTED. So I packed a few things. Secretly. And went.

HEDDA. Without telling anyone?

MRS. ELVSTED. Yes. I caught the train and came straight here.

HEDDA. But my dear Thea! How brave of you!

MRS. ELVSTED *gets up and walks across the room.* Well, what else could I do?

HEDDA. But what do you suppose your husband will say when you get back?

MRS. ELVSTED, *by the table, looks at her.* Back there? To him?

HEDDA. Yes. Surely—?

MRS. ELVSTED. I shall never go back to him.

HEDDA *gets up and goes closer.* You mean you've left your home for good?

MRS. ELVSTED. Yes. I didn't see what else I could do.

HEDDA. But to do it so openly!

MRS. ELVSTED. Oh, it's no use trying to keep a thing like that secret.

HEDDA. But what do you suppose people will say?

MRS. ELVSTED. They can say what they like.

Sits sadly, wearily on the sofa.

I had to do it.

HEDDA, *after a short silence.* What do you intend to do now? How are you going to live?

MRS. ELVSTED. I don't know. I only know that I must live wherever Eilert Loevborg is. If I am to go on living.

HEDDA *moves a chair from the table, sits on it near* MRS. ELVSTED *and strokes her hands.* Tell me, Thea, how did this —friendship between you and Eilert Loevborg begin?

MRS. ELVSTED. Oh, it came about gradually. I developed a kind of—power over him.

HEDDA. Oh?

MRS. ELVSTED. He gave up his old habits. Not because I asked him to. I'd never have dared to do that. I suppose he just noticed I didn't like that kind of thing. So he gave it up.

HEDDA *hides a smile.* So you've made a new man of him. Clever little Thea!

MRS. ELVSTED. Yes—anyway, he says I have. And he's made a—sort of—real person of me. Taught me to think—and to understand all kinds of things.

HEDDA. Did he give you lessons too?

MRS. ELVSTED. Not exactly lessons. But he talked to me. About —oh, you've no idea—so many things! And then he let me work with him. Oh, it was wonderful. I was so happy to be allowed to help him.

HEDDA. Did he allow you to help him!

MRS. ELVSTED. Yes. Whenever he wrote anything we always— did it together.

HEDDA. Like good pals?

MRS. ELVSTED, *eagerly.* Pals! Yes—why, Hedda, that's exactly the word he used! Oh, I ought to feel so happy. But I can't. I don't know if it will last.

HEDDA. You don't seem very sure of him.

MRS. ELVSTED, *sadly.* Something stands between Eilert Loevborg and me. The shadow of another woman.

HEDDA. Who can that be?

MRS. ELVSTED. I don't know. Someone he used to be friendly with in—in the old days. Someone he's never been able to forget.

HEDDA. What has he told you about her?

MRS. ELVSTED. Oh, he only mentioned her once, casually.

HEDDA. Well! What did he say?

MRS. ELVSTED. He said when he left her she tried to shoot him with a pistol.

HEDDA, *cold, controlled.* What nonsense. People don't do such things. The kind of people we know.

MRS. ELVSTED. No. I think it must have been that red-haired singer he used to—

HEDDA. Ah yes, very probably.

MRS. ELVSTED. I remember they used to say she always carried a loaded pistol.

HEDDA. Well then, it must be her.

MRS. ELVSTED. But Hedda, I hear she's come back, and is living here. Oh, I'm so desperate—!

HEDDA *glances towards the rear room.* Ssh! Tesman's coming.
Gets up and whispers.

Thea, we mustn't breathe a word about this to anyone.

MRS. ELVSTED *jumps up.* Oh, no, no! Please don't!

GEORGE TESMAN *appears from the right in the rear room with a letter in his hand, and comes into the drawing room.*

TESMAN. Well, here's my little epistle all signed and sealed.

HEDDA. Good. I think Mrs. Elvsted wants to go now. Wait a moment—I'll see you as far as the garden gate.

TESMAN. Er—Hedda, do you think Bertha could deal with this?

HEDDA *takes the letter.* I'll give her instructions.

BERTHA *enters from the hall.*

BERTHA. Judge Brack is here and asks if he may pay his respects to Madam and the Doctor.

HEDDA. Yes, ask him to be so good as to come in. And—wait a moment—drop this letter in the post box.

BERTHA *takes the letter.* Very good, madam.

She opens the door for JUDGE BRACK, and goes out. JUDGE BRACK is forty-five; rather short, but well-built, and elastic in his movements. He has a roundish face with an aristocratic profile. His hair, cut short, is still almost black, and is carefully barbered. Eyes lively and humorous. Thick eye-brows. His moustache is also thick, and is trimmed square at the ends. He is wearing outdoor clothes which are elegant but a little too youthful for him. He has a monocle in one eye; now and then he lets it drop.

BRACK, *hat in hand, bows.* May one presume to call so early?

HEDDA. One may presume.

TESMAN *shakes his hand.* You're welcome here any time. Judge Brack—Mrs. Rysing.

HEDDA *sighs.*

BRACK *bows.* Ah—charmed—

HEDDA *looks at him and laughs.* What fun to be able to see you by daylight for once, Judge.

BRACK. Do I look—different?

HEDDA. Yes. A little younger, I think.

BRACK. Obliged.

TESMAN. Well, what do you think of Hedda? What? Doesn't she look well? Hasn't she filled out—?

HEDDA. Oh, do stop it. You ought to be thanking Judge Brack for all the inconvenience he's put himself to—

BRACK. Nonsense, it was a pleasure—

HEDDA. You're a loyal friend. But my other friend is pining to get away. Au revoir, Judge. I won't be a minute.

Mutual salutations. MRS. ELVSTED *and* HEDDA *go out through the hall.*

BRACK. Well, is your wife satisfied with everything?

TESMAN. Yes, we can't thank you enough. That is—we may have to shift one or two things around, she tells me. And we're short of one or two little items we'll have to purchase.

BRACK. Oh? Really?

TESMAN. But you mustn't worry your head about that. Hedda says she'll get what's needed. I say, why don't we sit down? What?

BRACK. Thanks, just for a moment.

Sits at the table.

There's something I'd like to talk to you about, my dear Tesman.

TESMAN. Oh? Ah yes, of course.

Sits.

After the feast comes the reckoning. What?

BRACK. Oh, never mind about the financial side—there's no hurry about that. Though I could wish we'd arranged things a little less palatially.

TESMAN. Good heavens, that'd never have done. Think of Hedda, my dear chap. You know her. I couldn't possibly ask her to live like a suburban housewife.

BRACK. No, no—that's just the problem.

TESMAN. Anyway, it can't be long now before my nomination comes through.

BRACK. Well, you know, these things often take time.

TESMAN. Have you heard any more news? What?

BRACK. Nothing definite.

Changing the subject.

Oh, by the way, I have one piece of news for you.

TESMAN. What?

BRACK. Your old friend Eilert Loevborg is back in town.

TESMAN. I know that already.

BRACK. Oh? How did you hear that?

TESMAN. She told me. That lady who went out with Hedda.

BRACK. I see. What was her name? I didn't catch it.

TESMAN. Mrs. Elvsted.

BRACK. Oh, the magistrate's wife. Yes, Loevborg's been living up near them, hasn't he?

TESMAN. I'm delighted to hear he's become a decent human being again.

BRACK. Yes, so they say.

TESMAN. I gather he's published a new book, too. What?

BRACK. Indeed he has.

TESMAN. I hear it's created rather a stir.

BRACK. Quite an unusual stir.

TESMAN. I say, isn't that splendid news! He's such a gifted chap—and I was afraid he'd gone to the dogs for good.

BRACK. Most people thought he had.

TESMAN. But I can't think what he'll do now. How on earth will he manage to make ends meet? What?

As he speaks his last words, HEDDA *enters from the hall.*

HEDDA, *to* BRACK, *laughs slightly scornfully.* Tesman is always worrying about making ends meet.

TESMAN. We were talking about poor Eilert Loevborg, Hedda dear.

HEDDA *gives him a quick look.* Oh, were you?

Sits in the armchair by the stove and asks casually.

Is he in trouble?

TESMAN. Well, he must have run through his inheritance long ago by now. And he can't write a new book every year. What? So I'm wondering what's going to become of him.

BRACK. I may be able to enlighten you there.

TESMAN. Oh?

BRACK. You mustn't forget he has relatives who wield a good deal of influence.

TESMAN. Relatives? Oh, they've quite washed their hands of him, I'm afraid.

BRACK. They used to regard him as the hope of the family.

TESMAN. Used to, yes. But he's put an end to that.

HEDDA. Who knows?

With a little smile.

I hear the Elvsteds have made a new man of him.

BRACK. And then this book he's just published—

TESMAN. Well, let's hope they find something for him. I've just written him a note. Oh, by the way, Hedda, I asked him to come over and see us this evening.

BRACK. But my dear chap, you're coming to me this evening.

My bachelor party. You promised me last night when I met you at the boat.

HEDDA. Had you forgotten, Tesman?

TESMAN. Good heavens, yes, I'd quite forgotten.

BRACK. Anyway, you can be quite sure he won't turn up here.

TESMAN. Why do you think that? What?

BRACK, *a little unwillingly, gets up and rests his hands on the back of his chair.* My dear Tesman—and you, too, Mrs. Tesman—there's something I feel you ought to know.

TESMAN. Concerning Eilert?

BRACK. Concerning him and you.

TESMAN. Well, my dear Judge, tell us, please!

BRACK. You must be prepared for your nomination not to come through quite as quickly as you hope and expect.

TESMAN *jumps up uneasily.* Is anything wrong? What?

BRACK. There's a possibility that the appointment may be decided by competition—

TESMAN. Competition! By Jove, Hedda, fancy that!

HEDDA *leans further back in her chair.* Ah! How interesting!

TESMAN. But who else—? I say, you don't mean—?

BRACK. Exactly. By competition with Eilert Loevborg.

TESMAN *clasps his hands in alarm.* No, no, but this is inconceivable! It's absolutely impossible! What?

BRACK. Hm. We may find it'll happen, all the same.

TESMAN. No, but—Judge Brack, they couldn't be so inconsiderate towards me!

Waves his arms.

I mean, by Jove, I—I'm a married man! It was on the strength of this that Hedda and I *got* married! We ran up some pretty hefty debts. And borrowed money from Auntie Juju! I mean, good heavens, they practically promised me the appointment. What?

BRACK. Well, well, I'm sure you'll get it. But you'll have to go through a competition.

HEDDA, *motionless in her armchair*. How exciting, Tesman. It'll be a kind of duel, by Jove.

TESMAN. My dear Hedda, how can you take it so lightly?

HEDDA, *as before*. I'm not. I can't wait to see who's going to win.

BRACK. In any case, Mrs. Tesman, it's best you should know how things stand. I mean before you commit yourself to these little items I hear you're threatening to purchase.

HEDDA. I can't allow this to alter my plans.

BRACK. Indeed? Well, that's your business. Good-bye.

To TESMAN.

I'll come and collect you on the way home from my afternoon walk.

TESMAN. Oh, yes, yes. I'm sorry, I'm all upside down just now.

HEDDA, *lying in her chair, holds out her hand*. Good-bye, Judge. See you this afternoon.

BRACK. Thank you. Good-bye, good-bye.

TESMAN *sees him to the door*. Good-bye, my dear Judge. You will excuse me, won't you?

JUDGE BRACK *goes out through the hall*.

TESMAN, *pacing up and down*. Oh, Hedda! One oughtn't to go plunging off on wild adventures. What?

HEDDA *looks at him and smiles*. Like you're doing?

TESMAN. Yes. I mean, there's no denying it, it was a pretty big adventure to go off and get married and set up house merely on expectation.

HEDDA. Perhaps you're right.

TESMAN. Well, anyway, we have our home, Hedda. By Jove, yes. The home we dreamed of. And set our hearts on. What?

HEDDA *gets up slowly, wearily*. You agreed that we should enter society. And keep open house. That was the bargain.

TESMAN. Yes. Good heavens, I was looking forward to it all so much. To seeing you play hostess to a select circle! By Jove! What? Ah, well, for the time being we shall have to make do with each other's company, Hedda. Perhaps have Auntie

Juju in now and then. Oh dear, this wasn't at all what you had in mind—

HEDDA. I won't be able to have a liveried footman. For a start.

TESMAN. Oh no, we couldn't possibly afford a footman.

HEDDA. And that thoroughbred horse you promised me—

TESMAN, *fearfully*. Thoroughbred horse!

HEDDA. I mustn't even think of that now.

TESMAN. Heaven forbid!

HEDDA *walks across the room*. Ah, well. I still have one thing left to amuse myself with.

TESMAN, *joyfully*. Thank goodness for that. What's that, Hedda? What?

HEDDA, *in the open doorway, looks at him with concealed scorn*. My pistols, George darling.

TESMAN, *alarmed*. Pistols!

HEDDA, *her eyes cold*. General Gabler's pistols.

She goes into the rear room and disappears.

TESMAN *runs to the doorway and calls after her*. For heaven's sake, Hedda dear, don't touch those things. They're dangerous. Hedda—please—for my sake! What?

ACT TWO

The same as in Act One, except that the piano has been removed and an elegant little writing table, with a bookcase, stands in its place. By the sofa on the left a smaller table has been placed. Most of the flowers have been removed. MRS. ELVSTED's *bouquet stands on the larger table, downstage. It is afternoon.*

HEDDA, *dressed to receive callers, is alone in the room. She is standing by the open french windows, loading a revolver. The pair to it is lying in an open pistol case on the writing table.*

HEDDA *looks down into the garden and calls.* Good afternoon, Judge.

BRACK, *in the distance, below.* Afternoon, Mrs. Tesman.

HEDDA *raises the pistol and takes aim.* I'm going to shoot you, Judge Brack.

BRACK *shouts from below.* No, no, no! Don't aim that thing at me!

HEDDA. This'll teach you to enter houses by the back door. *Fires.*

BRACK, *below.* Have you gone completely out of your mind?

HEDDA. Oh dear! Did I hit you?

BRACK, *still outside.* Stop playing these silly tricks.

HEDDA. All right, Judge. Come along in.

JUDGE BRACK, *dressed for a bachelor party, enters through the french windows. He has a light overcoat on his arm.*

BRACK. For God's sake! Haven't you stopped fooling around with those things yet? What are you trying to hit?

HEDDA. Oh, I was just shooting at the sky.

BRACK *takes the pistol gently from her hand.* By your leave, ma'am.

Looks at it.

Ah, yes—I know this old friend well.

Looks around.

Where's the case? Oh, yes.

Puts the pistol in the case and closes it.

That's enough of that little game for today.

HEDDA. Well, what on earth *am* I to do?

BRACK. You haven't had any visitors?

HEDDA *closes the french windows.* Not one. I suppose the best people are all still in the country.

BRACK. Your husband isn't home yet?

HEDDA *locks the pistol away in a drawer of the writing table.* No. The moment he'd finished eating he ran off to his aunties. He wasn't expecting you so early.

BRACK. Ah, why didn't I think of that? How stupid of me.

HEDDA *turns her head and looks at him.* Why stupid?

BRACK. I'd have come a little sooner.

HEDDA *walks across the room.* There'd have been no one to receive you. I've been in my room since lunch, dressing.

BRACK. You haven't a tiny crack in the door through which we might have negotiated?

HEDDA. You forgot to arrange one.

BRACK. Another stupidity.

HEDDA. Well, we'll have to sit down here. And wait. Tesman won't be back for some time.

BRACK. Sad. Well, I'll be patient.

HEDDA *sits on the corner of the sofa.* BRACK *puts his coat over the back of the nearest chair and seats himself, keeping his hat in his hand. Short pause. They look at each other.*

HEDDA. Well?

BRACK, *in the same tone of voice.* Well?

HEDDA. I asked first.

BRACK *leans forward slightly.* Yes, well, now we can enjoy a nice, cosy little chat—Mrs. Hedda.

HEDDA *leans further back in her chair.* It seems such ages since we had a talk. I don't count last night or this morning.

BRACK. You mean: *à deux?*

HEDDA. Mm—yes. That's roughly what I meant.

BRACK. I've been longing so much for you to come home.

HEDDA. So have I.

BRACK. You? Really, Mrs. Hedda? And I thought you were having such a wonderful honeymoon.

HEDDA. Oh, yes. Wonderful!

BRACK. But your husband wrote such ecstatic letters.

HEDDA. He! Oh, yes! He thinks life has nothing better to offer than rooting around in libraries and copying old pieces of parchment, or whatever it is he does.

BRACK, *a little maliciously.* Well, that *is* his life. Most of it, anyway.

HEDDA. Yes, I know. Well, it's all right for him. But for me! Oh no, my dear Judge. I've been bored to death.

BRACK, *sympathetically.* Do you mean that? Seriously?

HEDDA. Yes. Can you imagine? Six whole months without ever meeting a single person who was one of us, and to whom I could talk about the kind of things we talk about.

BRACK. Yes, I can understand. I'd miss that, too.

HEDDA. That wasn't the worst, though.

BRACK. What was?

HEDDA. Having to spend every minute of one's life with—with the same person.

BRACK *nods.* Yes. What a thought! Morning; noon; and—

HEDDA, *coldly.* As I said: every minute of one's life.

BRACK. I stand corrected. But dear Tesman is such a clever fellow, I should have thought one ought to be able—

HEDDA. Tesman is only interested in one thing, my dear Judge. His special subject.

BRACK. True.

HEDDA. And people who are only interested in one thing don't make the most amusing company. Not for long, anyway.

BRACK. Not even when they happen to be the person one loves?

HEDDA. Oh, don't use that sickly, stupid word.

BRACK *starts.* But, Mrs. Hedda—!

HEDDA, *half laughing, half annoyed.* You just try it, Judge. Listening to the history of civilisation morning, noon and—

BRACK *corrects her.* Every minute of one's life.

HEDDA. All right. Oh, and those domestic industries of Brabant in the Middle Ages! That really is beyond the limit.

BRACK *looks at her searchingly.* But, tell me—if you feel like this why on earth did you—? Ha—

HEDDA. Why on earth did I marry George Tesman?

BRACK. If you like to put it that way.

HEDDA. Do you think it so very strange?

BRACK. Yes—and no, Mrs. Hedda.

HEDDA. I'd danced myself tired, Judge. I felt my time was up—
Gives a slight shudder.
No, I mustn't say that. Or even think it.

BRACK. You've no rational cause to think it.

HEDDA. Oh—cause, cause—
Looks searchingly at him.
After all, George Tesman—well, I mean, he's a very respectable man.

BRACK. Very respectable, sound as a rock. No denying that.

HEDDA. And there's nothing exactly ridiculous about him. Is there?

BRACK. Ridiculous? N-no, I wouldn't say that.

HEDDA. Mm. He's very clever at collecting material and all that, isn't he? I mean, he may go quite far in time.

BRACK *looks at her a little uncertainly.* I thought you believed, like everyone else, that he would become a very prominent man.

HEDDA *looks tired.* Yes, I did. And when he came and begged me on his bended knees to be allowed to love and to cherish me, I didn't see why I shouldn't let him.

BRACK. No, well—if one looks at it like that—

HEDDA. It was more than my other admirers were prepared to do, Judge dear.

BRACK *laughs.* Well, I can't answer for the others. As far as I myself am concerned, you know I've always had a considerable respect for the institution of marriage. As an institution.

HEDDA, *lightly.* Oh, I've never entertained any hopes of you.

BRACK. All I want is to have a circle of friends whom I can trust, whom I can help with advice or—or by any other means, and into whose houses I may come and go as a— trusted friend.

HEDDA. Of the husband?

BRACK *bows.* Preferably, to be frank, of the wife. And of the husband too, of course. Yes, you know, this kind of—triangle is a delightful arrangement for all parties concerned.

HEDDA. Yes, I often longed for a third person while I was away. Oh, those hours we spent alone in railway compartments—

BRACK. Fortunately your honeymoon is now over.

HEDDA *shakes her head.* There's a long, long way still to go. I've only reached a stop on the line.

BRACK. Why not jump out and stretch your legs a little, Mrs. Hedda?

HEDDA. I'm not the jumping sort.

BRACK. Aren't you?

HEDDA. No. There's always someone around who—

BRACK *laughs.* Who looks at one's legs?

HEDDA. Yes. Exactly.

BRACK. Well, but surely—

HEDDA, *with a gesture of rejection.* I don't like it. I'd rather stay where I am. Sitting in the compartment. *À deux.*

BRACK. But suppose a third person were to step into the compartment?

HEDDA. That would be different.

BRACK. A trusted friend—someone who understood—

HEDDA. And was lively and amusing—

BRACK. And interested in—more subjects than one—

HEDDA *sighs audibly.* Yes, that'd be a relief.

BRACK *hears the front door open and shut.* The triangle is completed.

HEDDA, *half under breath.* And the train goes on.

GEORGE TESMAN, *in grey walking dress with a soft felt hat, enters from the hall. He has a number of paper-covered books under his arm and in his pockets.*

TESMAN *goes over to the table by the corner sofa.* Phew! It's too hot to be lugging all this around.

Puts the books down.

I'm positively sweating, Hedda. Why, hullo, hullo! You here already, Judge? What? Bertha didn't tell me.

BRACK *gets up.* I came in through the garden.

HEDDA. What are all those books you've got there?

TESMAN *stands glancing through them.* Oh, some new publications dealing with my special subject. I had to buy them.

HEDDA. Your special subject?

BRACK. His special subject, Mrs. Tesman.

BRACK *and* HEDDA *exchange a smile.*

HEDDA. Haven't you collected enough material on your special subject?

TESMAN. My dear Hedda, one can never have too much. One must keep abreast of what other people are writing.

HEDDA. Yes. Of course.

TESMAN, *rooting among the books.* Look—I bought a copy of Eilert Loevborg's new book, too.

Holds it out to her.

Perhaps you'd like to have a look at it, Hedda? What?

HEDDA. No, thank you. Er—yes, perhaps I will, later.

TESMAN. I glanced through it on my way home.

BRACK. What's your opinion—as a specialist on the subject?

TESMAN. I'm amazed how sound and balanced it is. He never used to write like that.

Gathers his books together.

Well, I must get down to these at once. I can hardly wait to cut the pages. Oh, I've got to change, too.

To BRACK.

We don't have to be off just yet, do we? What?

BRACK. Heavens, no. We've plenty of time yet.

TESMAN. Good, I needn't hurry, then.

Goes with his books, but stops and turns in the doorway.

Oh, by the way, Hedda, Auntie Juju won't be coming to see you this evening.

HEDDA. Won't she? Oh—the hat, I suppose.

TESMAN. Good heavens, nó. How could you think such a thing of Auntie Juju? Fancy—! No, Auntie Rena's very ill.

HEDDA. She always is.

TESMAN. Yes, but today she's been taken really bad.

HEDDA. Oh, then it's quite understandable that the other one should want to stay with her. Well, I shall have to swallow my disappointment.

TESMAN. You can't imagine how happy Auntie Juju was in spite of everything. At your looking so well after the honeymoon!

HEDDA, *half beneath her breath, as she rises.* Oh, these everlasting aunts!

TESMAN. What?

HEDDA *goes over to the french windows.* Nothing.

TESMAN. Oh. All right.

Goes into the rear room and out of sight.

BRACK. What was that about the hat?

HEDDA. Oh, something that happened with Miss Tesman this morning. She'd put her hat down on a chair.

Looks at him and smiles.

And I pretended to think it was the servant's.

BRACK *shakes his head.* But my dear Mrs. Hedda, how could you do such a thing? To that poor old lady?

HEDDA, *nervously, walking across the room.* Sometimes a mood like that hits me. And I can't stop myself.

Throws herself down in the armchair by the stove.

Oh, I don't know how to explain it.

BRACK, *behind her chair.* You're not really happy. That's the answer.

HEDDA *stares ahead of her.* Why on earth should I be happy? Can you give me a reason?

BRACK. Yes. For one thing you've got the home you always wanted.

HEDDA *looks at him.* You really believe that story?

BRACK. You mean it isn't true?

HEDDA. Oh, yes, it's partly true.

BRACK. Well?

HEDDA. It's true I got Tesman to see me home from parties last summer—

BRACK. It was a pity my home lay in another direction.

HEDDA. Yes. Your interests lay in another direction, too.

BRACK *laughs.* That's naughty of you, Mrs. Hedda. But to return to you and Tesman—

HEDDA. Well, we walked past this house one evening. And poor Tesman was fidgeting in his boots trying to find something to talk about. I felt sorry for the great scholar—

BRACK *smiles incredulously.* Did you? Hm.

HEDDA. Yes, honestly I did. Well, to help him out of his misery,

I happened to say quite frivolously how much I'd love to live in this house.

BRACK. Was that all?

HEDDA. That evening, yes.

BRACK. But—afterwards?

HEDDA. Yes. My little frivolity had its consequences, my dear Judge.

BRACK. Our little frivolities do. Much too often, unfortunately.

HEDDA. Thank you. Well, it was our mutual admiration for the late Prime Minister's house that brought George Tesman and me together on common ground. So we got engaged, and we got married, and we went on our honeymoon, and— Ah well, Judge, I've—made my bed and I must lie in it, I was about to say.

BRACK. How utterly fantastic! And you didn't really care in the least about the house?

HEDDA. God knows I didn't.

BRACK. Yes, but now that we've furnished it so beautifully for you?

HEDDA. Ugh—all the rooms smell of lavender and dried roses. But perhaps Auntie Juju brought that in.

BRACK *laughs.* More likely the Prime Minister's widow, rest her soul.

HEDDA. Yes, it's got the odour of death about it. It reminds me of the flowers one has worn at a ball—the morning after. *Clasps her hands behind her neck, leans back in the chair and looks up at him.*

Oh, my dear Judge, you've no idea how hideously bored I'm going to be out here.

BRACK. Couldn't you find some kind of occupation, Mrs. Hedda? Like your husband?

HEDDA. Occupation? That'd interest me?

BRACK. Well—preferably.

HEDDA. God knows what. I've often thought—
Breaks off.

No, that wouldn't work either.

BRACK. Who knows? Tell me about it.

HEDDA. I was thinking—if I could persuade Tesman to go into politics, for example.

BRACK *laughs.* Tesman! No, honestly, I don't think he's quite cut out to be a politician.

HEDDA. Perhaps not. But if I could persuade him to have a go at it?

BRACK. What satisfaction would that give you? If he turned out to be no good? Why do you want to make him do that?

HEDDA. Because I'm bored.

After a moment.

You feel there's absolutely no possibility of Tesman becoming Prime Minister, then?

BRACK. Well, you know, Mrs. Hedda, for one thing he'd have to be pretty well off before he could become that.

HEDDA *gets up impatiently.* There you are!

Walks across the room.

It's this wretched poverty that makes life so hateful. And ludicrous. Well, it is!

BRACK. I don't think that's the real cause.

HEDDA. What is, then?

BRACK. Nothing really exciting has ever happened to you.

HEDDA. Nothing serious, you mean?

BRACK. Call it that if you like. But now perhaps it may.

HEDDA *tosses her head.* Oh, you're thinking of this competition for that wretched professorship? That's Tesman's affair. I'm not going to waste my time worrying about that.

BRACK. Very well, let's forget about that then. But suppose you were to find yourself faced with what people call—to use the conventional phrase—the most solemn of human responsibilities?

Smiles.

A new responsibility, little Mrs. Hedda.

HEDDA, *angrily.* Be quiet! Nothing like that's going to happen.

BRACK, *warily.* We'll talk about it again in a year's time. If not earlier.

HEDDA, *curtly.* I've no leanings in that direction, Judge. I don't want any—responsibilities.

BRACK. But surely you must feel some inclination to make use of that—natural talent which every woman—

HEDDA, *over by the french windows.* Oh, be quiet, I say! I often think there's only one thing for which I have any natural talent.

BRACK *goes closer.* And what is that, if I may be so bold as to ask?

HEDDA *stands looking out.* For boring myself to death. Now you know.

Turns, looks toward the rear room and laughs.

Talking of boring, here comes the Professor.

BRACK, *quietly, warningly.* Now, now, now, Mrs. Hedda!

GEORGE TESMAN, *in evening dress, with gloves and hat in his hand, enters through the rear room from the right.*

TESMAN. Hedda, hasn't any message come from Eilert? What?

HEDDA. No.

TESMAN. Ah, then we'll have him here presently. You wait and see.

BRACK. You really think he'll come?

TESMAN. Yes, I'm almost sure he will. What you were saying about him this morning is just gossip.

BRACK. Oh?

TESMAN. Yes. Auntie Juju said she didn't believe he'd ever dare to stand in my way again. Fancy that!

BRACK. Then everything in the garden's lovely.

TESMAN *puts his hat, with his gloves in it, on a chair, right.* Yes, but you really must let me wait for him as long as possible.

BRACK. We've plenty of time. No one'll be turning up at my place before seven or half past.

TESMAN. Ah, then we can keep Hedda company a little longer.
And see if he turns up. What?

HEDDA *picks up* BRACK'S *coat and hat and carries them over to
the corner sofa.* And if the worst comes to the worst, Mr.
Loevborg can sit here and talk to me.

BRACK, *offering to take his things from her.* No, please. What
do you mean by "if the worst comes to the worst"?

HEDDA. If he doesn't want to go with you and Tesman.

TESMAN *looks doubtfully at her.* I say, Hedda, do you think
it'll be all right for him to stay here with you? What? Remember Auntie Juju isn't coming.

HEDDA. Yes, but Mrs. Elvsted is. The three of us can have a
cup of tea together.

TESMAN. Ah, that'll be all right then.

BRACK *smiles.* It's probably the safest solution as far as he's
concerned.

HEDDA. Why?

BRACK. My dear Mrs. Tesman, you always say of my little
bachelor parties that they should be attended only by men
of the strongest principles.

HEDDA. But Mr. Loevborg is a man of principle now. You
know what they say about a reformed sinner—

BERTHA *enters from the hall.*

BERTHA. Madam, there's a gentleman here who wants to see
you—

HEDDA. Ask him to come in.

TESMAN, *quietly.* I'm sure it's him. By Jove. Fancy that!

EILERT LOEVBORG *enters from the hall. He is slim and lean,
of the same age as* TESMAN, *but looks older and somewhat
haggard. His hair and beard are of a blackish-brown; his
face is long and pale, but with a couple of reddish patches
on his cheekbones. He is dressed in an elegant and fairly
new black suit, and carries black gloves and a top hat in his
hand. He stops just inside the door and bows abruptly. He
seems somewhat embarrassed.*

TESMAN *goes over and shakes his hand.* My dear Eilert! How grand to see you again after all these years!

EILERT LOEVBORG *speaks softly.* It was good of you to write, George.

Goes nearer to HEDDA.

May I shake hands with you, too, Mrs. Tesman?

HEDDA *accepts his hand.* Delighted to see you, Mr. Loevborg. *With a gesture.*

I don't know if you two gentlemen—

LOEVBORG *bows slightly.* Judge Brack, I believe.

BRACK, *also with a slight bow.* Correct. We—met some years ago—

TESMAN *puts his hands on* LOEVBORG'S *shoulders.* Now you're to treat this house just as though it were your own home, Eilert. Isn't that right, Hedda? I hear you've decided to settle here again? What?

LOEVBORG. Yes, I have.

TESMAN. Quite understandable. Oh, by the bye—I've just bought your new book. Though to tell the truth I haven't found time to read it yet.

LOEVBORG. You needn't bother.

TESMAN. Oh? Why?

LOEVBORG. There's nothing much in it.

TESMAN. By Jove, fancy hearing that from you!

BRACK. But everyone's praising it.

LOEVBORG. That was exactly what I wanted to happen. So I only wrote what I knew everyone would agree with.

BRACK. Very sensible.

TESMAN. Yes, but my dear Eilert—

LOEVBORG. I want to try to re-establish myself. To begin again —from the beginning.

TESMAN, *a little embarrassed.* Yes, I—er—suppose you do. What?

LOEVBORG *smiles, puts down his hat and takes a package*

wrapped in paper from his coat pocket. But when this gets published—George Tesman—read it. This is my real book. The one in which I have spoken with my own voice.

TESMAN. Oh, really? What's it about?

LOEVBORG. It's the sequel.

TESMAN. Sequel? To what?

LOEVBORG. To the other book.

TESMAN. The one that's just come out?

LOEVBORG. Yes.

TESMAN. But my dear Eilert, that covers the subject right up to the present day.

LOEVBORG. It does. But this is about the future.

TESMAN. The future! But, I say, we don't know anything about that.

LOEVBORG. No. But there are one or two things that need to be said about it.

Opens the package.

Here, have a look.

TESMAN. Surely that's not your handwriting?

LOEVBORG. I dictated it.

Turns the pages.

It's in two parts. The first deals with the forces that will shape our civilisation.

Turns further on towards the end.

And the second indicates the direction in which that civilisation may develop.

TESMAN. Amazing! I'd never think of writing about anything like that.

HEDDA, *by the french windows, drumming on the pane.* No. You wouldn't.

LOEVBORG *puts the pages back into their cover and lays the package on the table.* I brought it because I thought I might possibly read you a few pages this evening.

TESMAN. I say, what a kind idea! Oh, but this evening—?

Glances at BRACK.

I'm not quite sure whether—

LOEVBORG. Well, some other time, then. There's no hurry.

BRACK. The truth is, Mr. Loevborg, I'm giving a little dinner this evening. In Tesman's honour, you know.

LOEVBORG *looks round for his hat.* Oh—then I mustn't—

BRACK. No, wait a minute. Won't you do me the honour of joining us?

LOEVBORG, *curtly, with decision.* No I can't. Thank you so much.

BRACK. Oh, nonsense. Do—please. There'll only be a few of us. And I can promise you we shall have some good sport, as Mrs. Hed—as Mrs. Tesman puts it.

LOEVBORG. I've no doubt. Nevertheless—

BRACK. You could bring your manuscript along and read it to Tesman at my place. I could lend you a room.

TESMAN. By Jove, Eilert, that's an idea. What?

HEDDA *interposes.* But Tesman, Mr. Loevborg doesn't want to go. I'm sure Mr. Loevborg would much rather sit here and have supper with me.

LOEVBORG *looks at her.* With you, Mrs. Tesman?

HEDDA. And Mrs. Elvsted.

LOEVBORG. Oh.

Casually.

I ran into her this afternoon.

HEDDA. Did you? Well, she's coming here this evening. So you really must stay, Mr. Loevborg. Otherwise she'll have no one to see her home.

LOEVBORG. That's true. Well—thank you, Mrs. Tesman, I'll stay then.

HEDDA. I'll just tell the servant.

She goes to the door which leads into the hall, and rings. BERTHA *enters.* HEDDA *talks softly to her and points towards the rear room.* BERTHA *nods and goes out.*

TESMAN, *to* LOEVBORG, *as* HEDDA *does this.* I say, Eilert. This
new subject of yours—the—er—future—is that the one you're
going to lecture about?

LOEVBORG. Yes.

TESMAN. They told me down at the bookshop that you're going to hold a series of lectures here during the autumn.

LOEVBORG. Yes, I am. I—hope you don't mind, Tesman.

TESMAN. Good heavens, no! But—?

LOEVBORG. I can quite understand it might queer your pitch a
little.

TESMAN, *dejectedly.* Oh well, I can't expect you to put them
off for my sake.

LOEVBORG. I'll wait till your appointment's been announced.

TESMAN. You'll wait! But—but—aren't you going to compete
with me for the post? What?

LOEVBORG. No. I only want to defeat you in the eyes of the
world.

TESMAN. Good heavens! Then Auntie Juju was right after all!
Oh, I knew it, I knew it! Hear that, Hedda? Fancy! Eilert
doesn't want to stand in our way.

HEDDA, *curtly.* Our? Leave me out of it, please.

She goes towards the rear room, where BERTHA *is setting a
tray with decanters and glasses on the table.* HEDDA *nods
approval, and comes back into the drawing room.* BERTHA
goes out.

TESMAN, *while this is happening.* Judge Brack, what do you
think about all this? What?

BRACK. Oh, I think honour and victory can be very splendid
things—

TESMAN. Of course they can. Still—

HEDDA *looks at* TESMAN *with a cold smile.* You look as if you'd
been hit by a thunderbolt.

TESMAN. Yes, I feel rather like it.

BRACK. There was a black cloud looming up, Mrs. Tesman. But
it seems to have passed over.

HEDDA *points towards the rear room.* Well, gentlemen, won't you go in and take a glass of cold punch?

BRACK *glances at his watch.* A stirrup cup? Yes, why not?

TESMAN. An admirable suggestion, Hedda. Admirable! Oh, I feel so relieved!

HEDDA. Won't you have one, too, Mr. Loevborg?

LOEVBORG. No, thank you. I'd rather not.

BRACK. Great heavens, man, cold punch isn't poison. Take my word for it.

LOEVBORG. Not for everyone, perhaps.

HEDDA. I'll keep Mr. Loevborg company while you drink.

TESMAN. Yes, Hedda dear, would you?

He and BRACK *go into the rear room, sit down, drink punch, smoke cigarettes and talk cheerfully during the following scene.* EILERT LOEVBORG *remains standing by the stove.* HEDDA *goes to the writing table.*

HEDDA, *raising her voice slightly.* I've some photographs I'd like to show you, if you'd care to see them. Tesman and I visited the Tyrol on our way home.

She comes back with an album, places it on the table by the sofa and sits in the upstage corner of the sofa. EILERT LOEVBORG *comes towards her, stops and looks at her. Then he takes a chair and sits down on her left, with his back towards the rear room.*

HEDDA *opens the album.* You see these mountains, Mr. Loevborg? That's the Ortler group. Tesman has written the name underneath. You see: "The Ortler Group near Meran."

LOEVBORG *has not taken his eyes from her; says softly, slowly.* Hedda—Gabler!

HEDDA *gives him a quick glance.* Ssh!

LOEVBORG *repeats softly.* Hedda Gabler!

HEDDA *looks at the album.* Yes, that used to be my name. When we first knew each other.

LOEVBORG. And from now on—for the rest of my life—I must teach myself never to say: Hedda Gabler.

HEDDA, *still turning the pages.* Yes, you must. You'd better start getting into practice. The sooner the better.

LOEVBORG, *bitterly.* Hedda Gabler married? And to George Tesman?

HEDDA. Yes. Well—that's life.

LOEVBORG. Oh, Hedda, Hedda! How could you throw yourself away like that?

HEDDA *looks sharply at him.* Stop it.

LOEVBORG. What do you mean?

TESMAN *comes in and goes towards the sofa.*

HEDDA *hears him coming and says casually.* And this, Mr. Loevborg, is the view from the Ampezzo valley. Look at those mountains.

Glances affectionately up at TESMAN.

What did you say those curious mountains were called, dear?

TESMAN. Let me have a look. Oh, those are the Dolomites.

HEDDA. Of course. Those are the Dolomites, Mr. Loevborg.

TESMAN. Hedda, I just wanted to ask you, can't we bring some punch in here? A glass for you, anyway. What?

HEDDA. Thank you, yes. And a biscuit or two, perhaps.

TESMAN. You wouldn't like a cigarette?

HEDDA. No.

TESMAN. Right.

He goes into the rear room and over to the right. BRACK *is sitting there, glancing occasionally at* HEDDA *and* LOEVBORG.

LOEVBORG, *softly, as before.* Answer me, Hedda. How could you do it?

HEDDA, *apparently absorbed in the album.* If you go on calling me Hedda I won't talk to you any more.

LOEVBORG. Mayn't I even when we're alone?

HEDDA. No. You can think it. But you mustn't say it.

LOEVBORG. Oh, I see. Because you love George Tesman.

HEDDA *glances at him and smiles.* Love? Don't be funny.

LOEVBORG. You don't love him?

HEDDA. I don't intend to be unfaithful to him. That's not what I want.

LOEVBORG. Hedda—just tell me one thing—

HEDDA. Ssh!

TESMAN *enters from the rear room, carrying a tray.*

TESMAN. Here we are! Here come the goodies!

Puts the tray down on the table.

HEDDA. Why didn't you ask the servant to bring it in?

TESMAN *fills the glasses.* I like waiting on you, Hedda.

HEDDA. But you've filled both glasses. Mr. Loevborg doesn't want to drink.

TESMAN. Yes, but Mrs. Elvsted'll be here soon.

HEDDA. Oh yes, that's true. Mrs. Elvsted—

TESMAN. Had you forgotten her? What?

HEDDA. We're so absorbed with these photographs.

Shows him one.

You remember this little village?

TESMAN. Oh, that one down by the Brenner Pass. We spent a night there—

HEDDA. Yes, and met all those amusing people.

TESMAN. Oh yes, it was there, wasn't it? By Jove, if only we could have had you with us, Eilert! Ah, well.

Goes back into the other room and sits down with BRACK.

LOEVBORG. Tell me one thing, Hedda.

HEDDA. Yes?

LOEVBORG. Didn't you love me either? Not—just a little?

HEDDA. Well now, I wonder? No, I think we were just good pals— Really good pals who could tell each other anything.

Smiles.

You certainly poured your heart out to me.

LOEVBORG. You begged me to.

HEDDA. Looking back on it, there was something beautiful and fascinating—and brave—about the way we told each other everything. That secret friendship no one else knew about.

LOEVBORG. Yes, Hedda, yes! Do you remember? How I used to come up to your father's house in the afternoon—and the General sat by the window and read his newspapers—with his back towards us—

HEDDA. And we sat on the sofa in the corner—

LOEVBORG. Always reading the same illustrated magazine—

HEDDA. We hadn't any photograph album.

LOEVBORG. Yes, Hedda. I regarded you as a kind of confessor. Told you things about myself which no one else knew about —then. Those days and nights of drinking and— Oh, Hedda, what power did you have to make me confess such things?

HEDDA. Power? You think I had some power over you?

LOEVBORG. Yes—I don't know how else to explain it. And all those—oblique questions you asked me—

HEDDA. You knew what they meant.

LOEVBORG. But that you could sit there and ask me such questions! So unashamedly—

HEDDA. I thought you said they were oblique.

LOEVBORG. Yes, but you asked them so unashamedly. That you could question me about—about that kind of thing!

HEDDA. You answered willingly enough.

LOEVBORG. Yes—that's what I can't understand—looking back on it. But tell me, Hedda—what you felt for me—wasn't that —love? When you asked me those questions and made me confess my sins to you, wasn't it because you wanted to wash me clean?

HEDDA. No, not exactly.

LOEVBORG. Why did you do it, then?

HEDDA. Do you find it so incredible that a young girl, given the chance to do so without anyone knowing, should want to be allowed a glimpse into a forbidden world of whose existence she is supposed to be ignorant?

LOEVBORG. So that was it?

HEDDA. One reason. One reason—I think.

LOEVBORG. You didn't love me, then. You just wanted—knowledge. But if that was so, why did you break it off?

HEDDA. That was your fault.

LOEVBORG. It was you who put an end to it.

HEDDA. Yes, when I realised that our friendship was threatening to develop into something—something else. Shame on you, Eilert Loevborg! How could you abuse the trust of your dearest friend?

LOEVBORG *clenches his fists.* Oh, why didn't you do it? Why didn't you shoot me dead? As you threatened to?

HEDDA. I was afraid. Of the scandal.

LOEVBORG. Yes, Hedda. You're a coward at heart.

HEDDA. A dreadful coward.

Changes her tone.

Luckily for you. Well, now you've found consolation with the Elvsteds.

LOEVBORG. I know what Thea's been telling you.

HEDDA. I dare say you told her about us.

LOEVBORG. Not a word. She's too silly to understand that kind of thing.

HEDDA. Silly?

LOEVBORG. She's silly about that kind of thing.

HEDDA. And I am a coward.

Leans closer to him, without looking him in the eyes, and says quietly.

But let me tell you something. Something you don't know.

LOEVBORG, *tensely.* Yes?

HEDDA. My failure to shoot you wasn't my worst act of cowardice that evening.

LOEVBORG *looks at her for a moment, realises her meaning and whispers passionately.* Oh, Hedda! Hedda Gabler! Now I see what was behind those questions. Yes! It wasn't knowledge you wanted! It was life!

HEDDA *flashes a look at him and says quietly.* Take care! Don't you delude yourself!

It has begun to grow dark. BERTHA, *from outside, opens the door leading into the hall.*

HEDDA *closes the album with a snap and cries, smiling.* Ah, at last! Come in, Thea dear!

MRS. ELVSTED *enters from the hall, in evening dress. The door is closed behind her.*

HEDDA, *on the sofa, stretches out her arms towards her.* Thea darling, I thought you were never coming!

MRS. ELVSTED *makes a slight bow to the gentlemen in the rear room as she passes the open doorway, and they to her. Then she goes to the table and holds out her hand to* HEDDA. EILERT LOEVBORG *has risen from his chair. He and* MRS. ELVSTED *nod silently to each other.*

MRS. ELVSTED. Perhaps I ought to go in and say a few words to your husband?

HEDDA. Oh, there's no need. They're happy by themselves. They'll be going soon.

MRS. ELVSTED. Going?

HEDDA. Yes, they're off on a spree this evening.

MRS. ELVSTED, *quickly, to* LOEVBORG. You're not going with them?

LOEVBORG. No.

HEDDA. Mr. Loevborg is staying here with us.

MRS. ELVSTED *takes a chair and is about to sit down beside him.* Oh, how nice it is to be here!

HEDDA. No, Thea darling, not there. Come over here and sit beside me. I want to be in the middle.

MRS. ELVSTED. Yes, just as you wish.

She goes round the table and sits on the sofa, on HEDDA's *right.* LOEVBORG *sits down again in his chair.*

LOEVBORG, *after a short pause, to* HEDDA. Isn't she lovely to look at?

HEDDA *strokes her hair gently.* Only to look at?

LOEVBORG. Yes. We're just good pals. We trust each other implicitly. We can talk to each other quite unashamedly.

HEDDA. No need to be oblique?

MRS. ELVSTED *nestles close to* HEDDA *and says quietly.* Oh, Hedda I'm so happy. Imagine—he says I've inspired him!

HEDDA *looks at her with a smile.* Dear Thea! Does he really?

LOEVBORG. She has the courage of her convictions, Mrs. Tesman.

MRS. ELVSTED. I? Courage?

LOEVBORG. Absolute courage. Where friendship is concerned.

HEDDA. Yes. Courage. Yes. If only one had that—

LOEVBORG. Yes?

HEDDA. One might be able to live. In spite of everything. *Changes her tone suddenly.*

Well, Thea darling, now you're going to drink a nice glass of cold punch.

MRS. ELVSTED. No, thank you. I never drink anything like that.

HEDDA. Oh. You, Mr. Loevborg?

LOEVBORG. Thank you, I don't either.

MRS. ELVSTED. No, he doesn't, either.

HEDDA *looks into his eyes.* But if I want you to?

LOEVBORG. That doesn't make any difference.

HEDDA *laughs.* Have I no power over you at all? Poor me!

LOEVBORG. Not where this is concerned.

HEDDA. Seriously, I think you should. For your own sake.

MRS. ELVSTED. Hedda!

LOEVBORG. Why?

HEDDA. Or perhaps I should say for other people's sake.

LOEVBORG. What do you mean?

HEDDA. People might think you didn't feel absolutely and unashamedly sure of yourself. In your heart of hearts.

MRS. ELVSTED, *quietly*. Oh, Hedda, no!

LOEVBORG. People can think what they like. For the present.

MRS. ELVSTED, *happily*. Yes, that's true.

HEDDA. I saw it so clearly in Judge Brack a few minutes ago.

LOEVBORG. Oh. What did you see?

HEDDA. He smiled so scornfully when he saw you were afraid to go in there and drink with them.

LOEVBORG. Afraid! I wanted to stay here and talk to you.

MRS. ELVSTED. That was only natural, Hedda.

HEDDA. But the Judge wasn't to know that. I saw him wink at Tesman when you showed you didn't dare to join their wretched little party.

LOEVBORG. Didn't dare! Are you saying I didn't dare?

HEDDA. I'm not saying so. But that was what Judge Brack thought.

LOEVBORG. Well, let him.

HEDDA. You're not going, then?

LOEVBORG. I'm staying here with you and Thea.

MRS. ELVSTED. Yes, Hedda, of course he is.

HEDDA *smiles, and nods approvingly to* LOEVBORG. Firm as a rock! A man of principle! That's how a man should be!
Turns to MRS. ELVSTED *and strokes her cheek.*
Didn't I tell you so this morning when you came here in such a panic—

LOEVBORG *starts*. Panic?

MRS. ELVSTED, *frightened*. Hedda! But—Hedda!

HEDDA. Well, now you can see for yourself. There's no earthly need for you to get scared to death just because—
Stops.
Well! Let's all three cheer up and enjoy ourselves.

LOEVBORG. Mrs. Tesman, would you mind explaining to me what this is all about?

MRS. ELVSTED. Oh, my God, my God, Hedda, what are you saying? What are you doing?

HEDDA. Keep calm. That horrid Judge has his eye on you.

LOEVBORG. Scared to death, were you? For my sake?

MRS. ELVSTED, *quietly, trembling.* Oh, Hedda! You've made me so unhappy!

LOEVBORG *looks coldly at her for a moment. His face is distorted.* So that was how much you trusted me.

MRS. ELVSTED. Eilert dear, please listen to me—

LOEVBORG *takes one of the glasses of punch, raises it and says quietly, hoarsely.* Skoal, Thea!

Empties the glass, puts it down and picks up one of the others.

MRS. ELVSTED, *quietly.* Hedda, Hedda! Why did you want this to happen?

HEDDA. I—want it? Are you mad?

LOEVBORG. Skoal to you too, Mrs. Tesman. Thanks for telling me the truth. Here's to the truth!

Empties his glass and refills it.

HEDDA *puts her hand on his arm.* Steady. That's enough for now. Don't forget the party.

MRS. ELVSTED. No, no, no!

HEDDA. Ssh! They're looking at you.

LOEVBORG *puts down his glass.* Thea, tell me the truth—

MRS. ELVSTED. Yes!

LOEVBORG. Did your husband know you were following me?

MRS. ELVSTED. Oh, Hedda!

LOEVBORG. Did you and he have an agreement that you should come here and keep an eye on me? Perhaps he gave you the idea? After all, he's a magistrate. I suppose he needed me back in his office. Or did he miss my companionship at the card table?

MRS. ELVSTED, *quietly, sobbing.* Eilert, Eilert!

LOEVBORG *seizes a glass and is about to fill it.* Let's drink to him, too.

HEDDA. No more now. Remember you're going to read your book to Tesman.

LOEVBORG, *calm again, puts down his glass.* That was silly of me, Thea. To take it like that, I mean. Don't be angry with me, my dear. You'll see—yes, and they'll see, too—that though I fell, I— I have raised myself up again. With your help, Thea.

MRS. ELVSTED, *happily.* Oh, thank God!

BRACK *has meanwhile glanced at his watch. He and* TESMAN *get up and come into the drawing room.*

BRACK *takes his hat and overcoat.* Well, Mrs. Tesman, it's time for us to go.

HEDDA. Yes, I suppose it must be.

LOEVBORG *gets up.* Time for me too, Judge.

MRS. ELVSTED, *quietly, pleadingly.* Eilert, please don't!

HEDDA *pinches her arm.* They can hear you.

MRS. ELVSTED *gives a little cry.* Oh!

LOEVBORG *to* BRACK. You were kind enough to ask me to join you.

BRACK. Are you coming?

LOEVBORG. If I may.

BRACK. Delighted.

LOEVBORG *puts the paper package in his pocket and says to* TESMAN. I'd like to show you one or two things before I send it off to the printer.

TESMAN. I say, that'll be fun. Fancy—! Oh, but Hedda, how'll Mrs. Elvsted get home? What?

HEDDA. Oh, we'll manage somehow.

LOEVBORG *glances over towards the ladies.* Mrs. Elvsted? I shall come back and collect her, naturally.

Goes closer.

About ten o'clock, Mrs. Tesman? Will that suit you?

HEDDA. Yes. That'll suit me admirably.

TESMAN. Good, that's settled. But you mustn't expect me back so early, Hedda.

HEDDA. Stay as long as you c— as long as you like, dear.

MRS. ELVSTED, *trying to hide her anxiety.* Well then, Mr. Loevborg, I'll wait here till you come.

LOEVBORG, *his hat in his hand.* Pray do, Mrs. Elvsted.

BRACK. Well, gentlemen, now the party begins. I trust that, in the words of a certain fair lady, we shall enjoy good sport.

HEDDA. What a pity the fair lady can't be there, invisible.

BRACK. Why invisible?

HEDDA. So as to be able to hear some of your uncensored witticisms, your honour.

BRACK *laughs.* Oh, I shouldn't advise the fair lady to do that.

TESMAN *laughs too.* I say, Hedda, that's good. By Jove! Fancy that!

BRACK. Well, good night, ladies, good night!

LOEVBORG *bows farewell.* About ten o'clock, then.

BRACK, LOEVBORG and TESMAN go out through the hall. As they do so, BERTHA *enters from the rear room with a lighted lamp. She puts it on the drawing-room table, then goes out the way she came.*

MRS. ELVSTED *has got up and is walking uneasily to and fro.* Oh Hedda, Hedda! How is all this going to end?

HEDDA. At ten o'clock, then. He'll be here. I can see him. With a crown of vine-leaves in his hair. Burning and unashamed!

MRS. ELVSTED. Oh, I do hope so!

HEDDA. Can't you see? Then he'll be himself again! He'll be a free man for the rest of his days!

MRS. ELVSTED. Please God you're right.

HEDDA. That's how he'll come!

Gets up and goes closer.

You can doubt him as much as you like. I believe in him! Now we'll see which of us—

MRS. ELVSTED. You're after something, Hedda.

HEDDA. Yes, I am. For once in my life I want to have the power to shape a man's destiny.

MRS. ELVSTED. Haven't you that power already?

HEDDA. No, I haven't. I've never had it.

MRS. ELVSTED. What about your husband?

HEDDA. Him! Oh, if you could only understand how poor I am. And you're allowed to be so rich, so rich!

Clasps her passionately.

I think I'll burn your hair off after all!

MRS. ELVSTED. Let me go! Let me go! You frighten me, Hedda!

BERTHA, *in the open doorway.* I've laid tea in the dining room, madam.

HEDDA. Good, we're coming.

MRS. ELVSTED. No, no, no! I'd rather go home alone! Now—at once!

HEDDA. Rubbish! First you're going to have some tea, you little idiot. And then—at ten o'clock—Eilert Loevborg will come. With a crown of vine-leaves in his hair!

She drags MRS. ELVSTED *almost forcibly towards the open doorway.*

ACT THREE

The same. The curtains are drawn across the open door-
way, and also across the french windows. The lamp, half
turned down, with a shade over it, is burning on the table.
In the stove, the door of which is open, a fire has been burn-
ing, but it is now almost out.

MRS. ELVSTED, *wrapped in a large shawl and with her feet*
resting on a footstool, is sitting near the stove, huddled in
the armchair. HEDDA *is lying asleep on the sofa, fully*
dressed, with a blanket over her.

MRS. ELVSTED, *after a pause, suddenly sits up in her chair*
and listens tensely. Then she sinks wearily back again and
sighs. Not back yet! Oh, God! Oh, God! Not back yet!

BERTHA *tiptoes cautiously in from the hall. She has a letter*
in her hand.

MRS. ELVSTED *turns and whispers.* What is it? Has someone
come?

BERTHA, *quietly.* Yes, a servant's just called with this letter.

MRS. ELVSTED, *quickly, holding out her hand.* A letter! Give it
to me!

BERTHA. But it's for the Doctor, madam.

MRS. ELVSTED. Oh. I see.

BERTHA. Miss Tesman's maid brought it. I'll leave it here on
the table.

MRS. ELVSTED. Yes, do.

BERTHA *puts down the letter.* I'd better put the lamp out. It's starting to smoke.

MRS. ELVSTED. Yes, put it out. It'll soon be daylight.

BERTHA *puts out the lamp.* It's daylight already, madam.

MRS. ELVSTED. Yes. Broad day. And not home yet.

BERTHA. Oh dear, I was afraid this would happen.

MRS. ELVSTED. Were you?

BERTHA. Yes. When I heard that a certain gentleman had returned to town, and saw him go off with them. I've heard all about him.

MRS. ELVSTED. Don't talk so loud. You'll wake your mistress.

BERTHA *looks at the sofa and sighs.* Yes. Let her go on sleeping, poor dear. Shall I put some more wood on the fire?

MRS. ELVSTED. Thank you, don't bother on my account.

BERTHA. Very good.

Goes quietly out through the hall.

HEDDA *wakes as the door closes and looks up.* What's that?

MRS. ELVSTED. It was only the maid.

HEDDA *looks round.* What am I doing here? Oh, now I remember.

Sits up on the sofa, stretches herself and rubs her eyes.

What time is it, Thea?

MRS. ELVSTED. It's gone seven.

HEDDA. When did Tesman get back?

ELVSTED. He's not back yet.

HEDDA. Not home yet?

MRS. ELVSTED *gets up.* No one's come.

HEDDA. And we sat up waiting for them till four o'clock.

MRS. ELVSTED. God! How I waited for him!

HEDDA *yawns and says with her hand in front of her mouth.* Oh, dear. We might have saved ourselves the trouble.

MRS. ELVSTED. Did you manage to sleep?

HEDDA. Oh, yes. Quite well, I think. Didn't you get any?

MRS. ELVSTED. Not a wink. I couldn't, Hedda. I just couldn't.

HEDDA *gets up and comes over to her.* Now, now, now. There's nothing to worry about. I know what's happened.

MRS. ELVSTED. What? Please tell me.

HEDDA. Well, obviously the party went on very late—

MRS. ELVSTED. Oh dear, I suppose it must have. But—

HEDDA. And Tesman didn't want to come home and wake us all up in the middle of the night.

Laughs.

Probably wasn't too keen to show his face either, after a spree like that.

MRS. ELVSTED. But where could he have gone?

HEDDA. I should think he's probably slept at his aunts'. They keep his old room for him.

MRS. ELVSTED. No, he can't be with them. A letter came for him just now from Miss Tesman. It's over there.

HEDDA. Oh?

Looks at the envelope.

Yes, it's Auntie Juju's handwriting. Well, he must still be at Judge Brack's, then. And Eilert Loevborg is sitting there, reading to him. With a crown of vine-leaves in his hair.

MRS. ELVSTED. Hedda, you're only saying that. You don't believe it.

HEDDA. Thea, you really are a little fool.

MRS. ELVSTED. Perhaps I am.

HEDDA. You look tired to death.

MRS. ELVSTED. Yes. I am tired to death.

HEDDA. Go to my room and lie down for a little. Do as I say, now; don't argue.

MRS. ELVSTED. No, no. I couldn't possibly sleep.

HEDDA. Of course you can.

MRS. ELVSTED. But your husband'll be home soon. And I must know at once—

HEDDA. I'll tell you when he comes.

MRS. ELVSTED. Promise me, Hedda?

HEDDA. Yes, don't worry. Go and get some sleep.

MRS. ELVSTED. Thank you. All right, I'll try.

She goes out through the rear room. HEDDA *goes to the french windows and draws the curtains. Broad daylight floods into the room. She goes to the writing table, takes a small hand mirror from it and arranges her hair. Then she goes to the door leading into the hall and presses the bell. After a few moments,* BERTHA *enters.*

BERTHA. Did you want anything, madam?

HEDDA. Yes, put some more wood on the fire. I'm freezing.

BERTHA. Bless you, I'll soon have this room warmed up.

She rakes the embers together and puts a fresh piece of wood on them. Suddenly she stops and listens.

There's someone at the front door, madam.

HEDDA. Well, go and open it. I'll see to the fire.

BERTHA. It'll burn up in a moment.

She goes out through the hall. HEDDA *kneels on the footstool and puts more wood in the stove. After a few seconds,* GEORGE TESMAN *enters from the hall. He looks tired, and rather worried. He tiptoes towards the open doorway and is about to slip through the curtains.*

HEDDA, *at the stove, without looking up.* Good morning.

TESMAN *turns.* Hedda!

Comes nearer.

Good heavens, are you up already? What?

HEDDA. Yes, I got up very early this morning.

TESMAN. I was sure you'd still be sleeping. Fancy that!

HEDDA. Don't talk so loud. Mrs. Elvsted's asleep in my room.

TESMAN. Mrs. Elvsted? Has she stayed the night here?

HEDDA. Yes. No one came to escort her home.

TESMAN. Oh. No, I suppose not.

HEDDA *closes the door of the stove and gets up.* Well. Was it fun?

TESMAN. Have you been anxious about me? What?

HEDDA. Not in the least. I asked if you'd had fun.

TESMAN. Oh yes, rather! Well, I thought, for once in a while—
The first part was the best; when Eilert read his book to
me. We arrived over an hour too early—what about that,
eh? By Jove! Brack had a lot of things to see to, so Eilert
read to me.

HEDDA *sits at the right-hand side of the table.* Well? Tell me
about it.

TESMAN *sits on a footstool by the stove.* Honestly, Hedda,
you've no idea what a book that's going to be. It's really one
of the most remarkable things that's ever been written. By
Jove!

HEDDA. Oh, never mind about the book—

TESMAN. I'm going to make a confession to you, Hedda. When
he'd finished reading a sort of beastly feeling came over me.

HEDDA. Beastly feeling?

TESMAN. I found myself envying Eilert for being able to write
like that. Imagine that, Hedda!

HEDDA. Yes. I can imagine.

TESMAN. What a tragedy that with all those gifts he should
be so incorrigible.

HEDDA. You mean he's less afraid of life than most men?

TESMAN. Good heavens, no. He just doesn't know the meaning of the word moderation.

HEDDA. What happened afterwards?

TESMAN. Well, looking back on it I suppose you might almost
call it an orgy, Hedda.

HEDDA. Had he vine-leaves in his hair?

TESMAN. Vine-leaves? No, I didn't see any of them. He made
a long, rambling oration in honour of the woman who'd inspired him to write this book. Yes, those were the words
he used.

HEDDA. Did he name her?

TESMAN. No. But I suppose it must be Mrs. Elvsted. You wait and see!

HEDDA. Where did you leave him?

TESMAN. On the way home. We left in a bunch—the last of us, that is—and Brack came with us to get a little fresh air. Well, then, you see, we agreed we ought to see Eilert home. He'd had a drop too much.

HEDDA. You don't say?

TESMAN. But now comes the funny part, Hedda. Or I should really say the tragic part. Oh, I'm almost ashamed to tell you. For Eilert's sake, I mean—

HEDDA. Why, what happened?

TESMAN. Well, you see, as we were walking towards town I happened to drop behind for a minute. Only for a minute —er—you understand—

HEDDA. Yes, yes—?

TESMAN. Well then, when I ran on to catch them up, what do you think I found by the roadside. What?

HEDDA. How on earth should I know?

TESMAN. You mustn't tell anyone, Hedda. What? Promise me that—for Eilert's sake.

Takes a package wrapped in paper from his coat pocket. Just fancy! I found this.

HEDDA. Isn't this the one he brought here yesterday?

TESMAN. Yes! The whole of that precious, irreplaceable manuscript! And he went and lost it! Didn't even notice! What about that? By Jove! Tragic.

HEDDA. But why didn't you give it back to him?

TESMAN. I didn't dare to, in the state he was in.

HEDDA. Didn't you tell any of the others?

TESMAN. Good heavens, no. I didn't want to do that. For Eilert's sake, you understand.

HEDDA. Then no one else knows you have his manuscript?

TESMAN. No. And no one must be allowed to know.

HEDDA. Didn't it come up in the conversation later?

TESMAN. I didn't get a chance to talk to him any more. As soon as we got into the outskirts of town, he and one or two of the others gave us the slip. Disappeared, by Jove!

HEDDA. Oh? I suppose they took him home.

TESMAN. Yes, I imagine that was the idea. Brack left us, too.

HEDDA. And what have you been up to since then?

TESMAN. Well, I and one or two of the others—awfully jolly chaps, they were—went back to where one of them lived, and had a cup of morning coffee. Morning-after coffee— what? Ah, well. I'll just lie down for a bit and give Eilert time to sleep it off, poor chap, then I'll run over and give this back to him.

HEDDA *holds out her hand for the package.* No, don't do that. Not just yet. Let me read it first.

TESMAN. Oh no, really, Hedda dear, honestly, I daren't do that.

HEDDA. Daren't?

TESMAN. No—imagine how desperate he'll be when he wakes up and finds his manuscript's missing. He hasn't any copy, you see. He told me so himself.

HEDDA. Can't a thing like that be rewritten?

TESMAN. Oh no, not possibly, I shouldn't think. I mean, the inspiration, you know—

HEDDA. Oh, yes. I'd forgotten that.

Casually.

By the way, there's a letter for you.

TESMAN. Is there? Fancy that!

HEDDA *holds it out to him.* It came early this morning.

TESMAN. I say, it's from Auntie Juju! What on earth can it be? *Puts the package on the other footstool, opens the letter, reads it and jumps up.*

Oh, Hedda! She says poor Auntie Rena's dying.

HEDDA. Well, we've been expecting that.

TESMAN. She says if I want to see her I must go quickly. I'll run over at once.

HEDDA *hides a smile*. Run?

TESMAN. Hedda dear, I suppose you wouldn't like to come with me? What about that, eh?

HEDDA *gets up and says wearily and with repulsion*. No, no, don't ask me to do anything like that. I can't bear illness or death. I loathe anything ugly.

TESMAN. Yes, yes. Of course.

In a dither.

My hat? My overcoat? Oh yes, in the hall. I do hope I won't get there too late, Hedda? What?

HEDDA. You'll be all right if you run.

BERTHA *enters from the hall.*

BERTHA. Judge Brack's outside and wants to know if he can come in.

TESMAN. At this hour? No, I can't possibly receive him now.

HEDDA. I can.

To BERTHA.

Ask his honour to come in.

BERTHA *goes.*

HEDDA *whispers quickly*. The manuscript, Tesman.

She snatches it from the footstool.

TESMAN. Yes, give it to me.

HEDDA. No, I'll look after it for now.

She goes over to the writing table and puts it in the book-case. TESMAN *stands dithering, unable to get his gloves on.* JUDGE BRACK *enters from the hall.*

HEDDA *nods to him*. Well, you're an early bird.

BRACK. Yes, aren't I?

To TESMAN.

Are you up and about, too?

TESMAN. Yes, I've got to go and see my aunts. Poor Auntie Rena's dying.

BRACK. Oh dear, is she? Then you mustn't let me detain you. At so tragic a—

TESMAN. Yes, I really must run. Good-bye! Good-bye!

Runs out through the hall.

HEDDA *goes nearer*. You seem to have had excellent sport last night—Judge.

BRACK. Indeed yes, Mrs. Hedda. I haven't even had time to take my clothes off.

HEDDA. *You* haven't either?

BRACK. As you see. What's Tesman told you about last night's escapades?

HEDDA. Oh, only some boring story about having gone and drunk coffee somewhere.

BRACK. Yes, I've heard about that coffee party. Eilert Loevborg wasn't with them, I gather?

HEDDA. No, they took him home first.

BRACK. Did Tesman go with him?

HEDDA. No, one or two of the others, he said.

BRACK *smiles*. George Tesman is a credulous man, Mrs. Hedda.

HEDDA. God knows. But—has something happened?

BRACK. Well, yes, I'm afraid it has.

HEDDA. I see. Sit down and tell me.

She sits on the left of the table, BRACK *at the long side of it, near her.*

HEDDA. Well?

BRACK. I had a special reason for keeping track of my guests last night. Or perhaps I should say some of my guests.

HEDDA. Including Eilert Loevborg?

BRACK. I must confess—yes.

HEDDA. You're beginning to make me curious.

BRACK. Do you know where he and some of my other guests spent the latter half of last night, Mrs. Hedda?

HEDDA. Tell me. If it won't shock me.

BRACK. Oh, I don't think it'll shock you. They found themselves participating in an exceedingly animated *soirée*.

HEDDA. Of a sporting character?

BRACK. Of a highly sporting character.

HEDDA. Tell me more.

BRACK. Loevborg had received an invitation in advance—as had the others. I knew all about that. But he had refused. As you know, he's become a new man.

HEDDA. Up at the Elvsteds', yes. But he went?

BRACK. Well, you see, Mrs. Hedda, last night at my house, unhappily, the spirit moved him.

HEDDA. Yes, I hear he became inspired.

BRACK. Somewhat violently inspired. And as a result, I suppose, his thoughts strayed. We men, alas, don't always stick to our principles as firmly as we should.

HEDDA. I'm sure you're an exception, Judge Brack. But go on about Loevborg.

BRACK. Well, to cut a long story short, he ended up in the establishment of a certain Mademoiselle Danielle.

HEDDA. Mademoiselle Danielle?

BRACK. She was holding the *soirée*. For a selected circle of friends and admirers.

HEDDA. Has she got red hair?

BRACK. She has.

HEDDA. A singer of some kind?

BRACK. Yes—among other accomplishments. She's also a celebrated huntress—of men, Mrs. Hedda. I'm sure you've heard about her. Eilert Loevborg used to be one of her most ardent patrons. In his salad days.

HEDDA. And how did all this end?

BRACK. Not entirely amicably, from all accounts. Mademoiselle Danielle began by receiving him with the utmost tenderness and ended by resorting to her fists.

HEDDA. Against Loevborg?

BRACK. Yes. He accused her, or her friends, of having robbed
him. He claimed his pocketbook had been stolen. Among
other things. In short, he seems to have made a bloodthirsty
scene.

HEDDA. And what did this lead to?

BRACK. It led to a general free-for-all, in which both sexes par-
ticipated. Fortunately, in the end the police arrived.

HEDDA. The police too?

BRACK. Yes. I'm afraid it may turn out to be rather an expensive joke for Master Eilert. Crazy fool!

HEDDA. Oh?

BRACK. Apparently he put up a very violent resistance. Hit
one of the constables on the ear and tore his uniform. He
had to accompany them to the police station.

HEDDA. Where did you learn all this?

BRACK. From the police.

HEDDA, *to herself.* So that's what happened. He didn't have a
crown of vine-leaves in his hair.

BRACK. Vine-leaves, Mrs. Hedda?

HEDDA, *in her normal voice again.* But, tell me, Judge, why
do you take such a close interest in Eilert Loevborg?

BRACK. For one thing it'll hardly be a matter of complete in-
difference to me if it's revealed in court that he came there
straight from my house.

HEDDA. Will it come to court?

BRACK. Of course. Well, I don't regard that as particularly
serious. Still, I thought it my duty, as a friend of the family,
to give you and your husband a full account of his nocturnal
adventures.

HEDDA. Why?

BRACK. Because I've a shrewd suspicion that he's hoping to
use you as a kind of screen.

HEDDA. What makes you think that?

BRACK. Oh, for heaven's sake, Mrs. Hedda, we're not blind.

You wait and see. This Mrs. Elvsted won't be going back to her husband just yet.

HEDDA. Well, if there were anything between those two there are plenty of other places where they could meet.

BRACK. Not in anyone's home. From now on every respectable house will once again be closed to Eilert Loevborg.

HEDDA. And mine should be too, you mean?

BRACK. Yes. I confess I should find it more than irksome if this gentleman were to be granted unrestricted access to this house. If he were superfluously to intrude into—

HEDDA. The triangle?

BRACK. Precisely. For me it would be like losing a home.

HEDDA *looks at him and smiles.* I see. You want to be the cock of the walk.

BRACK *nods slowly and lowers his voice.* Yes, that is my aim. And I shall fight for it with—every weapon at my disposal.

HEDDA, *as her smile fades.* You're a dangerous man, aren't you? When you really want something.

BRACK. You think so?

HEDDA. Yes, I'm beginning to think so. I'm deeply thankful you haven't any kind of hold over me.

BRACK *laughs equivocally.* Well, well, Mrs. Hedda—perhaps you're right. If I had, who knows what I might not think up?

HEDDA. Come, Judge Brack. That sounds almost like a threat.

BRACK *gets up.* Heaven forbid! In the creation of a triangle —and its continuance—the question of compulsion should never arise.

HEDDA. Exactly what I was thinking.

BRACK. Well, I've said what I came to say. I must be getting back. Good-bye, Mrs. Hedda.

Goes towards the french windows.

HEDDA *gets up.* Are you going out through the garden?

BRACK. Yes, it's shorter.

HEDDA. Yes. And it's the back door, isn't it?

BRACK. I've nothing against back doors. They can be quite in-triguing—sometimes.

HEDDA. When people fire pistols out of them, for example?

BRACK, *in the doorway, laughs.* Oh, people don't shoot tame cocks.

HEDDA *laughs too.* I suppose not. When they've only got one. *They nod good-bye, laughing. He goes. She closes the french windows behind him, and stands for a moment, looking out pensively. Then she walks across the room and glances through the curtains in the open doorway. Goes to the writing table, takes* LOEVBORG'S *package from the bookcase and is about to leaf through the pages when* BERTHA *is heard remonstrating loudly in the hall.* HEDDA *turns and listens. She hastily puts the package back in the drawer, locks it and puts the key on the inkstand.* EILERT LOEVBORG, *with his overcoat on and his hat in his hand, throws the door open. He looks somewhat confused and excited.*

LOEVBORG *shouts as he enters.* I must come in, I tell you! Let me pass!

He closes the door, turns, sees HEDDA, *controls himself im-mediately and bows.*

HEDDA, *at the writing table.* Well, Mr. Loevborg, this is rather a late hour to be collecting Thea.

LOEVBORG. And an early hour to call on you. Please forgive me.

HEDDA. How do you know she's still here?

LOEVBORG. They told me at her lodgings that she has been out all night.

HEDDA *goes to the table.* Did you notice anything about their behaviour when they told you?

LOEVBORG *looks at her, puzzled.* Notice anything?

HEDDA. Did they sound as if they thought it—strange?

LOEVBORG *suddenly understands.* Oh, I see what you mean. I'm dragging her down with me. No, as a matter of fact I didn't notice anything. I suppose Tesman isn't up yet?

HEDDA. No, I don't think so.

LOEVBORG. When did he get home?

HEDDA. Very late.

LOEVBORG. Did he tell you anything?

HEDDA. Yes. I gather you had a merry party at Judge Brack's last night.

LOEVBORG. He didn't tell you anything else?

HEDDA. I don't think so. I was so terribly sleepy—

MRS. ELVSTED *comes through the curtains in the open doorway.*

MRS. ELVSTED *runs towards him.* Oh, Eilert! At last!

LOEVBORG. Yes—at last. And too late.

MRS. ELVSTED. What is too late?

LOEVBORG. Everything—now. I'm finished, Thea.

MRS. ELVSTED. Oh, no, no! Don't say that!

LOEVBORG. You'll say it yourself, when you've heard what I—

MRS. ELVSTED. I don't want to hear anything!

HEDDA. Perhaps you'd rather speak to her alone? I'd better go.

LOEVBORG. No, stay.

MRS. ELVSTED. But I don't want to hear anything, I tell you!

LOEVBORG. It's not about last night.

MRS. ELVSTED. Then what—?

LOEVBORG. I want to tell you that from now on we must stop seeing each other.

MRS. ELVSTED. Stop seeing each other!

HEDDA, *involuntarily.* I knew it!

LOEVBORG. I have no further use for you, Thea.

MRS. ELVSTED. You can stand there and say that! No further use for me! Surely I can go on helping you? We'll go on working together, won't we?

LOEVBORG. I don't intend to do any more work from now on.

MRS. ELVSTED, *desperately.* Then what use have I for my life?

LOEVBORG. You must try to live as if you had never known me.

MRS. ELVSTED. But I can't!

LOEVBORG. Try to, Thea. Go back home—

MRS. ELVSTED. Never! I want to be wherever you are! I won't let myself be driven away like this! I want to stay here—and be with you when the book comes out.

HEDDA *whispers*. Ah, yes! The book!

LOEVBORG *looks at her*. Our book; Thea's and mine. It belongs to both of us.

MRS. ELVSTED. Oh, yes! I feel that, too! And I've a right to be with you when it comes into the world. I want to see people respect and honour you again. And the joy! The joy! I want to share it with you!

LOEVBORG. Thea—our book will never come into the world.

HEDDA. Ah!

MRS. ELVSTED. Not—?

LOEVBORG. It cannot. Ever.

MRS. ELVSTED. Eilert—what have you done with the manuscript? Where is it?

LOEVBORG. Oh Thea, please don't ask me that!

MRS. ELVSTED. Yes, yes—I must know. I've a right to know. Now!

LOEVBORG. The manuscript. I've torn it up.

MRS. ELVSTED *screams*. No, no!

HEDDA, *involuntarily*. But that's not—!

LOEVBORG *looks at her*. Not true, you think?

HEDDA *controls herself*. Why—yes, of course it is, if you say so. It just sounded so incredible—

LOEVBORG. It's true, nevertheless.

MRS. ELVSTED. Oh, my God, my God, Hedda—he's destroyed his own book!

LOEVBORG. I have destroyed my life. Why not my life's work, too?

MRS. ELVSTED. And you—did this last night?

LOEVBORG. Yes, Thea. I tore it into a thousand pieces. And scattered them out across the fjord. It's good, clean, salt water. Let it carry them away; let them drift in the current and the wind. And in a little while, they will sink. Deeper and deeper. As I shall, Thea.

MRS. ELVSTED. Do you know, Eilert—this book—all my life I shall feel as though you'd killed a little child?

LOEVBORG. You're right. It is like killing a child.

MRS. ELVSTED. But how could you? It was my child, too!

HEDDA, *almost inaudibly.* Oh—the child—!

MRS. ELVSTED *breathes heavily.* It's all over, then. Well—I'll go now, Hedda.

HEDDA. You're not leaving town?

MRS. ELVSTED. I don't know what I'm going to do. I can't see anything except—darkness.

She goes out through the hall.

HEDDA *waits a moment.* Aren't you going to escort her home, Mr. Loevborg?

LOEVBORG. I? Through the streets? Do you want me to let people see her with me?

HEDDA. Of course I don't know what else may have happened last night. But is it so utterly beyond redress?

LOEVBORG. It isn't just last night. It'll go on happening. I know it. But the curse of it is, I don't want to live that kind of life. I don't want to start all that again. She's broken my courage. I can't spit in the eyes of the world any longer.

HEDDA, *as though to herself.* That pretty little fool's been trying to shape a man's destiny.

Looks at him.

But how could you be so heartless towards her?

LOEVBORG. Don't call me heartless!

HEDDA. To go and destroy the one thing that's made her life worth living? You don't call that heartless?

LOEVBORG. Do you want to know the truth, Hedda?

HEDDA. The truth?

LOEVBORG. Promise me first—give me your word—that you'll never let Thea know about this.

HEDDA. I give you my word.

LOEVBORG. Good. Well; what I told her just now was a lie.

HEDDA. About the manuscript?

LOEVBORG. Yes. I didn't tear it up. Or throw it in the fjord.

HEDDA. You didn't? But where is it, then?

LOEVBORG. I destroyed it, all the same. I destroyed it, Hedda!

HEDDA. I don't understand.

LOEVBORG. Thea said that what I had done was like killing a child.

HEDDA. Yes. That's what she said.

LOEVBORG. But to kill a child isn't the worst thing a father can do to it.

HEDDA. What could be worse than that?

LOEVBORG. Hedda—suppose a man came home one morning, after a night of debauchery, and said to the mother of his child: "Look here. I've been wandering round all night. I've been to—such-and-such a place and such-and-such a place. And I had our child with me. I took him to—these places. And I've lost him. Just—lost him. God knows where he is or whose hands he's fallen into."

HEDDA. I see. But when all's said and done, this was only a book—

LOEVBORG. Thea's heart and soul were in that book. It was her whole life.

HEDDA. Yes. I understand.

LOEVBORG. Well, then you must also understand that she and I cannot possibly ever see each other again.

HEDDA. Where will you go?

LOEVBORG. Nowhere. I just want to put an end to it all. As soon as possible.

HEDDA *takes a step towards him.* Eilert Loevborg, listen to me. Do it—beautifully!

LOEVBORG. Beautifully?

Smiles.

With a crown of vine-leaves in my hair? The way you used to dream of me—in the old days?

HEDDA. No. I don't believe in that crown any longer. But—do it beautifully, all the same. Just this once. Good-bye. You must go now. And don't come back.

LOEVBORG. Adieu, madam. Give my love to George Tesman.

Turns to go.

HEDDA. Wait. I want to give you a souvenir to take with you.

She goes over to the writing table, opens the drawer and the pistol-case, and comes back to LOEVBORG *with one of the pistols.*

LOEVBORG *looks at her*. This? Is this the souvenir?

HEDDA *nods slowly*. You recognise it? You looked down its barrel once.

LOEVBORG. You should have used it then.

HEDDA. Here! Use it now!

LOEVBORG *puts the pistol in his breast pocket*. Thank you.

HEDDA. Do it beautifully, Eilert Loevborg. Only promise me that!

LOEVBORG. Good-bye, Hedda Gabler.

He goes out through the hall. HEDDA *stands by the door for a moment, listening. Then she goes over to the writing table, takes out the package containing the manuscript, glances inside it, pulls some of the pages half out and looks at them. Then she takes it to the armchair by the stove and sits down with the package in her lap. After a moment, she opens the door of the stove; then she opens the packet.*

HEDDA *throws one of the pages into the stove and whispers to herself*. I'm burning your child, Thea! You with your beautiful wavy hair!

She throws a few more pages into the stove.

The child Eilert Loevborg gave you.

Throws the rest of the manuscript in.

I'm burning it! I'm burning your child!

ACT FOUR

The same. It is evening. The drawing room is in darkness.
The small room is illuminated by the hanging lamp over the
table. The curtains are drawn across the french windows.
HEDDA, *dressed in black, is walking up and down in the*
darkened room. Then she goes into the small room and
crosses to the left. A few chords are heard from the piano.
She comes back into the drawing room.

BERTHA *comes through the small room from the right with*
a lighted lamp, which she places on the table in front of the
corner sofa in the drawing room. Her eyes are red with cry-
ing, and she has black ribbons on her cap. She goes quietly
out, right. HEDDA *goes over to the french windows, draws*
the curtains slightly to one side and looks out into the dark-
ness.

A few moments later, MISS TESMAN *enters from the hall.*
She is dressed in mourning, with a black hat and veil. HEDDA
goes to meet her and holds out her hand.

MISS TESMAN. Well, Hedda, here I am in the weeds of sorrow.
My poor sister has ended her struggles at last.

HEDDA. I've already heard. Tesman sent me a card.

MISS TESMAN. Yes, he promised me he would. But I thought,
no, I must go and break the news of death to Hedda myself
—here, in the house of life.

HEDDA. It's very kind of you.

MISS TESMAN. Ah, Rena shouldn't have chosen a time like this to pass away. This is no moment for Hedda's house to be a place of mourning.

HEDDA, *changing the subject.* She died peacefully, Miss Tesman?

MISS TESMAN. Oh, it was quite beautiful! The end came so calmly. And she was so happy at being able to see George once again. And say good-bye to him. Hasn't he come home yet?

HEDDA. No. He wrote that I mustn't expect him too soon. But please sit down.

MISS TESMAN. No, thank you, Hedda dear—bless you. I'd like to. But I've so little time. I must dress her and lay her out as well as I can. She shall go to her grave looking really beautiful.

HEDDA. Can't I help with anything?

MISS TESMAN. Why, you mustn't think of such a thing! Hedda Tesman mustn't let her hands be soiled by contact with death. Or her thoughts. Not at this time.

HEDDA. One can't always control one's thoughts.

MISS TESMAN *continues.* Ah, well, that's life. Now we must start to sew poor Rena's shroud. There'll be sewing to be done in this house too before long, I shouldn't wonder. But not for a shroud, praise God.

GEORGE TESMAN *enters from the hall.*

HEDDA. You've come at last! Thank heavens!

TESMAN. Are you here, Auntie Juju? With Hedda? Fancy that!

MISS TESMAN. I was just on the point of leaving, dear boy. Well, have you done everything you promised me?

TESMAN. No, I'm afraid I forgot half of it. I'll have to run over again tomorrow. My head's in a complete whirl today. I can't collect my thoughts.

MISS TESMAN. But George dear, you mustn't take it like this.

TESMAN. Oh? Well—er—how should I?

MISS TESMAN. You must be happy in your grief. Happy for what's happened. As I am.

TESMAN. Oh, yes, yes. You're thinking of Aunt Rena.

HEDDA. It'll be lonely for you now, Miss Tesman.

MISS TESMAN. For the first few days, yes. But it won't last long,
I hope. Poor dear Rena's little room isn't going to stay empty.

TESMAN. Oh? Whom are you going to move in there? What?

MISS TESMAN. Oh, there's always some poor invalid who needs
care and attention.

HEDDA. Do you really want another cross like that to bear?

MISS TESMAN. Cross! God forgive you, child. It's been no cross
for me.

HEDDA. But now—if a complete stranger comes to live with
you—?

MISS TESMAN. Oh, one soon makes friends with invalids. And
I need so much to have someone to live for. Like you, my
dear. Well, I expect there'll soon be work in this house too
for an old aunt, praise God!

HEDDA. Oh—please!

TESMAN. By Jove, yes! What a splendid time the three of us
could have together if—

HEDDA. If?

TESMAN, *uneasily*. Oh, never mind. It'll all work out. Let's hope
so—what?

MISS TESMAN. Yes, yes. Well, I'm sure you two would like to be
alone.
Smiles.
Perhaps Hedda may have something to tell you, George.
Good-bye. I must go home to Rena.
Turns to the door.
Dear God, how strange! Now Rena is with me and with poor
dear Joachim.

TESMAN. Fancy that. Yes, Auntie Juju! What?

MISS TESMAN *goes out through the hall.*

HEDDA *follows* TESMAN *coldly and searchingly with her eyes.*
I really believe this death distresses you more than it does
her.

TESMAN. Oh, it isn't just Auntie Rena. It's Eilert I'm so worried about.

HEDDA, *quickly*. Is there any news of him?

TESMAN. I ran over to see him this afternoon. I wanted to tell him his manuscript was in safe hands.

HEDDA. Oh? You didn't find him?

TESMAN. No. He wasn't at home. But later I met Mrs. Elvsted and she told me he'd been here early this morning.

HEDDA. Yes, just after you'd left.

TESMAN. It seems he said he'd torn the manuscript up. What?

HEDDA. Yes, he claimed to have done so.

TESMAN. You told him we had it, of course?

HEDDA. No.

Quickly.

Did you tell Mrs. Elvsted?

TESMAN. No, I didn't like to. But you ought to have told him. Think if he should go home and do something desperate! Give me the manuscript, Hedda. I'll run over to him with it right away. Where did you put it?

HEDDA, *cold and motionless, leaning against the armchair*. I haven't got it any longer.

TESMAN. Haven't got it? What on earth do you mean?

HEDDA. I've burned it.

TESMAN *starts, terrified*. Burned it! Burned Eilert's manuscript!

HEDDA. Don't shout. The servant will hear you.

TESMAN. Burned it! But in heaven's name—! Oh, no, no, no! This is impossible!

HEDDA. Well, it's true.

TESMAN. But Hedda, do you realise what you've done? That's appropriating lost property! It's against the law! By Jove! You ask Judge Brack and see if I'm not right.

HEDDA. You'd be well advised not to talk about it to Judge Brack or anyone else.

TESMAN. But how could you go and do such a dreadful thing?

What on earth put the idea into your head? What came over you? Answer me! What?

HEDDA *represses an almost imperceptible smile.* I did it for your sake, George.

TESMAN. For my sake?

HEDDA. When you came home this morning and described how he'd read his book to you—

TESMAN. Yes, yes?

HEDDA. You admitted you were jealous of him.

TESMAN. But, good heavens, I didn't mean it literally!

HEDDA. No matter. I couldn't bear the thought that anyone else should push you into the background.

TESMAN, *torn between doubt and joy.* Hedda—is this true? But —but—but I never realised you loved me like that! Fancy—

HEDDA. Well, I suppose you'd better know. I'm going to have— *Breaks off and says violently.*

No, no—you'd better ask your Auntie Juju. She'll tell you.

TESMAN. Hedda! I think I understand what you mean. *Clasps his hands.*

Good heavens, can it really be true! What?

HEDDA. Don't shout. The servant will hear you.

TESMAN, *laughing with joy.* The servant! I say, that's good! The servant! Why, that's Bertha! I'll run out and tell her at once!

HEDDA *clenches her hands in despair.* Oh, it's destroying me, all this—it's destroying me!

TESMAN. I say, Hedda, what's up? What?

HEDDA, *cold, controlled.* Oh, it's all so—absurd—George.

TESMAN. Absurd? That I'm so happy? But surely—? Ah, well —perhaps I won't say anything to Bertha.

HEDDA. No, do. She might as well know too.

TESMAN. No, no, I won't tell her yet. But Auntie Juju—I must let her know! And you—you called me George! For the first time! Fancy that! Oh, it'll make Auntie Juju so happy, all this! So very happy!

HEDDA. Will she be happy when she hears I've burned Eilert Loevborg's manuscript—for your sake?

TESMAN. No, I'd forgotten about that. Of course no one must be allowed to know about the manuscript. But that you're burning with love for me, Hedda, I must certainly let Auntie Juju know that. I say, I wonder if young wives often feel like that towards their husbands? What?

HEDDA. You might ask Auntie Juju about that too.

TESMAN. I will, as soon as I get the chance.

Looks uneasy and thoughtful again.

But I say, you know, that manuscript. Dreadful business. Poor Eilert!

MRS. ELVSTED, *dressed as on her first visit, with hat and overcoat, enters from the hall.*

MRS. ELVSTED *greets them hastily and tremulously.* Oh, Hedda dear, do please forgive me for coming here again.

HEDDA. Why, Thea, what's happened?

TESMAN. Is it anything to do with Eilert Loevborg? What?

MRS. ELVSTED. Yes—I'm so dreadfully afraid he may have met with an accident.

HEDDA *grips her arm.* You think so?

TESMAN. But, good heavens, Mrs. Elvsted, what makes you think that?

MRS. ELVSTED. I heard them talking about him at the boarding-house, as I went in. Oh, there are the most terrible rumours being spread about him in town today.

TESMAN. Fancy. Yes, I heard about them too. But I can testify that he went straight home to bed. Fancy that!

HEDDA. Well—what did they say in the boarding-house?

MRS. ELVSTED. Oh, I couldn't find out anything. Either they didn't know, or else— They stopped talking when they saw me. And I didn't dare to ask.

TESMAN *fidgets uneasily.* We must hope—we must hope you misheard them, Mrs. Elvsted.

MRS. ELVSTED. No, no, I'm sure it was he they were talking about. I heard them say something about a hospital—

TESMAN. Hospital!

HEDDA. Oh no, surely that's impossible!

MRS. ELVSTED. Oh, I became so afraid. So I went up to his rooms and asked to see him.

HEDDA. Do you think that was wise, Thea?

MRS. ELVSTED. Well, what else could I do? I couldn't bear the uncertainty any longer.

TESMAN. But *you* didn't manage to find him either? What?

MRS. ELVSTED. No. And they had no idea where he was. They said he hadn't been home since yesterday afternoon.

TESMAN. Since yesterday? Fancy that!

MRS. ELVSTED. I'm sure he must have met with an accident.

TESMAN. Hedda, I wonder if I ought to go into town and make one or two enquiries?

HEDDA. No, no, don't you get mixed up in this.

JUDGE BRACK *enters from the hall, hat in hand.* BERTHA, *who has opened the door for him, closes it. He looks serious and greets them silently.*

TESMAN. Hullo, my dear Judge. Fancy seeing you!

BRACK. I had to come and talk to you.

TESMAN. I can see Auntie Juju's told you the news.

BRACK. Yes, I've heard about that too.

TESMAN. Tragic, isn't it?

BRACK. Well, my dear chap, that depends how you look at it.

TESMAN *looks uncertainly at him.* Has something else happened?

BRACK. Yes.

HEDDA. Another tragedy?

BRACK. That also depends on how you look at it, Mrs. Tesman.

MRS. ELVSTED. Oh, it's something to do with Eilert Loevborg!

BRACK *looks at her for a moment.* How did you guess? Perhaps you've heard already—?

MRS. ELVSTED, *confused.* No, no, not at all—I—

TESMAN. For heaven's sake, tell us!

BRACK *shrugs his shoulders.* Well, I'm afraid they've taken him to the hospital. He's dying.

MRS. ELVSTED *screams.* Oh God, God!

TESMAN. The hospital! Dying!

HEDDA, *involuntarily.* So quickly!

MRS. ELVSTED, *weeping.* Oh, Hedda! And we parted enemies!

HEDDA *whispers.* Thea—Thea!

MRS. ELVSTED, *ignoring her.* I must see him! I must see him before he dies!

BRACK. It's no use, Mrs. Elvsted. No one's allowed to see him now.

MRS. ELVSTED. But what's happened to him? You must tell me!

TESMAN. He hasn't tried to do anything to himself? What?

HEDDA. Yes, he has. I'm sure of it.

TESMAN. Hedda, how can you—?

BRACK, *who has not taken his eyes from her.* I'm afraid you've guessed correctly, Mrs. Tesman.

MRS. ELVSTED. How dreadful!

TESMAN. Attempted suicide! Fancy that!

HEDDA. Shot himself!

BRACK. Right again, Mrs. Tesman.

MRS. ELVSTED *tries to compose herself.* When did this happen, Judge Brack?

BRACK. This afternoon. Between three and four.

TESMAN. But, good heavens—where? What?

BRACK, *a little hesitantly.* Where? Why, my dear chap, in his rooms of course.

MRS. ELVSTED. No, that's impossible. I was there soon after six.

BRACK. Well, it must have been somewhere else, then. I don't know exactly. I only know that they found him. He'd shot himself—through the breast.

MRS. ELVSTED. Oh, how horrible! That he should end like that!

HEDDA, *to* BRACK. Through the breast, you said?

BRACK. That is what I said.

HEDDA. Not through the head?

BRACK. Through the breast, Mrs. Tesman.

HEDDA. The breast. Yes; yes. That's good, too.

BRACK. Why, Mrs. Tesman?

HEDDA. Oh—no, I didn't mean anything.

TESMAN. And the wound's dangerous, you say? What?

BRACK. Mortal. He's probably already dead.

MRS. ELVSTED. Yes, yes—I feel it! It's all over. All over. Oh Hedda—!

TESMAN. But, tell me, how did you manage to learn all this?

BRACK, *curtly*. From the police. I spoke to one of them.

HEDDA, *loudly, clearly*. At last! Oh, thank God!

TESMAN, *appalled*. For God's sake, Hedda, what are you saying?

HEDDA. I am saying there's beauty in what he has done.

BRACK. Hm—Mrs. Tesman—

TESMAN. Beauty! Oh, but I say!

MRS. ELVSTED. Hedda, how can you talk of beauty in connection with a thing like this?

HEDDA. Eilert Loevborg has settled his account with life. He's had the courage to do what—what he had to do.

MRS. ELVSTED. No, that's not why it happened. He did it because he was mad.

TESMAN. He did it because he was desperate.

HEDDA. You're wrong! I know!

MRS. ELVSTED. He must have been mad. The same as when he tore up the manuscript.

BRACK *starts*. Manuscript? Did he tear it up?

MRS. ELVSTED. Yes. Last night.

TESMAN *whispers*. Oh, Hedda, we shall never be able to escape from this.

BRACK. Hm. Strange.

TESMAN *wanders round the room*. To think of Eilert dying like that. And not leaving behind him the thing that would have made his name endure.

MRS. ELVSTED. If only it could be pieced together again!

TESMAN. Yes, fancy! If only it could! I'd give anything—

MRS. ELVSTED. Perhaps it can, Mr. Tesman.

TESMAN. What do you mean?

MRS. ELVSTED *searches in the pocket of her dress*. Look! I kept the notes he dictated it from.

HEDDA *takes a step nearer*. Ah!

TESMAN. You kept them, Mrs. Elvsted! What?

MRS. ELVSTED. Yes, here they are. I brought them with me when I left home. They've been in my pocket ever since.

TESMAN. Let me have a look.

MRS. ELVSTED *hands him a wad of small sheets of paper*. They're in a terrible muddle. All mixed up.

TESMAN. I say, just fancy if we can sort them out! Perhaps if we work on them together—?

MRS. ELVSTED. Oh, yes! Let's try, anyway!

TESMAN. We'll manage it. We must! I shall dedicate my life to this.

HEDDA. *You*, George? Your life?

TESMAN. Yes—well, all the time I can spare. My book'll have to wait. Hedda, you do understand? What? I owe it to Eilert's memory.

HEDDA. Perhaps.

TESMAN. Well, my dear Mrs. Elvsted, you and I'll have to pool our brains. No use crying over spilt milk, what? We must try to approach this matter calmly.

MRS. ELVSTED. Yes, yes, Mr. Tesman. I'll do my best.

TESMAN. Well, come over here and let's start looking at these notes right away. Where shall we sit? Here? No, the other room. You'll excuse us, won't you, Judge? Come along with me, Mrs. Elvsted.

MRS. ELVSTED. Oh, God! If only we can manage to do it!

TESMAN *and* MRS. ELVSTED *go into the rear room. He takes off his hat and overcoat. They sit at the table beneath the hanging lamp and absorb themselves in the notes.* HEDDA *walks across to the stove and sits in the armchair. After a moment,* BRACK *goes over to her.*

HEDDA, *half aloud.* Oh, Judge! This act of Eilert Loevborg's— doesn't it give one a sense of release!

BRACK. Release, Mrs. Hedda? Well, it's a release for him, of course—

HEDDA. Oh, I don't mean him—I mean me! The release of knowing that someone can do something really brave! Something beautiful!

BRACK *smiles.* Hm—my dear Mrs. Hedda—

HEDDA. Oh, I know what you're going to say. You're a bourgeois at heart too, just like—ah, well!

BRACK *looks at her.* Eilert Loevborg has meant more to you than you're willing to admit to yourself. Or am I wrong?

HEDDA. I'm not answering questions like that from you. I only know that Eilert Loevborg has had the courage to live according to his own principles. And now, at last, he's done something big! Something beautiful! To have the courage and the will to rise from the feast of life so early!

BRACK. It distresses me deeply, Mrs. Hedda, but I'm afraid I must rob you of that charming illusion.

HEDDA. Illusion?

BRACK. You wouldn't have been allowed to keep it for long, anyway.

HEDDA. What do you mean?

BRACK. He didn't shoot himself on purpose.

HEDDA. Not on purpose?

BRACK. No. It didn't happen quite the way I told you.

HEDDA. Have you been hiding something? What is it?

BRACK. In order to spare poor Mrs. Elvsted's feelings, I permitted myself one or two small—equivocations.

HEDDA. What?

BRACK. To begin with, he is already dead.

HEDDA. He died at the hospital?

BRACK. Yes. Without regaining consciousness.

HEDDA. What else haven't you told us?

BRACK. The incident didn't take place at his lodgings.

HEDDA. Well, that's utterly unimportant.

BRACK. Not utterly. The fact is, you see, that Eilbert Loevborg was found shot in Mademoiselle Danielle's boudoir.

HEDDA *almost jumps up, but instead sinks back in her chair.* That's impossible. He can't have been there today.

BRACK. He was there this afternoon. He went to ask for something he claimed they'd taken from him. Talked some crazy nonsense about a child which had got lost—

HEDDA. Oh! So that was the reason!

BRACK. I thought at first he might have been referring to his manuscript. But I hear he destroyed that himself. So he must have meant his pocketbook—I suppose.

HEDDA. Yes, I suppose so. So they found him there?

BRACK. Yes; there. With a discharged pistol in his breast pocket. The shot had wounded him mortally.

HEDDA. Yes. In the breast.

BRACK. No. In the—hm—stomach. The—lower part—

HEDDA *looks at him with an expression of repulsion.* That too! Oh, why does everything I touch become mean and ludicrous? It's like a curse!

BRACK. There's something else, Mrs. Hedda. It's rather disagreeable, too.

HEDDA. What?

BRACK. The pistol he had on him—

HEDDA. Yes? What about it?

BRACK. He must have stolen it.

HEDDA *jumps up.* Stolen it! That isn't true! He didn't!

BRACK. It's the only explanation. He must have stolen it. Ssh!

TESMAN *and* MRS. ELVSTED *have got up from the table in in the rear room and come into the drawing room.*

TESMAN, *his hands full of papers.* Hedda, I can't see properly under that lamp. Think!

HEDDA. I am thinking.

TESMAN. Do you think we could possibly use your writing table for a little? What?

HEDDA. Yes, of course.

Quickly.

No, wait! Let me tidy it up first.

TESMAN. Oh, don't you trouble about that. There's plenty of room.

HEDDA. No, no, let me tidy it up first, I say. I'll take this in and put them on the piano. Here.

She pulls an object, covered with sheets of music, out from under the bookcase, puts some more sheets on top and carries it all into the rear room and away to the left. TESMAN *puts his papers on the writing table and moves the lamp over from the corner table. He and* MRS. ELVSTED *sit down and begin working again.* HEDDA *comes back.*

HEDDA, *behind* MRS. ELVSTED's *chair, ruffles her hair gently.* Well, my pretty Thea! And how is work progressing on Eilert Loevborg's memorial?

MRS. ELVSTED *looks up at her, dejectedly.* Oh, it's going to be terribly difficult to get these into any order.

TESMAN. We've got to do it. We must! After all, putting other people's papers into order is rather my speciality, what?

HEDDA *goes over to the stove and sits on one of the foot-stools.* BRACK *stands over her, leaning against the armchair.*

HEDDA *whispers.* What was that you were saying about the pistol?

BRACK, *softly*. I said he must have stolen it.

HEDDA. Why do you think that?

BRACK. Because any other explanation is unthinkable, Mrs. Hedda, or ought to be.

HEDDA. I see.

BRACK *looks at her for a moment*. Eilert Loevborg was here this morning. Wasn't he?

HEDDA. Yes.

BRACK. Were you alone with him?

HEDDA. For a few moments.

BRACK. You didn't leave the room while he was here?

HEDDA. No.

BRACK. Think again. Are you sure you didn't go out for a moment?

HEDDA. Oh—yes, I might have gone into the hall. Just for a few seconds.

BRACK. And where was your pistol-case during this time?

HEDDA. I'd locked it in that—

BRACK. Er—Mrs. Hedda?

HEDDA. It was lying over there on my writing table.

BRACK. Have you looked to see if both the pistols are still there?

HEDDA. No.

BRACK. You needn't bother. I saw the pistol Loevborg had when they found him. I recognised it at once. From yesterday. And other occasions.

HEDDA. Have you got it?

BRACK. No. The police have it.

HEDDA. What will the police do with this pistol?

BRACK. Try to trace the owner.

HEDDA. Do you think they'll succeed?

BRACK *leans down and whispers*. No, Hedda Gabler. Not as long as I hold my tongue.

HEDDA *looks nervously at him*. And if you don't?

BRACK *shrugs his shoulders.* You could always say he'd stolen it.

HEDDA. I'd rather die!

BRACK *smiles.* People say that. They never do it.

HEDDA, *not replying.* And suppose the pistol wasn't stolen? And they trace the owner? What then?

BRACK. There'll be a scandal, Hedda.

HEDDA. A scandal!

BRACK. Yes, a scandal. The thing you're so frightened of. You'll have to appear in court. Together with Mademoiselle Danielle. She'll have to explain how it all happened. Was it an accident, or was it—homicide? Was he about to take the pistol from his pocket to threaten her? And did it go off? Or did she snatch the pistol from his hand, shoot him and then put it back in his pocket? She might quite easily have done it. She's a resourceful lady, is Mademoiselle Danielle.

HEDDA. But I had nothing to do with this repulsive business.

BRACK. No. But you'll have to answer one question. Why did you give Eilert Loevborg this pistol? And what conclusions will people draw when it is proved you did give it to him?

HEDDA *bows her head.* That's true. I hadn't thought of that.

BRACK. Well, luckily there's no danger as long as I hold my tongue.

HEDDA *looks up at him.* In other words, I'm in your power, Judge. From now on, you've got your hold over me.

BRACK *whispers, more slowly.* Hedda, my dearest—believe me —I will not abuse my position.

HEDDA. Nevertheless, I'm in your power. Dependent on your will, and your demands. Not free. Still not free!

Rises passionately.

No. I couldn't bear that. No.

BRACK *looks half-derisively at her.* Most people resign themselves to the inevitable, sooner or later.

HEDDA *returns his gaze.* Possibly they do.

She goes across to the writing table.

HEDDA *represses an involuntary smile and says in* TESMAN's *voice.* Well, George. Think you'll be able to manage? What?

TESMAN. Heaven knows, dear. This is going to take months and months.

HEDDA, *in the same tone as before.* Fancy that, by Jove!

Runs her hands gently through MRS. ELVSTED's *hair.*

Doesn't it feel strange, Thea? Here you are working away with Tesman just the way you used to work with Eilert Loevborg.

MRS. ELVSTED. Oh—if only I can inspire your husband too!

HEDDA. Oh, it'll come. In time.

TESMAN. Yes—do you know, Hedda, I really think I'm beginning to feel a bit—well—that way. But you go back and talk to Judge Brack.

HEDDA. Can't I be of use to you two in any way?

TESMAN. No, none at all.

Turns his head.

You'll have to keep Hedda company from now on, Judge, and see she doesn't get bored. If you don't mind.

BRACK *glances at* HEDDA. It'll be a pleasure.

HEDDA. Thank you. But I'm tired this evening. I think I'll lie down on the sofa in there for a little while.

TESMAN. Yes, dear—do. What?

HEDDA *goes into the rear room and draws the curtains behind her. Short pause. Suddenly she begins to play a frenzied dance melody on the piano.*

MRS. ELVSTED *starts up from her chair.* Oh, what's that?

TESMAN *runs to the doorway.* Hedda dear, please! Don't play dance music tonight! Think of Auntie Rena. And Eilert.

HEDDA *puts her head out through the curtains.* And Auntie Juju. And all the rest of them. From now on I'll be quiet.

Closes the curtains behind her.

TESMAN, *at the writing table.* It distresses her to watch us doing this. I say, Mrs. Elvsted, I've an idea. Why don't you move in with Auntie Juju? I'll run over each evening, and we can sit and work there. What?

MRS. ELVSTED. Yes, that might be the best plan.

HEDDA, *from the rear room.* I can hear what you're saying, Tesman. But how shall I spend the evenings out here?

TESMAN, *looking through his papers.* Oh, I'm sure Judge Brack'll be kind enough to come over and keep you company. You won't mind my not being here, Judge?

BRACK, *in the armchair, calls gaily.* I'll be delighted, Mrs. Tesman. I'll be here every evening. We'll have great fun together, you and I.

HEDDA, *loud and clear.* Yes, that'll suit you, won't it, Judge? The only cock on the dunghill—!

A shot is heard from the rear room. TESMAN, MRS. ELVSTED *and* JUDGE BRACK *start from their chairs.*

TESMAN. Oh, she's playing with those pistols again.

He pulls the curtains aside and runs in. MRS. ELVSTED *follows him.* HEDDA *is lying dead on the sofa. Confusion and shouting.* BERTHA *enters in alarm from the right.*

TESMAN *screams to* BRACK. She's shot herself! Shot herself in the head! By Jove! Fancy that!

BRACK *half paralysed in the armchair.* But, good God! People don't do such things!